A Practical Guide for Teaching Science to Students with Special Needs in Inclusive Settings

Margo A. Mastropieri
Thomas E. Scruggs
(MISL Project)

8700 Shoal Creek Boulevard
Austin, Texas 78757

Table of Contents

Acknowledgements vii

Preface ix

**Part I: Characteristics of Disabilities and Implications
for Mainstreaming in Science Classes**

1. General Characteristics 1

2. Learning Disabilities 7

3. Communication Disorders 15

4. Mental Retardation 19

5. Emotional Disturbance 27

6. Hearing Impairments 35

7. Visual Impairments 45

8. Physical Disabilities 55

Part II: General Mainstreaming Strategies

9. Time and Resource Management 65

10. Effective Instruction 73

11. Cooperative Learning 77

12. Peer Assistance and Peer Tutoring 93

13. Evaluation 109

14. Strategies for Managing Classroom Behavior 121

15. Strategies for Improving Attention 139

16. Strategies for Improving Memory 145

17. Mainstreaming Students With Reading Difficulties 161

18. Improving Note-Taking, Study Skills,
    and Test-Taking Skills 179

19. Strategies for Improving Motivation and Affect 191

20. Instructional Media 199

21. Computer-Assisted Instruction 209

22. Field Trips and Demonstrations 217

**Part III: Guidelines for Implementing Specific Science Activities
in Mainstream Settings**

23. Introduction to Part III: Recommendations for *All*
    Activities 227

24. Measuring and Pouring 231

25. Charting, Graphing, and Recording Data 235

26. Observing, Classifying, and Predicting 239

27. Mapping Activities 243

28. Invention and Discovery Activities 247

29. Assembling Kits and Models 251

30. Human Anatomy 255

31. Activities With Plants and Animals 257

32. Activities With Microscopes 265

33. Water Activities 269

34. Powders, Mixtures, and Solutions 273

35. Weather Activities 277

36. Rocks, Minerals, and Fossils 279

37. Earth Science/Landform Activities 283

38. Astronomy Activities 285

39. Magnetism and Electricity Activities 289

40. Force and Motion Activities 291

41. Physics of Sound 295

42. Solids/Liquids/Gases 297

43. Light and Color 299

Relevant References 301

Index 315

Appendix A: Science Products/Adaptations 337

Appendix B: Related Organizations and Resources 345

**Appendix C: Guidelines for Curriculum Adoption Committees
and for Publishers of Science Curriculum** 355

Acknowledgments

We thank the following individuals for providing us with valuable assistance at various stages of the Mainstream Instruction for Scientific Literacy Project. Our acknowledgment of these individuals is not meant to imply that they, or their affiliated organizations, necessarily endorse this manual. Partial support for the development of these guidelines was provided by a cooperative agreement involving the authors, the Purdue University Research Foundation, and the U.S. Department of Education, Special Education Programs (No. H023D00010).

Dr. Tom Hanley, *U.S. Department of Education*

Dr. Alice Moses, *National Science Foundation*
Dr. Jane Kahle, *National Association for Research in Science Teaching*
Anthea Maton, *National Science Teachers Association*

Sally Shuler
Olive Covington
National Science Resource Center

Dr. Steve Forness, *University of California, Los Angeles*

Kathy Comfort, *California Assessment Project*
Tom Fiore, *Research Triangle Institute*

Ray Short, *Allyn & Bacon*
Dr. James Patton, *Pro-Ed Publishers*
Michael J. Kane, *Addison-Wesley Publishers*
Mike Dellefield, *Britannica Inc.*
Vickie Knight, *Brooks/Cole*

Linda DeLuccia
Larry Malone
Lawrence Hall of Science

Larry Small
Gerhardt C. Krohne
Rose Marie Mincey
School District 54, Schaumburg, Illinois

Dr. Hal McGrady
Marilyn Prehm
Robert Golden
Mae L. Johnson
Theresa M. Pasko
Karen Synder
Mary Foster
Arlington, Virginia Public Schools

Robert Foerster
Polly Honor
Sheryl Braile
West Lafayette, IN Public Schools

Dr. Susan Sprague
Jean Hamlin
Jack Terrio
Virginia Hollis Carter
Mary Kay Horn
Lisa Flook
Janet Morrow Carlson
Sandy Montoye
Paige Moore
Nick Parker
Lois Theilmann
Marilyn DeVan
Melanie Holmes
Mesa, Arizona Public Schools

Donna Daily
Jeffrey P. Bakken
G. Sharon Sullivan, osu
Frederick J. Brigham
Sharlene Shiah
Alice Stevens
Kara Meadows
Cheryl Deluca
Shanna Weagle
Kelly Lawson
Renee Daly
Anne Bisaha
Purdue University

Keith Butz, *Lafayette, IN*

Dr. Richard Wood
Mary Lu Smith
Mark Bruns
Deborah Grady-Ruth
Nancy Ann Sattler
Mary Schwartz
Kirstine K. Sharp
Mary Taylor
Tippecanoe County Schools, IN

Sources and Publishers

In preparation for this book, we consulted a wide variety of sources including opinions of expert teachers, curriculum developers, and personnel from national professional organizations. In addition, we consulted a large number of published material, all of which contributed in a general way to the overall development of this book. In order not to interrupt the flow of the book, we included these works in the *Relevant References* section at the end of this book and made only infrequent reference to them in the text. However, we wish to acknowledge particularly the contribution of the following sources: Bleck & Nagel (1982); Bybee (1972); Corn & Torres (1990); Corrick (1981); DeLucchi, Malone, & Thier (1980); Ehly & Larsen (1980); Hadary & Cohen (1978); Hallahan & Kauffman (1991); Hoffman & Ricker (1979); Johnson & Johnson (1991); Kerr & Nelson (1989); Lewis & Doorlag (1991); Malone & DeLucchi (1979); Mastropieri & Scruggs (1987, 1994); Mastropieri & Scruggs (1991); Metropolitan Museum of Art (1979); Moores (1987); Pierce, Stahlbrand, & Armstrong (1984); Salend (1990); Scruggs & Mastropieri (1992); and Slavin (1983). We would also like to acknowledge the important contribution of the publishers of science curriculum and adaptive materials, listed in the appendix.

The following illustrations were reprinted with permission:

1. *Trichina* mnemonic (p. 149). *Exceptional Children*, 1992, *58*, 219–229.

2. *Three parts of the earth* mnemonic (p. 151). *Teaching students ways to remember: Strategies for learning mnemonically.* Cambridge, MA: Brookline Books.

3. *Attributes of mammals* mnemonic (p. 152). *Teaching students ways to remember: Strategies for learning mnemonically.* Cambridge, MA: Brookline Books.

4. *Crocoite* mnemonic (p. 155). *Journal of Educational Psychology*, 1987, *79*, 27–34. Copyright 1987 by the American Psychological Association.

5. *Radial symmetry* mnemonic (p. 152). *Exceptional Children*, 1992, *58*, 219–229.

6. Types of vertebrates mnemonic (p. 158). *Teaching students ways to remember: Strategies for learning mnemonically.* Cambridge, MA: Brookline Books.

How to Use this Manual

This manual is intended to be a resource for teachers who have special education students in their mainstream science classes. The manual is also intended to be helpful to members of school district curriculum adoption committees and to publishers of science curriculum materials. The manual is divided into three major parts. The first part, ''Characteristics of Disabilities and Implications for Mainstreaming in Science Classes,'' describes general characteristics of students with disabilities. This section also provides general mainstreaming strategies and general laboratory suggestions for students of each respective disability area. The second part, General Mainstreaming Strategies, presents information related to instructional procedures that have proven effective for working with students with disabilities in mainstream settings. Topics include time and resource management, behavior management, cooperative learning, and adapting reading activities. The final section, ''Guidelines for Implementing Specific Science Activities in Mainstream Settings,'' presents adaptations that teachers can use when using specific activities during science instruction. General information is presented regarding all activities, and specific information is provided on activities such as measuring and pouring, using microscopes, activities with plants and animals, and astronomy activities.

The manual also contains an extensive indexing system that can assist teachers in locating specific information. The manual is indexed based both on individual words and concepts. Therefore sometimes the concept will be found in the referred page instead of the specific word which appears in the index. This system should facilitate the location of specific mainstreaming strategies for certain disability areas and for adaptations for specific science activities.

In an attempt to provide guidance to curriculum adoption committee members and publishers, an Appendix has been provided that has the major information contained from the manual in a tabular form. This form is intended to be used as a guideline when evaluating science curriculum materials for possible adoption or for revision. Although no specific criteria are presented, general suggestions are provided to guide both curriculum adoption committee members and publishers for use during the evaluation process. Information from the forms can then be beneficial for making more informed decisions regarding how well particular science curriculum materials address the needs of students with disabilities.

In order to provide additional information for teachers who may want to obtain specific adaptive materials suggested in this manual or who want to contact some of the professional organizations in special education or in science education, relevant extensive appendices have been added. Since addresses and phone numbers do frequently change, however, the accuracy of some of this information may need to be updated on a regular basis.

Part I

Characteristics of Disabilities and Implications for Mainstreaming in Science Classes

1

General Characteristics

What Are Common Characteristics of Students With Disabilities?

Students with disabilities include a wide variety of learner types. In fact, it may be said that students with disabilities constitute a population at least as divergent as the population of nondisabled students. Nevertheless, there are several areas of functioning which inhibit school success for a large number of students with disabilities, regardless of "category" of disability. These areas of functioning interact most specifically with classroom environments, and include the following:

1. **Language and Literacy**. Most students referred for special education services have some problem with language or basic literacy skills. Language deficits are particularly common in students with mental retardation, learning disabilities, and hearing impairments. However, they are also seen in many visually impaired or physically handicapped students who have had more limited experiences with which to develop language, or severely emotionally handicapped students whose emotional difficulties may have inhibited appropriate language development. Language cards, verbal elaboration, and other vocabulary-enhancing techniques (see also "Strategies for Improving Memory," in Part II) can be helpful with almost all groups of students. Likewise, most special education students have moderate to severe problems with basic literacy skills. "Mainstreaming Students with Reading Difficulties" in Part II, addresses these problems. Although exceptions certainly exist, language and literacy deficits are likely to exist in most mainstreamed handicapped students.

2. **Intellectual and Cognitive Development**. Deficits in these areas are characteristics of all students with mental retardation. However, milder intellectual or cognitive deficits are also observed in many students with learning disabilities,

emotional handicaps, and physical or sensory impairments. Organization and presentation strategies given in the section on learning disabilities can be helpful for these problems.

3. **Attention and Memory**. Problems with sustaining attention to task, or in remembering procedures, deadlines, or verbal information are characteristic of most disability areas, but may be particular problems with students characterized as learning disabled, mentally retarded, or emotionally handicapped. These problems can result in poor organizational skills. Strategies given in the relevant sections on attention and memory in Part II of this manual can be helpful.

4. **Affect and Social Behavior**. This is a particular problem for students with emotional handicaps; however, most students with disabilities have had at least some problems adjusting to society, and many have had a frustrating history of school failure. As a consequence, some students may exhibit low self-esteem, or negative affect toward the area of failure. Sometimes students have inappropriate attributions. These students view themselves as failures in school rather than attributing success and failure in school to effort and motivation. In some students, including some students with mental retardation, social interaction is developmentally immature. In addition, social acceptance of some individuals with disabilities is limited. "Strategies for Managing Classroom Behavior," and "Strategies for Improving Motivation and Affect," provide information for addressing these concerns.

5. **Physical or sensory functioning**. Students with physical or sensory impairments exhibit a great deal of difficulty in these areas. However, students with learning disabilities, mental retardation, or emotional handicaps often exhibit delays in gross motor or fine motor functioning. Physical clumsiness and lack of manual dexterity are often found in students from many disability areas. Strategies for addressing physical or sensory limitations are provided in the sections on physical disabilities, visual and hearing impairments in Part II, and in the specific science activities sections in Part III.

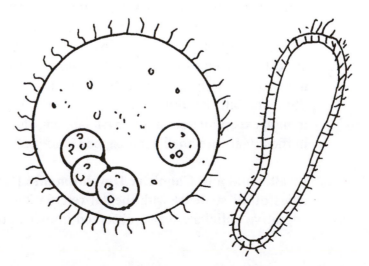

What Are the Implications for Mainstream Instruction?

In this manual, a variety of specific techniques are outlined and described for dealing with specific problems in the above mentioned five critical areas for school success. We describe some very general, overall recommendations that apply to any student mainstreamed into any regular classroom:

1. **Remember that, first and foremost, each student, disabled or nondisabled is an individual.** Specific techniques based on disability area, such as those listed in this manual, can be helpful, but they will not succeed if teachers do not consider the specific characteristics of the individual student. Remember, the student thinks of him or herself as an individual: "Bob," "Cindy," or "Ramon," and not "blind kid," "deaf kid," or "retarded kid." In most cases, they have long been used to having a particular characteristic that others see as a "handicap." To them, it is often only one of a variety of their personal characteristics. Parent conferences can help teachers get to know a student as an individual.

2. **With appropriate support, most students can succeed in at least some mainstream settings**. For others, the mainstream classroom may not prove to be the optimal instructional environment. However, before any specific decisions have been made, make sure you **give the student a good chance** to succeed in this new environment. Many students with disabilities may not learn in exactly the same way as other students; many may not learn as much. Some students, at first, may seem very different to you (and you may wonder why others were characterized as "disabled" at all). But, before you make a final decision regarding the suitability of mainstream placement, give yourself a chance to get to know the student, and become familiar with his or her idiosyncracies. Some problems may not seem so large once you get to know the student.

3. **Consult the special education teacher whenever possible**. The special education teacher probably has a wealth of information regarding the student's history, personal characteristics, and effective teaching strategies. Your job will be to find out how to best use this information in your own classroom. Most special education teachers openly welcome opportunities to discuss "their" students. Such collaboration can make the task of mainstreaming much easier. Arrange regular meetings on a weekly or biweekly basis. Often the special education teacher can help set behavioral expectations. Ask the special education teacher to observe the mainstreamed student in your room.

4. **Consider IEP objectives**. All students included in special education have an IEP, or Individualized Education Program. This IEP includes all important objectives to be mastered by the student (it does not typically include teaching or intervention strategies). At the end of the year, the student's progress is evaluated with respect to IEP objectives, so be certain your program for the student is serving these needs.

5. **Keep your expectations high**. Most special education students want to participate fully in all class activities; however, they may be shy or unsure of themselves and consequently allow others (including yourself) to do their work for them. In some cases it may seem easier for you or for classroom peers to simply do the task for the student. In order for the student with disabilities to develop optimally, however, you should avoid doing this as much as possible. Whenever you can, prompt the student to do the work, and reward **effort** and **perseverance**, two critical qualities for students with disabilities to develop. Don't give praise or reward that is not deserved. When you or classroom peers need to help, do so, but make sure the student has had some important role in the completion of the task.

6. **Do not single the student out more than necessary**. It is important to take a matter-of-fact approach to the student's disability. It is also important that all students in the class be aware of the student's disability and the steps being taken (by yourself and the class) to help the student compensate. It is also helpful to bring in the student's special experiences, whenever relevant. (For instance, electrical switches on assistive devices can be demonstrated during a unit on electricity.) However, the student should not be defined to the class as "disabled," and the disability should not be treated in such a way that serves to distance the student from the rest of the class. Students with disabilities should not be "taught" to expect special treatment, or that they need special treatment to succeed.

7. **Prepare your class for the student with disabilities.** Discuss the disability with students. Have a special educator present a disability awareness session. Explain that the disability is not a contagious condition.

8. **Use effective instructional techniques**. Although specific instructional techniques may be needed for specific disability areas, there are some general instructional guidelines that can help <u>all</u> students learn better. Some of these guidelines are given in the accompanying table.

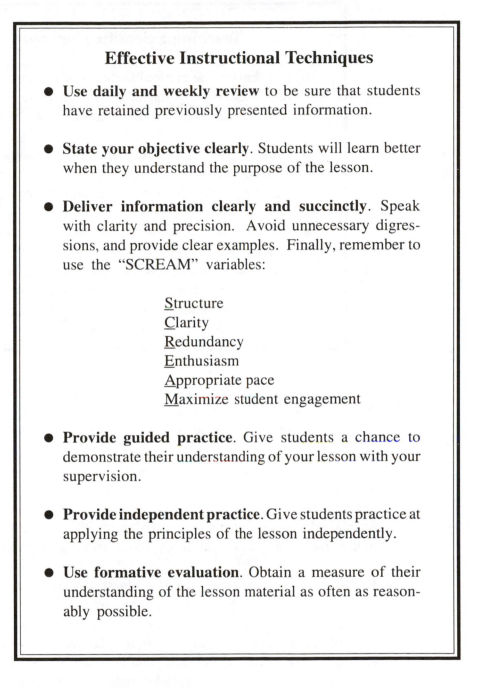

Effective Instructional Techniques

- **Use daily and weekly review** to be sure that students have retained previously presented information.

- **State your objective clearly**. Students will learn better when they understand the purpose of the lesson.

- **Deliver information clearly and succinctly**. Speak with clarity and precision. Avoid unnecessary digressions, and provide clear examples. Finally, remember to use the "SCREAM" variables:

  <u>S</u>tructure
  <u>C</u>larity
  <u>R</u>edundancy
  <u>E</u>nthusiasm
  <u>A</u>ppropriate pace
  <u>M</u>aximize student engagement

- **Provide guided practice**. Give students a chance to demonstrate their understanding of your lesson with your supervision.

- **Provide independent practice**. Give students practice at applying the principles of the lesson independently.

- **Use formative evaluation**. Obtain a measure of their understanding of the lesson material as often as reasonably possible.

Many students have difficulty learning new science concepts. When teaching new concepts, remember, in addition to the "effective teaching" guidelines, the recommendations in the accompanying table.

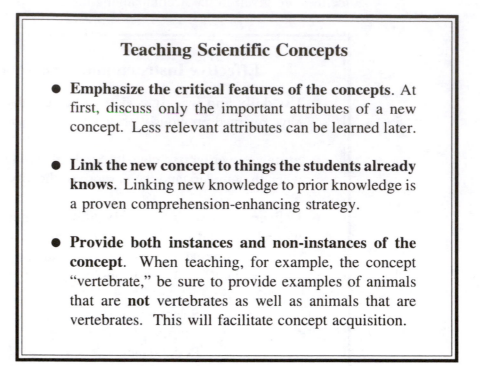

Teaching Scientific Concepts

- **Emphasize the critical features of the concepts**. At first, discuss only the important attributes of a new concept. Less relevant attributes can be learned later.

- **Link the new concept to things the students already knows**. Linking new knowledge to prior knowledge is a proven comprehension-enhancing strategy.

- **Provide both instances and non-instances of the concept**. When teaching, for example, the concept "vertebrate," be sure to provide examples of animals that are **not** vertebrates as well as animals that are vertebrates. This will facilitate concept acquisition.

9. **Prioritize objectives.** Many science activities and learning experiences are not necessary for the attainment of central instructional objectives. For example, many computer programs, individualized activities, or readings in science provide "enrichment" that may be useful for some students but not necessary for understanding the main concepts. Ask yourself, "Would this student be better off learning from these additional activities, or reviewing the central content?" Special education students generally benefit greatly from repeated presentations of lesson content. This redundancy may be more helpful than additional activities.

10. **Remember that diversity in the classroom is a positive experience for everyone**. Since we spend so much time in classrooms studying and discussing the enormous variety in cultures, customs, religions, and economics throughout the world, the fact of diversity within the classroom should be treated as a living example of individual differences and how we interact with them as a society. Overall, classrooms which include students with disabilities provide a richer environment than those that do not.

2

Learning Disabilities

What Is a Learning Disability?

The term "learning disabilities" (LD) refers to a cluster of **problems of learning** not caused by other handicapping conditions, or other factors such as cultural deprivation (although it has been argued that learning disabilities can co-exist with these other disability areas). It is therefore sometimes referred to as an "exclusionary" definition, because it describes what LD is by excluding alternative sources of learning failure. Nevertheless, the general presumption is that LD is often the result of some type of dysfunction of the central nervous system that allows normal functioning in general areas, but inhibits effective learning. Learning disabilities is generally considered an "umbrella" term for a variety of learning problems. It is the most common handicapping condition in schools. Other terms are given in the accompanying table.

Other Terms for Learning Disabilities:

- Educational Handicaps
- Minimal Brain Dysfunction (MBD)
- Minimal Brain Injury
- Perceptual Handicaps,
- Dyslexia (reading disability)
- Dyscalculia (mathematics disability)
- Word Blindness or Strephosymbolia
- Sometimes thought to include:
- Attention Deficit Disorder (ADD), with or without hyperactivity.

In schools, students with learning disabilities are often **identified** by referral from the classroom teacher, and confirmation by the school psychologist and other members of the multidisciplinary team (the teachers and staff who work with the student). The student with learning disabilities exhibits serious academic learning problems in the face of normal intelligence, emotional stability, adequate sensory and physical ability, and reasonable previous opportunities to learn. Learning disabilities are often supported by the computation of a **discrepancy**, or mismatch, between academic achievement and general intelligence. That is, if a student has a standard score IQ of 100 (indicating 50th percentile in intelligence) and a standard score reading achievement of 70 (indicating 2nd percentile in reading), **and** no obvious alternative explanation can be found, the student may be characterized as "learning disabled," and provided with special education services. Although the extent of the discrepancy varies from state to state, most states mandate a discrepancy in the range of 15-20 standard score points.

Although estimates vary, students with LD comprise about **5% of the student population**, or about 1-2 students in every "regular" classroom. Most students with LD are boys.

What Are the Characteristics of Students With Learning Disabilities?

Students with learning disabilities are the students most likely to be "mainstreamed" in science classes, therefore most regular education teachers are likely to be familiar with at least some of the general characteristics of these students.

All students with LD exhibit some serious **academic problems**. These problems are generally thought to lie in the area of reading, but problems in math and language arts are common. Difficulties with spelling are very common among students with LD. It can be generally stated that most students are struggling to learn the basic skills, and are less able to use these skills to help them learn. In other words, most students with LD are "learning to read," not "reading to learn." They may frequently miss assignment completion dates, or turn in messy or sloppy papers, or fail to follow assignment directions.

Many (but not all) students with LD also have difficulty **sustaining attention**. Attention problems are thought to be at the heart of **hyperactivity** disorders, which are also found among populations of students with LD. Such students have difficulty staying quietly seated and academically focused during instruction.

In perhaps even greater numbers, students with LD exhibit problems with **memory**. Students with LD may have great difficulty remembering new vocabulary or terminology, important factual information, or directions presented in sequence. In some cases, memory problems may occur because reading disorders prevent studying or reviewing new information. It may also be that semantic memory problems are the cause of some reading problems.

Many students with LD have difficulty with **organizational skills**.

Many students with LD have difficulties making **generalizations** and **applying** previously learned information to new situations.

Finally, a subgroup of students with LD may exhibit problems with **social behavior**. These problems may be the result of an inability to read social cues, the result of problems brought on because of hyperactive or impulsive behavior, or inappropriate social behaviors which result from feelings of personal inadequacy which have arisen from school failure, or difficulties with problem-solving and generating effective alternative solutions.

Students with LD may get along well with other students on the playground or after school, but may appear frustrated and unhappy in your class. Whether the student admits it or not (or even cooperates particularly well), the student would very much like to improve his or her school functioning to the point where it is more like that of other students. With the right kind of attention and effort (including his or her own), this goal often can be achieved.

What Are Mainstreaming Techniques?

How Should the Classroom Be Organized?

Probably the greatest threat to successful mainstreaming of LD students in science classes is a **reading disability**. The more your class is based on independent reading and studying of science textbooks, and independent completion of end-of-chapter exercises, the more difficult it will be for students with LD to succeed independently. If your class is oriented this way, it may be helpful to tape-record the textbook (or have students help you tape record it), so that students with reading problems can listen to the tape of the text, or listen as they read along. Perhaps a peer or the resource teacher can help the student write down the answers of chapter questions or workbook assignments as the student dictates to others or on tape. For additional information on this subject, see "Strategies for Mainstreaming Students with Reading Difficulties," in Part II of this manual.

If students with LD exhibit problems sustaining **attention**, or have persistent memory problems, or exhibit behavior problems during seatwork activities, you may wish to consider some of the strategies described in the "Attention", "Memory", or "Behavior Management" sections in Part II of this manual.

The more you **include class discussion, group projects, demonstrations, activities, and audio-visual presentations**, the easier it will be for students with LD to succeed. You might also find (as research has found) that all students enjoy science more, and learn more, when it is more activity-oriented and less textbook-oriented. Group-oriented learning activities such as cooperative learning and peer tutoring are described in Part II of this manual. Although these approaches to science education are likely to improve learning, the lessened structure of some of these activities may result in some **behavior problems**. Some strategies for dealing with such problems are also given in the "Strategies for Managing Classroom Behavior" section in Part II of this manual.

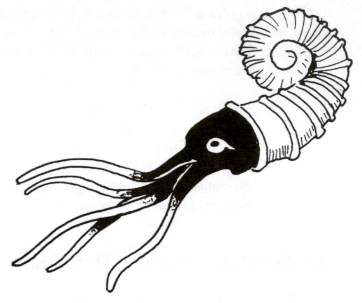

What Are Teacher Presentation Ideas?

When you speak to the class, be sure to **speak clearly and directly**, and be sure that mainstreamed students with LD have understood you. **Redundancy** in emphasizing concepts or providing directions can be very helpful for students with LD or for your class in general. It also may be helpful to provide information to students in both written and oral form. Provide outlines of lectures or of content to be mastered. Use **pictures** whenever possible. **List** important information. Keep the blackboard or overhead projector well **organized**, and erase irrelevant marks. Speak in an enthusiastic, motivating and engaging style. When presenting important information, simultaneously teach students elaborative strategies that help them learn how to remember key concepts. Finally, provide many opportunities for students to practice learned information in new situations. Such generalization and application activities help reinforce learning.

List and repeat any new **vocabulary**, **terminology**, or other **verbal labels** that may not be immediately familiar to students. Assimilation of new, key vocabulary is very important for understanding of lesson content, so you should try to make sure that these words have been learned. Provide sufficient opportunities for practice. Review, restate, and question key concepts periodically. Language cards may be helpful in reinforcing acquisition of new vocabulary. Provide opportunities for the student to answer questions during class. For strategies to improve memory for vocabulary or factual information, refer to the "Strategies for Improving Memory" section in Part II of this manual.

Testing Students With Learning Disabilities

When you give **tests**, you may wish to create a special format for students with reading disabilities. This can take the form of **individual oral questioning** of the student by the teacher or another student who has already completed the test, who then records the student's responses. A tape-recorded copy of the test, to which the student records answers on tape, could also be used. Often, questions may need to be reworded for clearer understanding. Involve the special education teacher in designing the best methods for testing.

Other recommendations for testing include use of **charts or drawings** instead of written responses, providing **partial credit** for partially correct answers, allowing close approximations in **spelling**, and allowing **extra time**. If you believe knowledge of the content is most important, it may be possible to make these modifications. If you feel that standard writing, spelling, etc. are also essential to grade, consider grading these mechanical aspects **separately** from the content.

Performance-based tests, which require active manipulation of scientific phenomena, such as completing electrical circuits or testing for the presence of calcite in a rock, require less reading and writing of all students. More information on performance-based tests, and other types of testing is given in the "Testing" section in Part II of this manual.

Many students with learning disabilities have poor **test-taking skills**. Test-taking skills include such things as allowing appropriate time for certain items, considering all alternative answers, and marking answers carefully. Students with LD can benefit from training in these skills, as described in Part II of this manual.

Mainstreaming Suggestions

Classroom Organization

- De-emphasize reading, and use strategies for non-readers.

- Monitor attention and behavior.

- Include class discussions, group projects, and multi-media presentations.

- Use behavior management strategies.

Teacher Presentation

- Speak clearly and directly, and repeat important points.

- Provide outlines of lectures.

- Enhance vocabulary and terminology.

- Use pictures whenever possible.

- Use well-organized blackboard or projection screen.

- Use elaborative strategies during presentations.

- Teach "generalization" and "application" objectives.

Testing

- Provide individual oral testing.

- Tape record responses.

- Allow charts or drawings, give partial credit, allow spelling, grammatical errors.

- Allow extra time.

- Use performance-based tests.

- Promote test-taking skills.

What are Some Laboratory Techniques?

Whenever possible, break larger tasks into **smaller steps**. Make sure students understand what they are to do (have them repeat directions) before they undertake a laboratory activity. List steps on the board, and picture the steps if possible, for students to refer to throughout the activity. **Self-monitoring sheets** (see Study Skills section in Part II) may be helpful for students to execute procedures systematically.

When possible, break activities into discrete 15-20 minute **segments**. Have alternative or additional activities available for students who may finish sooner than others, or for whom the task proves inappropriate. Pair the student with another with good motor skills or reading ability when needed.

Hands-on materials will increase motivation, interest and attention to task. Since many students with LD are **impulsive**, however, expect them to manipulate and explore materials as soon as they are received. **Do not pass out materials** until (a) it is time for students to use them, (b) students are very familiar with the expectations and rules associated with their use, and (c) students display understanding of the activity to be undertaken. Build in some structured **opportunity for movement** for highly active or impulsive students. Assign students the job of equipment getter.

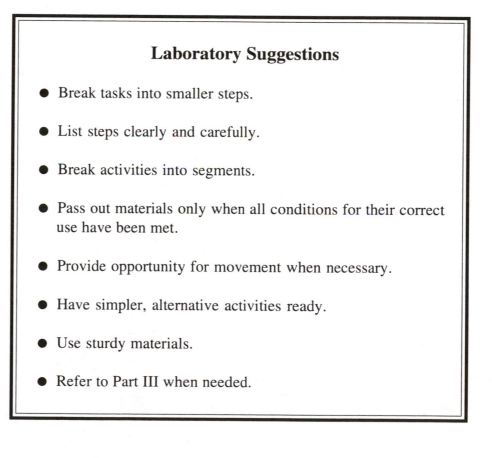

Laboratory Suggestions

- Break tasks into smaller steps.

- List steps clearly and carefully.

- Break activities into segments.

- Pass out materials only when all conditions for their correct use have been met.

- Provide opportunity for movement when necessary.

- Have simpler, alternative activities ready.

- Use sturdy materials.

- Refer to Part III when needed.

Whenever possible, use materials and apparatus that are **sturdy** and less likely to break. Some of these materials are described in Part III of this manual. Be very careful with potentially dangerous materials such as glass, mirrors, nails, etc.

Some specific laboratory activities used in science classes have specific implications for students with learning disabilities. Before undertaking these activities, refer to the appropriate section in Part III of this manual for possible suggestions.

3

Communication Disorders

What Are Communication Disorders?

The category "communication disorders" covers a variety of disability areas, all having to do with problems in interpersonal communication. As many as 10% of the general population have some problem with communication, and approximately 25% of all students identified for special education are characterized as having communication disorders. Further, many students from other categories of exceptionality (e.g., mental retardation, learning disabilities, hearing impairments) receive services in the area of speech and language.

According to the American Speech-Language-Hearing Association (ASHA), communication disorders include both **speech disorders** and **language disorders**.

What Are the Characteristics of Students With Communication Disorders?

Speech disorders include disorders of **voice**, **articulation**, and **fluency**. More than one of these disorders can occur together in one individual. The specific causes of most speech disorders are unknown. Different types of speech disorders and their causes are shown in the accompanying table.

Two factors contributing to speech disorders are **cleft palate** and **neurological damage**. Cleft palate can almost always be corrected by surgery, usually soon after birth. Speech disorders due to brain injury (e.g., **dysarthria** or **apraxia**) can be caused by oxygen deprivation, physical injury, disease, or stroke. **Cerebral palsy** (see Physical Disabilities/Other Health Impairments) is often associated with dysarthria and apraxia.

Types of Speech Disorders

- **Voice disorders** affect the pitch, volume, or quality of speech. Voice problems affect about 6% of the school population, and occur more frequently in younger children, and students with other handicapping conditions.

- **Articulation** disorders involve errors in pronouncing individual words, and include such problems as lisping, or omissions or additions of word sounds. Articulation disorders characterize about 75% of the children characterized as having communication disorders.

- **Fluency disorders** involve interruptions of the normal flow of speech. The most common type of fluency disorder is stuttering, which occurs in about one percent of the general population, more often in boys. Many children "outgrow" their disfluencies, but some do not. The specific cause of stuttering is unknown.

Language Disorders

Over half of the students seen by speech-language pathologists have some type of language disorder. Language disorders are viewed as potentially more damaging than speech disorders because they are central to communication. Disorders of language are classified into five forms: **phonology** (sounds), **morphology** (the forms of words), **syntax** (word order and sentence structure), **semantics** (the meanings of words and sentences), and **pragmatics** (the social use of language).

Additional language disorders include **elective mutism**, in which the student, for emotional reasons, may refuse to speak in school, **echolalia**, where the student simply repeats the words he or she previously heard spoken, and the nonverbal student. Some students may be unable to speak, but can communicate with the use of speech synthesizers, picture communication boards, and personal computers.

What Are Mainstreaming Techniques?

The vast majority of students characterized as having communication disorders receive most of their instruction in the regular classroom, and receive support services from the **speech-language** teacher. Like the special education teacher, the speech-language teacher can provide you with information regarding the best way of interacting with specific students with communication disorders. In addition, some overall guidelines can be given:

Be **patient and attentive** when the student wishes to speak, and do not attempt to "finish" the statement for the student. Advise all students in your class of the nature of the disorder, and appropriate ways of encouraging good communication. If the student speaks incorrectly, and correction at this point in the student's development is appropriate, simply restate the phrase or sentence correctly, rather than correct the student. For instance, if the student says, *"Weptiles are cold-blooded,"* you could reply, *"That's correct, reptiles are cold-blooded."*

In situations in which you simply wish to monitor understanding, in which time is a factor, or in which you particularly wish to build confidence in the student, **phrase the question so that only a brief response is required**. For example, instead of asking, *"What can you tell me about photosynthesis?"*, try, *"A plant uses a process called photosynthesis to produce....what?"*

If students have difficulty with syntax and semantics and they are required to complete large amounts of written work, they may experience difficulties. Provide assistance with writing either as a specific study strategy or in collaboration with a Resource Teacher.

Mainstreaming Suggestions

- Be patient and attentive.

- Provide appropriate feedback.

- Phrase questions for brief responses.

- Provide special assistance for oral and written reports.

- Use vocabulary-enhancing strategies when needed.

- Provide adaptive communication devices.

If students are expected to make science reports in front of the class, check with the speech-language teacher or the student in question regarding the best way to proceed. If the communication disorder is very serious, perhaps the student could communicate the report to a **classroom peer** (see Part II), who could give the report for the student. Perhaps the student could also use the **overhead projector** for outlines or other visual aides that reduce the amount of speaking necessary for the report to be understood.

If the student's language problems extend to difficulties with vocabulary learning, use **language cards**, **vocabulary lists**, or **mnemonic strategies**, of the type described in Part II.

If students are totally **nonverbal**, special **adaptive communication devices** can be provided to allow the student to communicate. Some students who are unable to speak are capable of comprehending the complete lesson. Teachers can check for understanding by allowing students to respond with the use of speech synthesizers, picture boards, and personal computers.

Testing Students With Communication Disorders

For recommended testing procedures, refer to Chapter 13, "Evaluation."

What Are Laboratory Techniques?

Students with communication disorders, if they do not also exhibit other learning problems, may find their greatest problem lies in communicating with other students in small group work. Be certain that other group members are appropriately **sensitized** to the specific communication problem in question and how to best ensure the student's participation. Again, the special education teacher may be helpful and present relevant information to all students.

Some group activities require specific students to lead the group by reading directions and outlining procedures to be followed in the activity. In some cases, you may find it best not to select the particular student with communication disorders to assume this role. In others, it may be particularly helpful for the student to assume a position of leadership and practice effective communication skills. However, be certain that in such cases, the other group members do not feel that they may be penalized in their grade for having a group leader with a communication problem. Rather, they should be encouraged to feel very positively that they are learning science, learning important interpersonal skills, and helping a student overcome a particular problem. More information on group or cooperative learning techniques is in Part II of this manual.

Laboratory Suggestions

- Sensitize group members.

- Choose appropriate group roles.

- Use adaptive communication devices.

4

Mental Retardation

What Is Mental Retardation?

Students with mental retardation (MR) make up about **2%** of the general population, and constitute about **15%** of the special education population. Students who are suspected of having mental retardation are given **intelligence tests** and tests of **"adaptive behavior"** -- that is, tests of everyday living skills -- in addition to standardized achievement tests. The most commonly used definition of mental retardation is that of the American Association on Mental Retardation (AAMR): "Mental retardation refers to significantly subaverage intellectual functioning resulting in or associated with impairments in adaptive behavior and manifested during the developmental period." "Significantly subaverage" usually means an IQ score lower than 70 (about the 2nd percentile), although scores as high as 75 may be considered in some cases. Tests such as the AAMR Adaptive Behavior Scale or the Adaptive Behavior Inventory for Children are frequently used to assess adaptive behavior.

Mental Retardation Components

- "Significantly subaverage" intellectual functioning (that is, IQ less than 70).

- Impairments in adaptive behavior.

Mental retardation is also referred to as **mental deficiency**, **mental disability**, **mental handicaps**, and **intellectual impairment**.

Most students with mental retardation who are mainstreamed into regular classes are characterized as **mildly retarded**. This usually means that the intelligence test scores are between 50-55 and about 70. These students are often capable of acquiring academic skills up to about the sixth grade level, during their school years.

Students who score lower than 50 on intelligence tests are characterized as **moderately**, **severely**, or **profoundly retarded**. Students with moderate mental retardation usually can learn some relevant information about science, but it may be very difficult for them to learn at the pace and level of complexity found in the age-equivalent regular classroom. The regular classroom may not be the most appropriate environment for students with severe or profound mental retardation to learn science, although in some cases such mainstreaming may serve a socialization objective, and be used to broaden the experiences of nonhandicapped students, and their understanding of disability.

Levels of Mental Retardation

1. Mild (IQ 50-55 to 70-75); can be very capable of academic achievement.

2. Moderate (IQ 35-40 to 50-55); can learn some relevant science information, but may have difficulty with pace and level of regular classroom instruction.

3. Severe-profound (IQ below 35-40); will have great difficulty with typical classroom instruction.

Although many specific syndromes have been identified that cause mental retardation, most causes of mental retardation are unknown.

What Are the Characteristics of Students With Mental Retardation?

Students with **mild mental retardation** may be very similar in appearance to other students in the regular classroom, although in some cases they may be more careless in dress and general appearance. They typically have less well-developed **language and communication skills** than their peers, and have difficulty **understanding complex concepts**. Their **academic skills** will almost certainly be well below average, and they will probably exhibit **memory deficits**. Students with MR often become good at decoding words, but often experience great difficulties in comprehending the written material.

A particular problem with most students with mental retardation is in the ability to **generalize** what they have learned to other situations.

Many students with mild mental retardation are very eager to please teachers and classmates; however, **social immaturity** may cause them to go about seeking approval in inappropriate ways. Because of this, they may have more difficulty making and sustaining friendships than, for example, students with learning disabilities. In addition, students with mild mental retardation may have difficulty in **sustaining attention**, and exhibiting **persistence of effort**, especially on difficult tasks.

In some cases, **motor coordination** is delayed, and students may need some assistance on tasks requiring manipulation of laboratory apparatus.

Most students with mild mental retardation are very much aware that they are "different" from other students, and they frequently feel **frustrated** that they have so much difficulty with things that seem to come so easily to others.

Nevertheless, students with mild mental retardation, with appropriate educational support, can be very successful in science class, and find it an exciting and rewarding experience.

What Are Mainstreaming Techniques?

Teaching Students With Mental Retardation

When **presenting new information**, speak clearly and directly, and check for comprehension. Students with MR will probably have difficulty acquiring new concepts the first time they experience them. They usually benefit from repeated presentations, direct explanations, and frequent review. Always be as **concrete** as possible when providing new information. Show **pictures** or **illustrations**, or bring in real **examples** of the things or concepts being studied whenever possible. Relate any new information to **familiar** information from the students' own personal experience.

Students with MR will also generally perform better when time for completion of assignments or activities is not fixed, and they are allowed **additional time**, perhaps with the assistance of a peer, to absorb important concepts. Repeated exposures to the new information will facilitate learning.

Students with mental retardation will have difficulty **generalizing** or transferring their newly-acquired science knowledge to general knowledge of the world outside the classroom, unless you make this information very explicit. For instance, you should underline the relevance of information about levers or the pendulum by demonstrating the principles on familiar objects, such as playground see-saws and swings. Question students and provide feedback to ensure they understand the general meaning of the concepts being taught, not just the classroom application.

Emphasize only the **most important concepts**, and review them frequently. Avoid introducing a number of different concepts in one lesson. Maintain a record of key concepts in lists or language cards, using pictures whenever possible, for student review. **Mnemonic techniques**, if appropriately structured, can be very helpful in facilitating memory for basic facts and concepts (See "Strategies for Improving Memory," in Part II of this manual).

If reading is required, you may wish to **tape-record**, in simple, direct language, the most important points in the text. Be sure the student is familiar with tape recorders and how to use them. It may also be helpful to direct the listener to pictures in the text, to provide focus for listening. See also the "Mainstreaming Students with Reading Difficulties" section in Part II.

It may also be helpful to develop instructional packages for parents, to inform them of the content and provide materials for home studying.

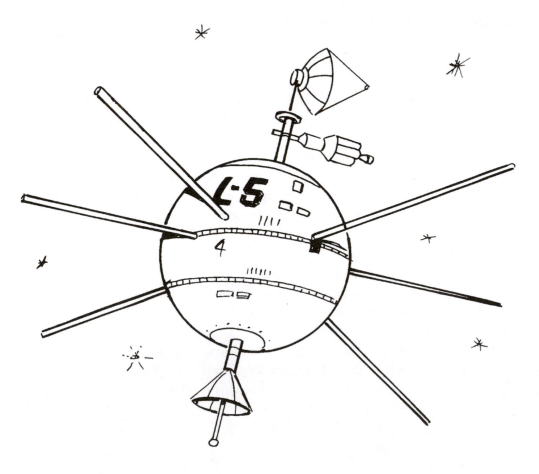

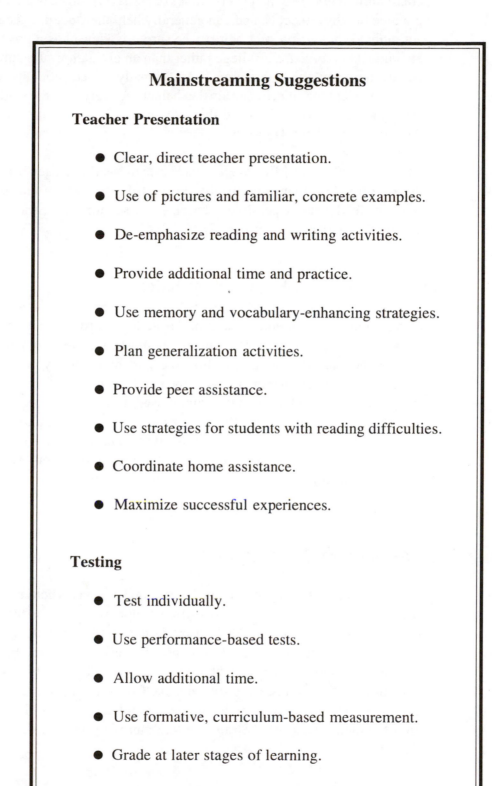

Mainstreaming Suggestions

Teacher Presentation

- Clear, direct teacher presentation.

- Use of pictures and familiar, concrete examples.

- De-emphasize reading and writing activities.

- Provide additional time and practice.

- Use memory and vocabulary-enhancing strategies.

- Plan generalization activities.

- Provide peer assistance.

- Use strategies for students with reading difficulties.

- Coordinate home assistance.

- Maximize successful experiences.

Testing

- Test individually.

- Use performance-based tests.

- Allow additional time.

- Use formative, curriculum-based measurement.

- Grade at later stages of learning.

Students with mental retardation will almost always benefit from **assistance from classroom peers**. Peer helpers (buddies or assisters) can be used to provide necessary practice on key concepts, and can generally help the student execute various science activities. When using peer helpers, be sure it is viewed as a positive experience for all students involved, a privilege rather than an obligation. Be sure the helper is also benefiting from the interaction. Additionally, since students with MR may be overdependent for help, be certain that helpers actively help the student with MR learn. For more information, turn to the sections on "Cooperative Learning" and "Peer Assistance and Peer Tutoring" in Part II.

Many students with MR have low self-esteem, and may get frustrated and give up easily. Provide as many **potentially successful experiences**, and as much appropriate positive feedback as possible. See also the section on "Strategies for Improving Motivation and Affect" in Part II.

Testing Students With Mental Retardation

Use formative evaluation to monitor the students' progress and determine as soon as possible when learning is not occurring. In most cases, **testing** will be more profitable when conducted individually. Allow the student to show you what he or she knows about the content, rather than relying too much on verbal or written descriptions of the information (individual **performance-based testing** may be very helpful). Design one or two essay questions that cover the main concepts and then record dictated answers or drawings. Students with MR will do best if they are tested at **later**, rather than earlier, stages of learning, and are allowed sufficient **time** for responding. Additional information on testing techniques is provided in the "Evaluation" section in Part II.

What Are Laboratory Techniques?

Students with MR will generally be able to cope with tasks better when they are broken into **smaller steps** and provided sufficient opportunities for practice. Provide very clear and explicit directions, demonstrate steps and ask the student to repeat directions prior to activity. Even if students have peer helpers, they should be aware of the nature of the task, and share responsibility for its completion. If possible, give written directions with pictures. Give students a **self-monitoring** sheet, so they can check off each step in the activity when it has been completed, and monitor completion of each step for themselves (see "Strategies for Improving Note-Taking, Study Skills, and Test-Taking Skills," Part II).

Provide students with MR instruction in the pre-skills necessary for succeeding at laboratory tasks. For example, if graphing data is a necessary skill, then provide ample opportunities for students to practice graphing skills <u>prior</u> to the laboratory activity.

Provide students with MR opportunities to learn the appropriate social interaction skills necessary for collaborating on science activities. Specific skills such as asking for assistance and sharing materials may need initial instruction, modeling, and practice.

It will generally be helpful to utilize the assistance of appropriately trained **classroom peers** in the execution of laboratory tasks (see "Peer Assistance and Peer Tutoring," Part II).

For individual observation activities, it may be helpful to **tell students what to look for**, and how to recognize it when they see it. For example, before having students examine onion cells through a microscope, show them a picture, or provide them with a good description of what the cell will look like, so that they will know what to observe. They may lack a well-developed sense of what to look for, and waste time, for example, studying dust particles or water drops, rather than onion cells.

Some open-ended "discovery" methods, often recommended by science educators, may place inappropriately high demands on the prior knowledge and insight of students with mental retardation (see the "Invention and Discovery Activities" section in Part III of this manual). As a result, some students may respond very negatively to such approaches, and learn little or nothing from the exercise. On the other hand, complete reliance on "direct instruction" approaches, often recommended by special educators, may inhibit development of thinking skills by emphasizing only rote responses. A suitable compromise for students with MR is to question and prompt students to "discover" the key concept in a highly systematic, structured fashion. For instance, in the "Black Boxes" lesson (FOSS), students are given small black rectangular plastic containers in which a loose marble and maze-like patterns have been placed inside and asked to "discover" what is inside the boxes. While many students may be able to independently approach this task with such minimal guidelines, students with MR may benefit from structured questioning, as shown in the table below.

Structured Questioning

1. *"Can you slowly roll the marble along each side of the box?"*
2. *"What does the marble hit?"*
3. *"Does the marble hit each corner?"*
4. *"Does the marble hit something in the corner?"*
5. *"What shape is the thing the marble hit?"*

Teachers can proceed with such coaching techniques and questioning until the necessary generalizations can be made. The important component is that one open-ended question is subdivided into several simpler questions directed toward the same final goal.

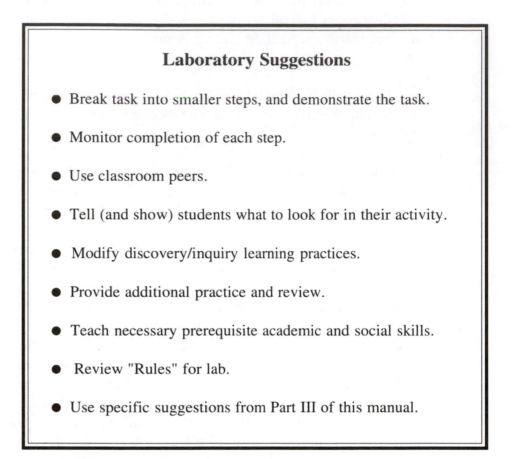

Laboratory Suggestions

- Break task into smaller steps, and demonstrate the task.

- Monitor completion of each step.

- Use classroom peers.

- Tell (and show) students what to look for in their activity.

- Modify discovery/inquiry learning practices.

- Provide additional practice and review.

- Teach necessary prerequisite academic and social skills.

- Review "Rules" for lab.

- Use specific suggestions from Part III of this manual.

Whenever possible, it would be helpful to provide students with MR **additional practice** or review at the end of the laboratory activity, followed by a summary of the important concepts. Employ the use of a peer tutor to assist with practice activities.

Students with **moderate, severe or profound** mental retardation may present particular problems with science education in regular classes, and individual student needs may vary widely. If students from these categories are intended to be mainstreamed in science classes, first determine the specific purposes of mainstreaming, and the specific objectives for the student. Consult carefully with the special education teacher, school psychologist, and school nurse for special techniques for meeting these objectives. This information is on students' IEPs. It may be necessary for some of these personnel to be present in the classroom during mainstreaming.

Some specific laboratory activities used in science classes have specific implications for students with mental retardation. Before undertaking these activities, refer to the appropriate section in Part III of this manual for possible suggestions.

5

Emotional Disturbance

What Is Emotional Disturbance?

Emotional disturbance (ED), as other disability areas, resists easy and precise definition, and is in reality an umbrella term for a group of disorders of social-emotional functioning. The federal government defined emotional disturbance as one or more social-emotional characteristics which are exhibited over an extended period of time and adversely affect school performance, including: (a) problems with learning or interpersonal relationships, (b) exhibiting inappropriate behavior under normal circumstances, (c) disorders of affect such as depression or pervasive unhappiness, or (d) exhibiting fears or physical symptoms in response to school or personal problems.

ED, according to the federal definition, is not intended to include "**social maladjustment**" unless it is accompanied by emotional disturbance (this issue is presently being debated). The federal definition does not now include (although it once did) students characterized as "autistic," but does still include students characterized as "schizophrenic."

Emotional Disturbance Defined

● A cluster of possible social-emotional characteristics.

● Exhibited over time, adversely affecting school performance.

● May include problems with affect as well as interpersonal relations.

● Not intended to include social maladjustment.

Government officials have estimated that about **2%** of the school-aged population are affected by ED, but other professionals feel the actual number is between 6 and 10 percent. Recent data indicate that only about **1%** of the students with these disorders are identified for special education services, so you may find some students in your classes with social or emotional problems who are not receiving special services. Additionally, many students with other types of disabilities suffer some emotional distress as a consequence of coping with that disability.

What Are Characteristics of Students With Emotional Disturbance?

Students with ED are among the least popular students with teachers. Most commonly, students with emotional disturbance exhibit acting out, **aggressive** actions toward their peers or their teachers. Students with these conduct disorders may display little or no obvious remorse for actions which may be hurtful toward others. (They may also be hurtful to themselves.) Often this behavior does not appear to be changed by discipline or consequences and students may appear to be noncompliant most of the time. Most (about 5 to 1) of the students with ED are boys. They may display affect inappropriate to the situation, such as anger or pleasure at inappropriate times. These students are usually not well liked by people they regularly come into contact with, and they often bring with them a history of criticism and punishment from others.

Another group of students with ED is characterized by **withdrawal**. They may be overly fearful of interactions or situations which appear nonthreatening to others. They may have a great deal of difficulty developing positive relationships with others. They may feel psychosomatic illnesses (illnesses with no obvious physical cause), or develop "real" illnesses as a result of personal stress. They may daydream and fantasize excessively and have severe anxieties. Students with ED may be prone to suicide.

The condition of emotional disturbance elicits less sympathy from other people than other disability categories do, partly because these students are often negative and aggressive toward others, and partly because others are less likely to believe the disability is beyond the individual's control (compared with, e.g., visual impairment). People often feel the student would do much better if he or she really tried to "get his (or her) act together," or "get on the ball." People often believe strict discipline alone will solve the problems, not realizing that many of these students have been punished continuously throughout their lives.

Emotional disturbance typically inhibits progress in basic academic areas, and as a consequence, many students with ED exhibit **academic deficiencies**, often as serious as students with learning disabilities, in such areas as reading, writing, spelling and mathematics. ED also inhibits learning from a variety of new situations, and can result in an **impoverished knowledge base**. New learning can be inhibited by lack of previous meaningful experience and the numerous mental distractions imposed by the nature of the disorder.

Students with ED may exhibit **difficulty interacting appropriately** with teachers and other students, avoiding eye contact, or not responding to social initiations. Also, irrational fears or fantasies may distract the student and inhibit learning. Fears can include fear of failure, fear of group interaction, or fear of adults. Depression or persistent negative affect may inhibit motivation or desire to succeed, encourage school phobia, and psychosomatic physical problems, such as stomach aches, head-aches, or fainting spells.

What Are Mainstreaming Techniques?

The most important strategy for mainstreaming a student with ED is to **create a positive, supportive classroom environment**. Most students with ED have a history of failed, unpleasant, negative relationships with others. They will probably expect the same from you. If the student gets the message that you (and the rest of the class) support the student and really want him or her to succeed, you will have a much greater chance of success.

Nevertheless, **inappropriate behavior** should not be tolerated, and information in Part II of this manual, "Strategies for Managing Classroom Behavior," will describe some strategies for dealing with behavior problems. The student must learn (most likely, through experience) that **classroom rules** are systematic, predictable, and consistent. It is the choice of the student, not the teacher, whether the student will enjoy class and gain rewards. The teacher (and other students) are there to help the student with ED make good choices.

Other ways of creating a positive and supportive classroom environment for the student with ED is to try to **ensure some success** on a relevant school activity each day.

Try, especially at first, to call on the student whenever he or she volunteers appropriate responses. As the student develops a history of successful interaction and successful task completion, he or she will feel more positive, more confident, and more a part of the classroom enviroment.

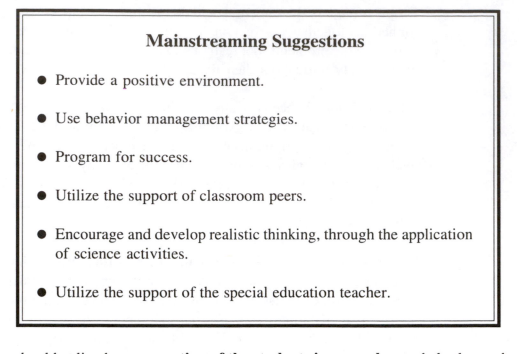

Mainstreaming Suggestions

- Provide a positive environment.

- Use behavior management strategies.

- Program for success.

- Utilize the support of classroom peers.

- Encourage and develop realistic thinking, through the application of science activities.

- Utilize the support of the special education teacher.

You should enlist the **cooperation of the students in your class** to help the student with ED. These students should be made aware that the mainstreamed student has a problem, and that the mainstreamed student needs their help in dealing with it, whether or not he or she appears to seek such help. Under no circumstances should class members laugh at, provoke or otherwise encourage inappropriate behaviors on the part of the student with ED. They should be positive and helpful whenever possible, and ignore negative behaviors whenever they can. More information on the effective use of classroom peers in behavior management is in Part II.

Science is a potentially beneficial subject for many students with ED. Science can demonstrate to students prone to fantasy or irrational fear the regularities and cause-and-effect nature of the universe, can provide structure to their school day, can motivate and interest through the nature of the subject matter (micro-organisms, animals, machines), and can provide opportunities for success. Further, manipulation of scientific phenomena and apparatus can empower the student, who rarely feels in control of the classroom environment.

Special education teachers can be used as resource personnel in facilitating mainstreaming of students with ED. They can provide information on how to foster successful peer interactions during science activities. Additionally, they may help with coordinating behavioral contracts or level systems with ED students (see behavior management section for details).

Testing Students With Emotional Disturbance

For recommended testing procedures, refer to chapter 13, "Evaluation."

What Are Laboratory Techniques?

Science experiments and other activities are usually very rewarding for students, and it is very likely that they will be enjoyable to students with ED. Make sure that the student is aware that his or her continued participation in the activities is **directly contingent** upon the display of appropriate behavior during these activities (make sure you are very clear about your expectations). When behavior becomes inappropriate, the student should be immediately removed from the activity, and given a less rewarding task (e.g., written seatwork). Make sure the task is perceived to be less rewarding by the student, not just yourself: if the task is perceived by the student as more rewarding, the student may act out deliberately in order to be placed in this activity.

Although the student with ED needs to work on self-control and appropriate behavior, it is nonetheless prudent to structure classroom activities in order to avoid unnecessary opportunity for conflict. If the student does not seem presently able to work in a group situation, try assigning the student to a **"group" of one**. (You may also consider assigning other students to their own group, so the student with ED does not feel singled out).

Be cautious with materials or apparatus that may be harmful to self or others. Ensure that students have demonstrated the ability to handle such apparatus appropriately.

If you do assign the student to group work, try to include others in the group who are likely to work well with this student. Try to identify which students the student with ED likes most and works most cooperatively with. It may be helpful to assign a "buddy" to the student to model appropriate behavior and help in other ways, such as presenting reports to the class. If the particular student exhibits withdrawn behavior, try to find peers whom the student likes, and who will encourage his participation, yet still be sensitive to his needs. In group activities, be particularly attentive to situations which require sharing, taking turns, or handling objects. Sometimes ED students have been successfully paired with students with visual impairments or students with physical disabilities.

Laboratory Suggestions

- Make desired activities directly contingent upon appropriate behavior.

- Carefully select group partners, or make student a "group" of one.

- Avoid use of potentially dangerous apparatus or materials, unless supervised.

- Consider using the student as a tutor.

- Be aware of specific fears, overt or covert, the student might have.

- Prepare alternate activities.

- Post "lab rules" and review at beginning of class.

- Prepare an activity checklist.

- Refer to Part III for specific activities.

In some cases, it may be helpful to assign the student with ED to be a peer assistant or tutor of some other student, perhaps another special education student with a different type of disability. If the relationship works well, it could enhance the role of the student with ED, and improve his or her attitude toward the class.

Remember that many students with ED exhibit aggressive behavior to cover or cope with inner fears they may have. Try to plan activities which are unlikely to elicit a fearful response. Be aware of any **specific fears** the student might have (e.g., dirty or wet hands, water, adults, dark). You can learn about these through conversations with the special education teacher or the student's parents. The student him or herself will rarely volunteer specific fears; but be sensitive to any subtle request to avoid a particular activity.

Have alternative activities ready. Some students with ED may choose to express opposition, or otherwise divorce themselves from the planned activity. In some cases, this is because of an unrealistic desire to "control" the classroom agenda; in other cases, it is simply because of student's fear of failure. If literal compliance with the planned activity is not immediately necessary, it may be possible to assign an alternative activity to the student, simply to avoid conflict and allow the student a chance to choose a positive alternative. In other cases, the student may finish a given task early, and the consequent idle time may foster unwanted behavior. Alternative activities for earlier finishers can help relieve this situation. Finally, events may occur which make it necessary for the student to be removed from the activity. When choosing alternative activities for this purpose, however, be sure it is an appropriate learning activity, not obvious "busy work."

Students who do poorly in science often rush through the activities. Prepare a checklist containing all the tasks that are to be completed in an activity. Have students use the checklist as they complete the activity. The checklist can help students stay on task, review the work they have completed, and self-evaluate their own performance on the activity. The checklist may be very much like the direction list which is distributed at the beginning of the activity.

For recommendations for specific science activities with ED students, consult Part III of this manual.

6

Hearing Impairments

What Are Hearing Impairments?

The most common distinction in characterizing hearing impairments is between **deaf** and **hard of hearing**. Generally speaking, **deaf** refers to a hearing disability which is sufficiently severe to preclude processing of language, when presented auditorily, with or without a hearing aid. **Hard of hearing** generally refers to hearing impairments which allow at least some processing of spoken language, often with the use of a hearing aid.

Hearing ability is often assessed with a **pure-tone audiometer**. Tones of different pitch and volume are presented through headphones to students who indicate (e.g., by raising their hands) which sounds they have heard. Pitch is referred to as **frequency**, and is measured in **Hertz (Hz)** units. Most speech sounds occur in the 500 (low) - 2,000 (high) Hz range. Volume is measured in **decibels** (dB), whereby zero decibels indicates the quietest sound a person with normal hearing can detect. Levels of hearing

---

Levels of Hearing Impairments

1. Mild (26-54 dB); may have difficulty with faint speech and some normal speech.

2. Moderate (55-69 dB); may often have difficulty understanding normal speech.

3. Severe (70-89 dB); may understand only amplified speech.

4. Profound (90 and above); may not understand amplified speech.

---

impairment based on audiometric evidence are presented in the accompanying table. Hearing loss above 90 decibels is often characterized as deafness, and below 90 decibels as hard of hearing. In general, students with the least severe hearing impairments are the most likely to receive instruction in mainstream classes.

About **.12%**, or a little more than one student in a thousand, are identified as hearing impaired.

Because of the vital role hearing plays in language acquisition, professionals often discriminate between **adventitiously deaf** (acquired) and **congenitally deaf** (from birth) individuals. Also, **prelingual** and **postlingual** deafness refers to occurrence before or after language development. Individuals who were born deaf or who acquired deafness before language developed usually have much more difficulty acquiring spoken language.

The **causes** of hearing impairments include heredity, prematurity, prenatal infections, oxygen deprivation, ear infections, head trauma, and excessive noise. In many cases, the specific cause is unknown.

Although most nonhandicapped people feel they would rather be deaf than blind, deafness is in many ways a more severe handicap for school age populations, because the ability to communicate with others can be severely impaired.

What Are Characteristics of Students With Hearing Impairments?

In general, students with hearing impairments exhibit severe deficits in the area of **language development**. Many have learned very little about language by the beginning of the school years, and so are at a great disadvantage with respect to their peers. Although some students may become fluent in sign language, a great majority have difficulty producing and understanding spoken language. Although many profoundly deaf students do not speak intelligibly, the majority of students with lesser hearing losses can be understood.

Most hearing impaired students are taught either by **oral techniques**, in which students are taught "speechreading" (i.e., lipreading) and taught to use the hearing they do possess; or they are taught by **total communication**, in which use of sign language is paired with oral techniques. Today, about two thirds of hearing impaired students are taught by total communication, and about one third are taught by oral techniques.

If the hearing impairment is not associated with another handicapping condition, such as mental retardation, there is little reason to believe that students with hearing impairments differ from the general hearing population in overall native **intelligence**.

Most students with hearing impairments exhibit **delayed performance in academic achievement**. Even math achievement, the overall strongest area for most students with hearing impairments, typically is several years' below grade level. Written work may appear disorganized or lack proper construction, particularly in use of prepositions, possessives, articles, and verb tense. Reading deficits are also usually very pronounced, although these can be improved by systematic and intensive instruction. Hearing impaired students who have benefitted from excellent instruction, particularly if their parents were heavily involved, may exhibit good language and academic skills.

Although some students with hearing impairments exhibit **social and personality characteristics** that are different from their hearing peers (e.g., excessively shy, or easily frustrated), they are generally not severe, and often predictable given the important role of language and communication in our society. Social maladjustment is relatively more common in students with multiple handicapping conditions (e.g., visual impairment), in addition to hearing impairment. As with other disability areas, positive social adjustment has much to do with how well the disability is accepted by others. If parents, other adults and peers, are cheerful, positive, and accepting of the disability area, and students are given a chance to succeed, there is little reason to expect social or emotional problems. Nevertheless, given the severe communication problems of students with hearing impairments, they typically have more difficulty establishing friendships with other students, and as a group, are more likely to seek out friendships among others with the same disability.

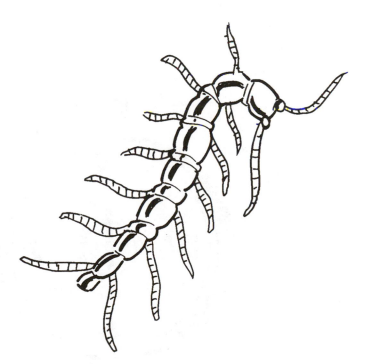

What Are Mainstreaming Techniques?

Classroom Organization

Students with hearing impairments generally use some type of **hearing aid**, and it is important to learn from special education teachers or other specialists how it is most effectively used, and whom to contact if a problem with the device occurs. In today's classrooms, it is common for students with hearing impairments to wear wireless FM systems. The teacher attaches a small microphone to his or her clothing, and the teacher's words are amplified for the student. Make sure you know how to check that it is working properly.

During the 1980s, **closed caption television and videos** became available. With a special decoder, many television programs and videos, including educational programs, can be viewed with written captions. Use captioned audio-visual material whenever possible, but also remember that many students with hearing impairments may have difficulty reading the captions. It is generally a good rule (for all students) to preview and review content from an audiovisual presentation. Many televisions have built in closed caption systems which can be special ordered, and by 1993, all new televisions will come equipped with the system.

Classrooms that accommodate students with hearing impairments are often **carpeted** to reduce background noises.

It is also important to **make yourself easily visible** to hearing impaired students, using the recommendations in the table. Remember, a good speechreader (lipreader) generally can understand only about 50% of what is spoken, and must infer the rest from context, so make sure that students have every chance to see your face.

Making Yourself Visible

- Face students directly.

- Be sure your face is well-lighted, with the light in front of you.

- Stand in front of a dark, uncluttered background.

- Seat hearing impaired students to face you (teachers should not stand in between the window and the student).

- Stand still unless students can continue to watch as you move.

- Keep book down and head up when reading.

- Keep all objects (pencil, papers, fingers, hair, etc.) away from your face when talking.

- Wear clothes that contrast with your hand color, so your hands will be clearly visible.

- Attempt to have your mouth near the level of the student's eyes.

- Do not speak while writing on the chalkboard.

A problem hearing impaired students often face in large classes is the ability to **see other students when they speak**. If the hearing impaired student cannot watch the speaker, comprehension will be impossible. Allow the student room to turn to see other students when speaking, or set the desk at an angle to see you and the class. If possible, seat the class in a circle, partial circle, or similar arrangement that allows the hearing impaired student to observe as many other students as possible. Always verify that the student's hearing aid is turned on and working properly.

Teacher Presentation

When using lecture and discussion formats, it is helpful to **preview new concepts** with students with hearing impairments, or have the special education teacher preview these concepts before the class begins. You could also have a peer tutor or partner, special education resource teacher, or speech clinician "preteach" selected lessons. This approach will lessen the information processing difficulties that students with hearing impairments generally encounter with new information. Use **language cards** before the concept is introduced, during the lesson, and afterwards for review.

Language cards should contain a picture, or other visual aid that represents the word, especially for very specific vocabulary (see table). Use them also as an introduction to related experiences that follow. Have the student make a "book" of language cards or flashcards for science class, containing all relevant concepts and vocabulary, and review it often. Abstract concepts, particularly those involving **time** and **space** may need special emphasis.

Following are examples of specific vocabulary words encountered in science which will probably require preteaching, modeling, role playing, or pictured language for their effective acquisition by students with hearing impairments:

Science Vocabulary

Vocabulary word	Comments
energy transfer	Demonstrations.
diatomaceous earth	Label samples of the compound.
compare	Highlight word whenever things are compared. Use concrete instances and non instances of the examples.
saturation	Provide several examples of things (cotton, sponge, soil) when saturated and when not saturated.
life cycle	Use a symbolic, thematic graphic display of different organisms going through life cycles. Relate it directly to classroom examples (e.g., mealworms, butterflies). Use enough examples so that students understand that life cycles are not unique to particular organisms.
environments	Use the word throughout the school year whenever a different environment is discussed. Cut pictures (or have students cut pictures) of different environments from magazines.
aquatic	Provide simple definition (e.g., "lives in water"), and several examples observable in classroom or around school (e.g., tadpoles, water plants, newts, fish).

Also, words such as: object, property, liquid, buoyancy, solubility, evaporation, subsystems, transformation, interaction, effective, origin, germinate, etc., may require additional elaboration.

Speak clearly and directly, but do not overenunciate, and do not raise your voice. Speak in simple, complete sentences, not in single words. Hearing impaired students will probably find slow or unnaturally pronounced speech difficult to understand. Speak directly to the student whenever possible, and be sure the student is looking at you. Simplify and shorten your sentences, and repeat the main points.

When calling on other students, use the student's name, and indicate location, so the student with hearing impairments can locate the student in the room. Repeat the question asked or the statement made before responding. Ask students to raise their hand before speaking, and allow only one student to speak at a time. Encourage the student with hearing impairments to answer the question for him or herself. Likewise, tell hearing impaired students when the **intercom** has come on, and report what is being said. If students misunderstand, try restating the statement or phrase in other words.

Use **non-verbal cues** whenever possible, such as facial expressions, gestures, and larger body movements. Role-play or act out new words, point to specific objects in the class for examples, and avoid vocabulary that can not be visualized (e.g., "compare," "presence"), or is vague (e.g., "better than this"). Remember (or imagine) attempts you might have made to communicate to someone who does not speak your language. Students with hearing impairments often use pantomime to communicate their thoughts. Try to avoid using irrelevant hand movements and gestures.

Use an **overhead projector**, when possible. Students can benefit from the visual information you present, and, unlike using a blackboard, you can remain facing the students. Write simply and clearly on the overhead projector, and use **simple pictures and diagrams** when possible to underscore your points. **It is impossible to place too much stress on the necessity to use visual aids to understanding whenever possible; they cannot be used too much**. Many published textbook series contain colored pictures and diagrams for the overhead projector. Use these for presentation and review. They can be very helpful for all students in your class.

Check for comprehension. Students with hearing impairments may nod their heads and pretend to understand when they do not. If you feel you are singling out the hearing impaired student by too many questions, review the content with the student at a later time. Or, ask for assistance from the special education teacher, or peer assistant. Make it a practice of asking students (both hearing impaired and normal hearing) to repeat directions for the benefit of the whole class. Use **listening partners** to verify understanding. When directions or information is presented, students understanding is increased when they listen with a partner and are given set times to check their understanding with that partner.

In some mainstream classes, students with hearing impairments may have an **interpreter**, who repeats in sign language what you have said in spoken English. When you are speaking to a hearing impaired student with an interpreter, be sure to speak **to the student,** not to the interpreter. Use whatever signs, fingerspelling or miming that you do know or can pick up. The "oral" child depends more on visual cues, while the total communication child relies on the interpreter for vocabulary development and concentration. Align yourself, the necessary instructional materials, the student, and the interpreter so the student is not required to focus in on several points simultaneously.

It is a myth that students with hearing impairments are more visually observant than others. Students with hearing impairments rely on visual input, either from the teacher or interpreter. Because of the additional effort that must be placed on attending and concentrating, they are likely to **fatigue** faster than other students. Try to build some breaks into the schedule so they can rest. Avoid lengthy lectures and explanations if possible. Hearing impaired students do not hear as well when they are tired, or if they have a cold.

Have special procedures arranged for fire, tornado, and other emergencies. Students can be assigned to assist the hearing impaired student during emergency procedures. Back up assistant students can be arranged in case of absences.

If you use appropriate instructional strategies, and you do not insist that students with hearing impairments communicate all they have learned to you in proper English, you should be able to hold very high expectations for the learning success of students with hearing impairments in your classroom.

Testing

Students with hearing impairments may have difficulty expressing what they have learned. **Individual oral assessment** may be helpful, and **performance-based assessment**, in which the student demonstrates his or her knowledge by interacting with science materials, may also be helpful. Students may also benefit from **identification**, rather than production formats. For more information, consult the "Evaluation" section in Part II.

If the student has an interpreter present, follow the same guidelines listed above. Spend time with the interpreter to ensure the interpreter can clearly sign appropriate information. Additionally, arrange suitable space for the interpreter and verify that the student with HI is "watching" the interpreter. The interpreter can be used to assist with "checking for understanding" during science tasks.

Mainstreaming Suggestions

Classroom Organization

- Become familiar with special equipment.

- Make yourself easily visible.

- Position hearing impaired students so they can see other students.

Teacher Presentation

- Preview new concepts; use language cards.

- Enhance new vocabulary.

- Speak clearly and directly

- Identify other students when they speak; repeat their questions.

- Alert students when the intercom comes on; repeat the information.

- Use non-verbal cues, such as role-play and pantomime.

- Use the overhead projector.

- Use pictures and diagrams whenever possible.

- Actively monitor comprehension.

- Use interpreters appropriately.

- Watch for fatigue.

Testing

- Provide individual oral assessment.

- Use performance-based assessment.

- Use identification formats.

- Consult "Evaluation," in Part II, for additional information.

What Are Laboratory Techniques?

In making a demonstration to the class, don't use a "look AND listen" approach. Rather, use a "**listen, THEN look, THEN listen**" approach. Remember, students with hearing impairments can not watch you closely and watch your demonstration at the same time. Tell students what you are going to demonstrate and what to look for. Then conduct the demonstration, and review what you have done.

Make **cards** for the hearing impaired student that outline the sequence of steps to be followed in a laboratory activity. Use as many pictures as possible, and review the cards with the student before initiating the activity.

It may often be helpful to identify a permanent place in the classroom where **directions and assignments** are always posted. Use pictures or drawings of steps involved when possible, as in the activity cards. Also, include a calendar which lists project due dates. Keep a running chart of acquired language posted and review the list continually.

Use **cooperative learning or peer assistants** when possible. A good group size may be three, with one hearing impaired and two hearing students. If your groups are normally larger than this, gradually increase the number of the group over time. It is generally wise to include only one student with hearing impairments in a group. Make sure that hearing peers only help the student understand what to do. They should not do activities for the hearing impaired student. Refer to Part II of this manual for more specific information.

Many science activities have very specific implications for students with hearing impairments, particularly those dealing with sound, and those enforcing more abstract concepts. Refer to the appropriate section in Part III for these activities.

Laboratory Suggestions

● Use listen, THEN look, THEN listen approach in demonstrations.

● Prepare sequence of steps on cards, using pictures whenever possible.

● Post directions and assignments in a special permanent place.

● Use cooperative learning and peer assistants.

● Consult Part III for specific activities.

7

Visual
Impairments

What Are Visual Impairments?

When asked to choose, most adults say they would rather be deaf than blind. However, prelingually deaf students often have more difficulty in school (because of communication problems), than do visually impaired students. One thing that is generally not known is that the majority of "blind" people can see! Up to 85% of students with visual impairments can benefit to some extent from their remaining sense of sight.

Visual impairment is one of the least common disabling conditions, affecting only about **1 in 2,000** students. However, the incidence of visual impairment is about **ten times higher** in the adult population (1 in 200). Some general information about visual impairment is provided next.

Information About Visual Impairments

The **legally blind** student has, with correction, vision no better than 20/200. This means the student sees at 20 feet what a normally sighted person can see at 200 feet. The vision of **partially sighted individuals** lies generally between 20/70 and 20/200.

There is no necessary link between visual impairment and **intelligence**, **social adjustment** or **language development**.

Visually impaired students may function below average in **academic achievement**. Students with visual impairments **do not automatically develop a "sixth sense,"** or greater acuity in other senses, to compensate for their sensory disadvantage. However, they can learn to use their senses more efficiently.

What Are Characteristics of Students With Visual Impairments?

As with any other handicapping condition, students with visual impairments present a wide variety of abilities and personalities, and generally prefer others to consider their **similarities** with, rather than their differences from, other students. Nevertheless, the following characteristics are relatively more common in visually impaired students:

Visually impaired students may use **tactual** sense to replace visual observations. If objects are small enough to fit into the student's hands, most physical attributes can be observed simultaneously (**synthetic touch**); but if the objects are much bigger, **analytic touch** is necessary. This means the student must touch different parts sequentially, and then attempt to combine these observations mentally. In this way, students with visual impairments may have more difficulty developing integrated concepts.

There is a great deal of variability in the relative **mobility** of students with visual impairments, although generally those who lost their sight at a later age are more mobile than those who lost their sight early, or were never sighted. Mobility often depends on spatial ability, and visually impaired students may use **cognitive mapping** to create a mental sense of a physical environment.

Some students with visual impairments develop **stereotypies** or **stereotypic behaviors** (sometimes referred to as **blindisms**), such as rocking or rubbing the eyes. It is generally the repetitiveness of the behavior, rather than the behavior itself, which is unusual.

The most common travel aid for individuals with visual impairments is the **long cane**, but extensive training is necessary for it to be used properly. Other travel aids include human guides, guide dogs (not commonly used with children), and electronic devices, such as laser canes.

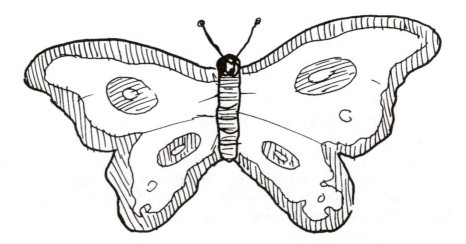

What Are Mainstreaming Techniques?

Classroom Organization

It is generally wise to allow visually impaired students to **explore the physical environment** of the classroom, so that they will be familiar with the surroundings. Identify the barriers verbally. For example, say *"we are coming to 5 steps,"* or *"we are approaching a downhill ramp"*.

Many visually impaired students, when using **adult guides**, prefer to take your arm just above the elbow, and walk about 1/2 step behind you (small children may prefer to hold your wrist). The natural movement of your body will help the student know when you are stepping up, down, turning, or going forward. It is important that the **visually impaired student holds** onto the guide's arm or body.

Be sure that there is **easy access** from the door of the classroom to the students' desk and any other areas they may need to get to.

Have a special procedure ready for fire, tornado, bomb scares, or other **emergencies**. Have a student assigned to provide any needed assistance under such circumstances, and a "back-up" assistant if the assigned student happens to be absent.

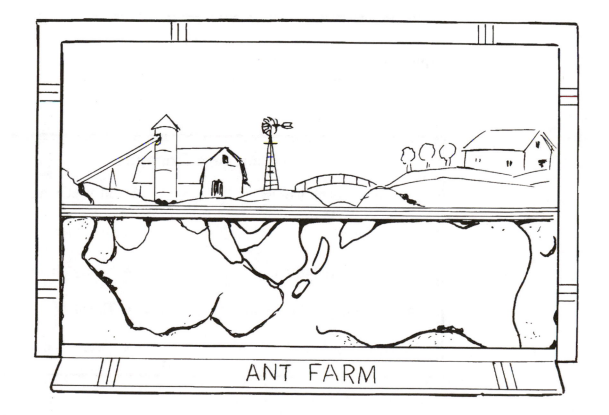

ANT FARM

Teacher Presentation

Most students with visual impairments appreciate the use of a few sensible guidelines when interacting with them, as shown in the table below.

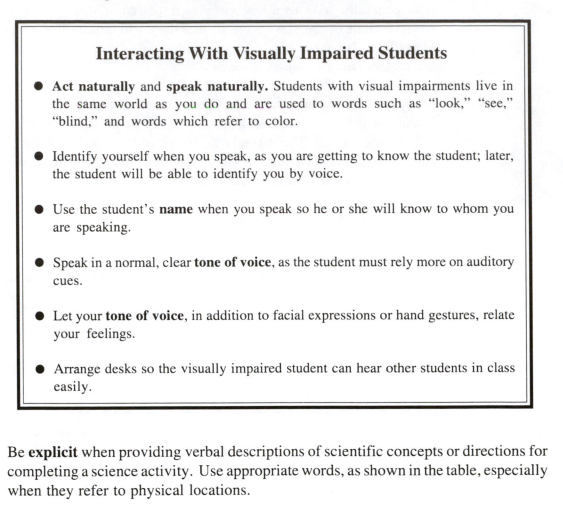

Interacting With Visually Impaired Students

- **Act naturally** and **speak naturally.** Students with visual impairments live in the same world as you do and are used to words such as "look," "see," "blind," and words which refer to color.

- Identify yourself when you speak, as you are getting to know the student; later, the student will be able to identify you by voice.

- Use the student's **name** when you speak so he or she will know to whom you are speaking.

- Speak in a normal, clear **tone of voice**, as the student must rely more on auditory cues.

- Let your **tone of voice**, in addition to facial expressions or hand gestures, relate your feelings.

- Arrange desks so the visually impaired student can hear other students in class easily.

Be **explicit** when providing verbal descriptions of scientific concepts or directions for completing a science activity. Use appropriate words, as shown in the table, especially when they refer to physical locations.

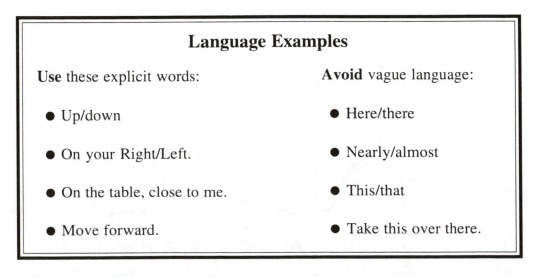

Language Examples

Use these explicit words:	**Avoid** vague language:
● Up/down	● Here/there
● On your Right/Left.	● Nearly/almost
● On the table, close to me.	● This/that
● Move forward.	● Take this over there.

When making demonstrations, make sure your language **clearly describes your activities** so that visually impaired students can understand what you are demonstrating, as shown in the table below. Tape record your demonstration, so students can replay it later. Provide only the information meant to be available to all students. If in the following example all students are not told that the seltzer tablet contains carbon dioxide, then the teacher should say *"the tablet is white and about the same size as a checker piece."* This will ensure that students with visual disabilities will have the same opportunities as other students to draw conclusions.

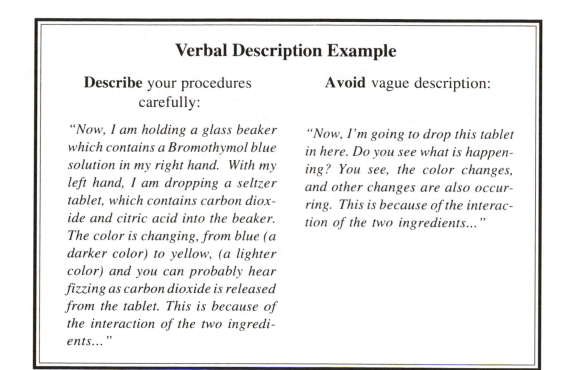

Verbal Description Example

Describe your procedures carefully:

"Now, I am holding a glass beaker which contains a Bromothymol blue solution in my right hand. With my left hand, I am dropping a seltzer tablet, which contains carbon dioxide and citric acid into the beaker. The color is changing, from blue (a darker color) to yellow, (a lighter color) and you can probably hear fizzing as carbon dioxide is released from the tablet. This is because of the interaction of the two ingredients..."

Avoid vague description:

"Now, I'm going to drop this tablet in here. Do you see what is happening? You see, the color changes, and other changes are also occurring. This is because of the interaction of the two ingredients..."

Use **"time" orientations**, relative to the visually impaired student's position, e.g., "The tape is on your table, at 11 o'clock."

Students with visual impairments must be provided with **appropriate methods for reading**. There are several possibilities, as shown in the section later in this book, "Strategies for Mainstreaming Students with Reading Difficulties". If you use a textbook-centered approach to science instruction, you will probably need to rely heavily on one of these methods.

Students with visual impairments generally understand concepts much better when they are allowed to interact physically with examples or representations of these concepts. Students who remember the language but do not completely understand the related concepts may employ **verbalisms**, that is, they use words they do not completely understand. Monitor comprehension regularly, and provide physical examples whenever possible.

Present multiple concepts **individually**, and allow sufficient time for each one to be acquired before proceeding to the next.

When using movies, or other audio-visual aides, try to obtain versions that include descriptive video components. Descriptive video provides verbal descriptions of events seen on the video, but not discussed in the dialogue. When those formats are unavailable try to preview audio-video materials and tape record a descriptive component, or ask a special education teacher or another student to tape record that component.

Testing

When testing, consider allowing students to use tape recorders. If performance-based testing is used, provide the student with sufficient assistance to locate apparatus and equipment, and sufficient time to demonstrate knowledge. Additional information is provided in the "Testing" section in Part II.

Mainstreaming Suggestions

Classroom Organization

- Help students explore the classroom environment.

- Use appropriate guiding techniques, when necessary, and promote their use with classroom peers.

- Provide easy access into, out of, and around the classroom.

- Plan for emergencies.

Teacher Presentation

- Use explicit language.

- Describe activities clearly; provide essential information.

- Use time orientations.

- Provide appropriate methods for reading.

- Check for comprehension.

- Present multiple concepts individually.

- Use videos and movies with descriptive video components.

- Enlarge all materials.

Testing

- Use tape recorders.

- Provide assistance for performance based tests.

- Allow sufficient time.

What Are Laboratory Techniques for Students With Visual Impairments?

Label all equipment or materials according to student abilities, either with Braille labels or large print. (Braille labelers can be obtained from the American Printing House for the Blind.) Black print on yellow may be helpful for students with low vision. Be sure that labels are always in the same relative position on the equipment, so students will know where to look for them. Use labels to identify experimental condition (e.g., plants with salt water, plants with distilled water).

Students with visual impairments may be "**tactually defensive**," and avoid touching or manipulating unfamiliar or unknown things. Provide encouragement and reward, if necessary, for "getting their hands messy."

During demonstrations or discussions, allow the student to **hold relevant materials**, in segmented trays, when possible. When describing the relative positions of objects on a laboratory tray, ask students to locate them as you describe them, or guide their hands with yours.

Closed circuit television (CCTV) can be very helpful for partially sighted students in observing almost anything, including reading and recording data. In many instances CCTV is preferable to magnifying lenses. CCTV can show enlarged examples of anything the class is studying.

Assign **peer assistants** when necessary, to identify colors or describe events during any observation activity (refer to the section on peer mediation later on in this book).

Arrange the room for easy **movement** around the classroom to obtain materials or equipment, to examine exhibits, or separate work areas. It is generally better to attempt to find a way for students with visual impairments to become a part of normal classroom activities, than to allow others to do all the movement.

Stabilize materials for the visually impaired student. Cover the student's desk with felt or with slotted trays so materials, including paper and pencils, won't slide.

Develop **Brailled laboratory manuals** and recording sheets, when appropriate.

Prepare the work area for spills. Anchor equipment when possible, so it can not be casually knocked over. Use a laboratory tray that has separate compartments for different materials. If the tray has sides on it, it will contain spills more easily. Tell students what materials are on the tray, and what position (compartment) they are in. Keep paper towels handy. (These precautions are also appropriate for younger or physically handicapped students).

Order special adaptive equipment. Extra large monitors for computers are available. Larger screens provide easier reading for students with visual impairment. Microprojectors can display enlarged views of objects typically only seen with microscopes. Light sensors can be used to help visually impaired students detect light changes, as well as motion, during science activities, such as those using pendulums.

There are important guidelines for many specific science activities when employed with visually impaired students. Refer to Part III of this manual for specific science activities, and look for specific recommendations for students with visual impairments.

Laboratory Suggestions

- Label all exhibits, equipment, and apparatus appropriately.

- Provide encouragement when needed for active manipulation of new or unusual phenomena.

- Provide tactual experiences whenever possible.

- Use closed circuit television with partially sighted students, when appropriate.

- Assign peer assistants when necessary.

- Provide for easy movement around the classroom.

- Provide Brailled laboratory manuals.

- Prepare the work area for spills.

- Order adaptive equipment such as extra large screen monitors, light sensors and projecting microscopes.

- Refer to Part III for specific activities.

- Stabilize all equipment.

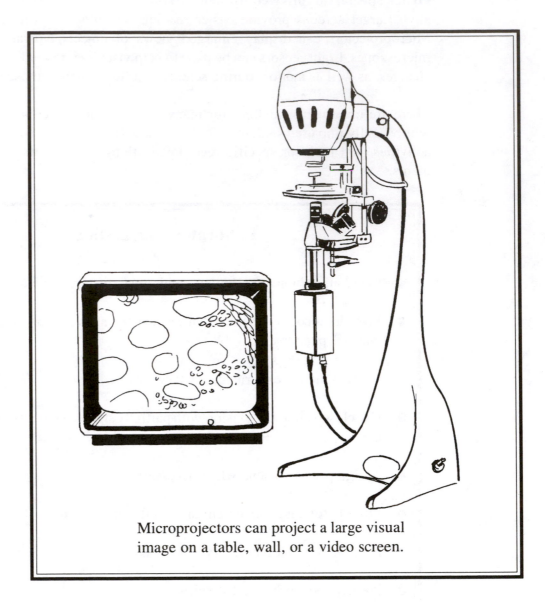

Microprojectors can project a large visual image on a table, wall, or a video screen.

8

Physical Disabilities

What Are Physical Disabilities?

Physical disabilities may be, overall, the **broadest** category of disability. Physical disabilities and health impairments can assume many forms, and each may carry some specific but unique implications for instruction. There is enormous **variation** in these handicapping conditions, from relatively mild and short-lived, to progressive, incapacitating, and life-threatening. Because of this, it is possible to discuss physical disabilities and other health impairments only in a very general way in this manual; interested readers can consult other texts, particularly Bleck and Nagel (1982), and Hallahan and Kauffman (1991, chapter 9) for further information.

About **.5%** (1 in 200) of the school-age population have physical disabilities. About half of these students have cerebral palsy or other crippling conditions; another half may suffer from severe chronic illness. Some general information about the most common physical disabilities are given in the table on the next page.

Students with physical disabilities or other health impairments often benefit from the use of **prosthetics**, **orthotics**, and **adaptive devices**. Prosthetics replace a missing body part (e.g., arm or leg), while orthotics enhance the function of a body part (e.g., leg braces). Adaptive devices can be used to more easily cope with ordinary tasks (e.g., specialized grips).

Some students with physical disabilities are positioned on **wedges**, which free their arms and hands for movement. Wedges require large amounts of floor space.

Common Types of Physical Disabilities

● **Cerebral palsy** is a disabling condition in which paralysis or other motor dysfunction is caused by damage to the child's developing brain, by such factors as infection, diseases, trauma, lack of oxygen, or problems during the birth process. The neurological damage is permanent, but not progressive. Involved individuals may also have seizures, psychological problems, impaired intellectual ability, communication problems, or visual and hearing problems; however, many individuals with cerebral palsy do not have these additional problems.

● **Epilepsy** (or seizure disorder) results from an abnormal discharge of electrical energy in certain brain cells. When enough cells are effected, the individual may lose consciousness, move involuntarily, or experience abnormal sensory phenomena. Individuals are characterized as epileptic only if they have repeated seizures.

● **Spina bifida** is a condition which results when the spinal column does not close completely during fetal development, resulting in paralysis. The protruding nerve fibers are referred to as a **myelomeningocele**, or **meningomyelocele**. Spina bifida may be associated with hydrocephalus (excessive pressure of cerebrospinal fluid) which could lead to attention or learning problems, or mental retardation. Sometimes hydrocephalus can be treated surgically, so the fluid drains away from the head.

● **Traumatic head injury** is frequently the result of vehicular accidents or near drownings. Students with such injuries may have difficulty sustaining attention, learning new things, remembering, and organizing their thoughts and their work. They may also have difficulty with social behavior.

● **Muscular Dystrophy** refers to a progressive and hereditary weakening and wasting away of muscle tissue. At present, the specific cause is unknown, and there is no cure. Some forms are generally fatal, but other forms may allow for a relatively normal life span with few obvious symptoms. Intelligence does not seem to be affected.

● **Rheumatoid arthritis** involves mild to severe inflammation, swelling, and/or stiffness in the joints or connective tissues. In most cases of the juvenile form, individuals improve completely over time. **Osteoarthritis** can occur among students with other physical disabilities, such as cerebral palsy, or when joints have been dislocated.

● Other conditions include **scoliosis** (curvature of the spine), **Osteomyelitis** (bacterial bone infection), **Osteogenesis imperfecta** (improper and brittle bone formation), and **Arthrogryposis** (missing or weakened limb muscles).

What are Mainstreaming Techniques?

Mainstream teachers who have physically handicapped or other health impaired students in their classrooms should familiarize themselves with appropriate **medical considerations**, and stay in contact with the school nurse or other appropriate school personnel. A checklist is given in the following table (see also Hallahan and Kauffman, 1991; Lewis and Doorlag, 1987, Chapter 13). The items on this checklist are typically the responsibility of a school nurse or other specialist. However, it is recommended that the general educator be familiar with the information on it.

It is also necessary to confer with the physical or occupational therapist and special education teacher (as well as students themselves) regarding such matters as (a) **transportation and movement** of the student, (b) how the student is able to or prefers to **communicate**, (c) what type of **self-care** help, such as eating and going to the toilet, is needed, and (d) the type of **positions** the student prefers for various activities, and the **positioning devices** (such as braces or wedges) that are most helpful. It is also important to develop a **plan for emergencies**, such as fire or tornado warning, in which the student may need to leave the classroom quickly. Assign a peer helper to assist the student in such a case, and assign a "back-up" student for cases in which the peer

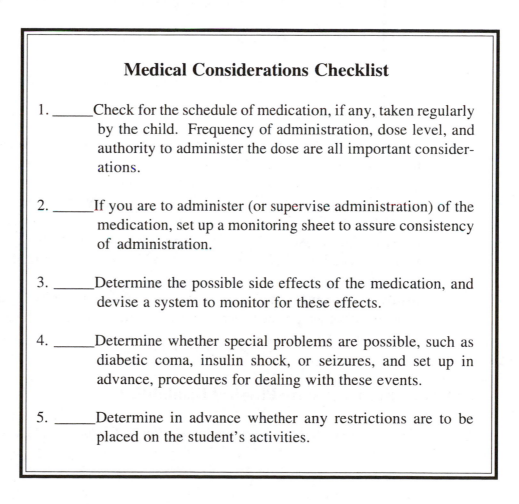

Medical Considerations Checklist

1. _____ Check for the schedule of medication, if any, taken regularly by the child. Frequency of administration, dose level, and authority to administer the dose are all important considerations.

2. _____ If you are to administer (or supervise administration) of the medication, set up a monitoring sheet to assure consistency of administration.

3. _____ Determine the possible side effects of the medication, and devise a system to monitor for these effects.

4. _____ Determine whether special problems are possible, such as diabetic coma, insulin shock, or seizures, and set up in advance, procedures for dealing with these events.

5. _____ Determine in advance whether any restrictions are to be placed on the student's activities.

helper is absent. Practice executing the exit procedure. Some students, such as those with **osteogenesis imperfecta**, are vulnerable to serious injury and must be treated very carefully by teachers and classmates; others may be quite robust. Be sure you and your other students are very familiar with the best ways of interacting physically. In many cases, the students themselves can provide very helpful information, and the special education teachers will assume some of the responsibilities for transporting students.

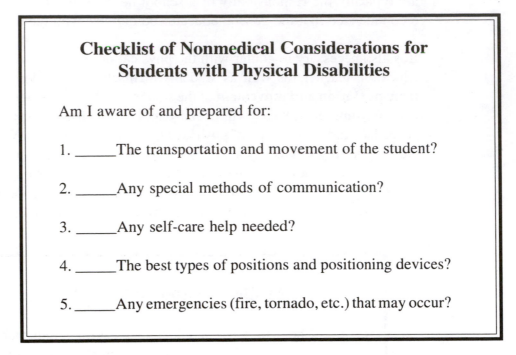

Checklist of Nonmedical Considerations for Students with Physical Disabilities

Am I aware of and prepared for:

1. _____The transportation and movement of the student?

2. _____Any special methods of communication?

3. _____Any self-care help needed?

4. _____The best types of positions and positioning devices?

5. _____Any emergencies (fire, tornado, etc.) that may occur?

Many students with physical disabilities have difficulty **moving** into, out of, or throughout the classroom. Make sure the classroom provides not only for easy access to the student's desk, but also for easy movement to any areas of the class in which science activities or materials are located. Generally, this means providing **plenty of space** for mobility. It is important to involve students with physical disabilities in as many routine classroom activities as possible, so that as little distinction as possible will be created between mainstreamed and regular class students.

Student assistants can also be helpful in extending mobility. Speak with the special education teacher, physical therapist, nurse, or the students themselves about how their mobility can be facilitated.

Testing Students With Physical Disabilities

For recommended testing procedures, refer to Chapter 13, "Evaluation."

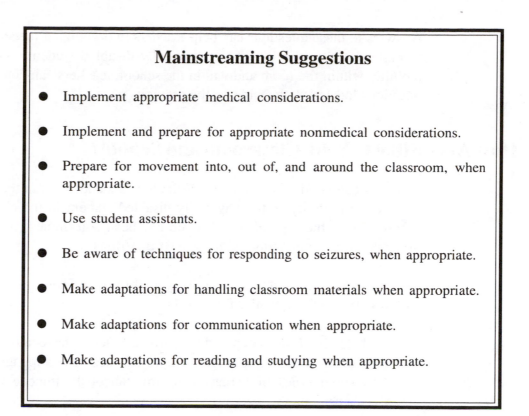

Mainstreaming Suggestions

- Implement appropriate medical considerations.

- Implement and prepare for appropriate nonmedical considerations.

- Prepare for movement into, out of, and around the classroom, when appropriate.

- Use student assistants.

- Be aware of techniques for responding to seizures, when appropriate.

- Make adaptations for handling classroom materials when appropriate.

- Make adaptations for communication when appropriate.

- Make adaptations for reading and studying when appropriate.

What Type of Mobility Aid Is Necessary?

Since there is such a variety of physical disabilities, it is difficult to state specifically what types of mobility difficulties students with physical disabilities might encounter. Teachers should use the listing of questions as potential considerations when planning for mainstreaming a student with physical disabilities.

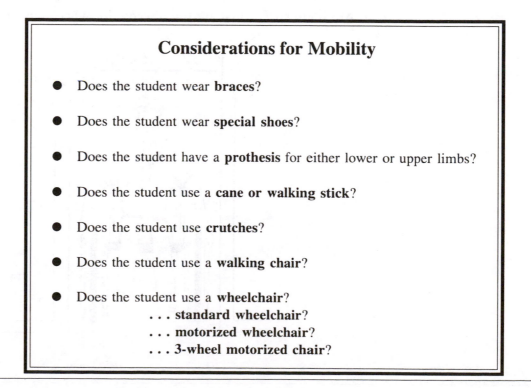

Considerations for Mobility

- Does the student wear **braces**?

- Does the student wear **special shoes**?

- Does the student have a **prothesis** for either lower or upper limbs?

- Does the student use a **cane or walking stick**?

- Does the student use **crutches**?

- Does the student use a **walking chair**?

- Does the student use a **wheelchair**?
  - . . . **standard wheelchair**?
  - . . . **motorized wheelchair**?
  - . . . **3-wheel motorized chair**?

Answers to these questions can help teachers in organizing the space and classroom to maximize the mobility of the physically disabled student. In order to increase mobility within the room and within the school, teachers can consider the following questions located in the table on the previous page.

How Accessible Is Your Classroom and School?

Teachers can conduct an analysis of the barriers and hazards that could potentially impede the mobility of the physically disabled student in the classroom and in the school. Once the type of mobility aid has been determined, teachers can use that information in conjunction with the next questions.

Teachers should carefully monitor the type of floor and determine the levels of safety and mobility with particular floor surfaces.

1. Is the **floor carpeted**? Carpeted floors have advantages and disadvantages. Carpeted floors can decrease slippage, however, some types of carpets can simultaneously impede mobility of wheelchairs.

2. Is the **floor surface slippery**? Tile floors can be dangerously slippery when using some types of assistive devices for increasing mobility.

Teachers should monitor the spaces necessary for mobility throughout the classroom with respect to the particular mobility needs of students with physical disabilities.

3. Are there spaces that are **too narrow** for wheelchair accessibility?

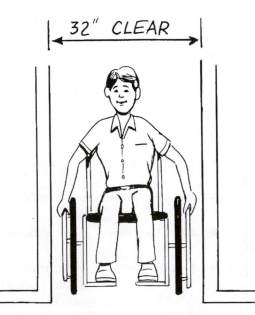

4. Are the **door knobs and door handles at a height** that students in wheelchairs can reach?

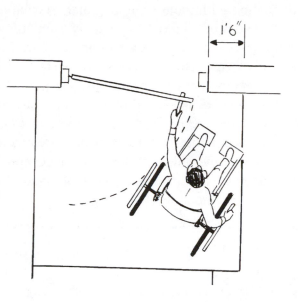

5. Are **restrooms and water fountains accessible**?

6. Have **emergency procedures** been established that allow quick and easy access for students with physical disabilities?

7. Are **alternatives to curbs and stairs** available?

Particular consideration can be made to classroom arrangements. Remember that students who are in wheelchairs have a different viewing height from students in regular desks or students who are standing. Consider the next questions when arranging scientific displays and lessons.

8. Are the **display tables at appropriate viewing heights**?

9. Are classroom **exhibits containing animals, rocks and minerals, and the like** at an appropriate viewing level?

10. Are **class computers and printers** at the level necessary for students with physical disabilities?

11. Are **labels and signs for directions to activities** at appropriate levels?

12. Are **presentations** by teachers and other students at the appropriate level for students with physical disabilities?

What Are Possible Medical Considerations?

If the student has epilepsy, and is subject to **seizures**, find out the appropriate method of dealing with them from the nurse, special education teacher, or other specialized staff. Types of seizures vary widely, from a few seconds to several minutes duration; from several times a day to once a year; from minor motor symptoms to major convulsive movements; and are caused by a variety of conditions, known or unknown. They may be completely, or only partially controlled by drugs. Although epileptic seizures may be anxiety-provoking, they last only a few minutes and generally do not require expert care. It may be important to ensure that all students have relevant information about seizures and their treatment. However, it may be wise to avoid singling out individual students. Some general considerations in dealing with seizures are given in the accompanying table (see also Hallahan & Kauffman, Chapter 9; Epilepsy Foundation of America).

Attending to Epileptic Seizures

1. Once a seizure has begun, it cannot be stopped. Be **calm**, and allow the seizure to run its course.

2. **Help** the student to the floor, and loosen his or her clothing.

3. Do not interfere with the student's physical movements, other than to **protect the head or body** from striking hard or dangerous objects.

4. **Turn the student's face** sidewise, to allow saliva to flow out.

5. **Do not insert objects** between the student's teeth.

6. Sometimes **breathing** stops momentarily during seizures. Do not be alarmed.

7. After the seizure has stopped, the student may need to **rest or sleep**.

8. Unless the seizure is repeated, or lasts more than ten minutes, it may not be necessary to call a doctor. However, be sure to **notify parents or guardians**, and other relevant school personnel. All seizure activity should be reported and charted.

What Are Additional Teacher Concerns?

Many students with physical disabilities have difficulty with manual grasp of classroom materials. Some possible adaptations include use of **pads of paper** or clipboard, rather than loose paper, and keeping loose paper in place with **tape or magnets**. Writing implements can be made easier to hold with **rubber bands** (twist them around pencil or pen), corrugated **cardboard** taped on, rubber or plastic **tubing**, or a **practice golf ball** over the pen or pencil. Soft lead pencils and felt tip pens require less pressure. Rubber stamps with handles can be used to "write names" or indicate correct answers on multiple choice questions. Typewriters can also be adapted.

Electric typewriters require less pressure. **Pointer sticks**, attached to head or mouthpiece, can help students strike the keys. **Eraser buttons** on the typewriter make correction much easier. Rather than require extensive writing when this presents difficulty, allow students to tape record verbal information. Calculators can be helpful for computation.

For manipulating other classroom materials, consider placing instructional materials (vocabulary cards, etc.) in **clear photograph cubes**. The student may be able to handle them more easily, and can turn them to indicate specific responses, if needed. Photo albums with sticky backings and plastic cover sheets may also be helpful for managing instructional materials.

Some students with physical disabilities may have difficulty with oral communication. They may have **communication boards**, which contain pictures, symbols, or numbers, and allow the student to communicate more easily by pointing to, or otherwise indicating selected responses. The special education teacher, physical therapist, or speech therapist can help show the teacher and the class how communication devices are used. In some cases, it may be helpful to name objects as the student identifies responses. It may also be helpful to identify some easily manipulated objects to represent common responses, such as "yes" or "no"; "true" or "false"; or "agree"/"disagree"/"I don't know". **Speech synthesizers** can be used to produce speech that students type on the computer.

Many students with physical disabilities are able to **read and study** from books, if they are properly positioned. Book holders and page turners are available to help students with physical disabilities manipulate books. Other devices, such as talking books, audiotapes, and compressed speech machines, are described in Part II in the section entitled "Mainstreaming Students with Reading Difficulties".

Sitting in a wheel chair for extended time periods can be very uncomfortable. Teachers or aids may need to provide a change of position using adaptive equipment during long science classes.

Some students with physical disabilities may have a drooling problem. In such cases, materials can be covered with clear plastic and students can use permanent markers instead of water-soluble ones.

What Are Laboratory Techniques for Students With Physical Disabilities?

Many of the guidelines suggested under the other special education categories would be useful to attend to for students with physical disabilities, too. Major considerations for laboratory use concern mobility and accessibility.

The classroom should be arranged so that **mobility around and within the room is easily accessible** for students with physical disabilities.

Laboratory equipment should be available at **appropriate heights** for students with physical disabilities.

Handouts for the activity can be placed **in a clear plastic folder** with a hard plastic binder. Students with poor fine motor skills can hold the paper more easily because they can grasp the plastic binder.

Lab tables containing appropriate materials should be **stable** and provide opportunities for students with physical disabilities to interact with equipment. All materials should be sufficiently immobilized to allow students sufficient access without fears of mishaps. **Velcro**, **felt pads**, and **slatted trays** might help facilitate the stabilizing of necessary equipment for students with physical disabilities.

Peer assistants can be assigned to help collect necessary materials if the student with physical disabilities has difficulty moving around and carrying items. Peer assistants can also help with **recording data** and execute **secretarial tasks** if students have difficulties with hand control.

Adaptive materials should be ordered and used whenever possible if necessary. For example, some students may require the use of a head stick or light beam in order to be able to participate in class activities. Velcro can be placed around various materials to increase gripping and grasping. The special education team (special educator, physical therapist, speech therapist, occupational therapist) can usually obtain any of the necessary adaptive devices. **Flap switches** are available (Prentke Romich Company) and are single movement switches that allow students more accessibility. **Reachers** can be obtained to attach to a pencil or dowel rod to extend the grasp of an individual (Prentke Romich Co.). Materials are available that can be **molded to an individual hand shape** to assist with gripping and grasping tasks (Beok Grip Kit from Wendell Foster). **Non-slip materials** and **little octopus suction holders** and **stay put suction disks** are available to assist with stabilizing materials (Wendell Foster). Use **felt boards** or **magnetic boards** for charting and recording data.

Laboratory Suggestions

- Arrange desks and chairs to maximize accessibility and mobility.

- Have laboratory equipment available at appropriate heights.

- Place handouts for the activity in a clear plastic folder.

- Stabilize all materials.

- Use peer assistants.

- Use adaptive materials.

Part II

General Mainstreaming Strategies

Time and Resource Management

What Are Strategies for Maximizing Time and Resources?

A big challenge for the general education science teacher is managing time and resources to effectively mainstream the special education student and still meet the needs of the remaining regular education students. A number of resources at your school or within your community may be available to assist you in completing some of the adaptations necessary to make the mainstream environment successful for the student with disabilities. Some of these resources are listed next.

```
╔══════════════════════════════════════════════╗
║                                                ║
║      Possible Resources for the Science Teacher ║
║                                                ║
║   ● Maximize Available Time                    ║
║   ● Team Teach With Other Grade Level Teachers ║
║   ● Team Teach With the Special Education Teacher ║
║   ● Enlist Support of:                         ║
║           Special Education Teachers           ║
║           General Educators                    ║
║           University Personnel                 ║
║           Media Specialists                    ║
║           Students (Older and Same Aged)       ║
║           School Specialists                   ║
║           Senior Citizens                      ║
║           Parent Volunteers                    ║
║           University Faculty                   ║
║           University Volunteer Students        ║
║           University Practicum Students        ║
║           University Student Teachers          ║
║                                                ║
╚══════════════════════════════════════════════╝
```

What Are Strategies for Maximizing Available Time?

Since a limited number of minutes in the day exist, it is important to use all of those minutes wisely. One activity that can help teachers monitor available time is to record the amount of time that currently exists in the day. A simple time tracking sheet may be helpful in recording what actually occurs from the beginning to the end of each day. This time tracking sheet can be used to determine how much time in a day is allocated to various instructional and noninstructional activities. For example, in the next sample a teacher arrives at school at 7:30 and leaves at 4:00.

```
┌──────────────────────────────────────┐
│            Sample Schedule             │
│                                        │
│   7:30    Arrive at School             │
│   8:00    Home room begins             │
│   8:15    First period                 │
│   9:15    Second period                │
│   10:15   Third period                 │
│   11:15   Fourth period                │
│   12:15   Lunch                        │
│   12:45   Fifth period                 │
│   1:45    Sixth period                 │
│   2:45    Seventh period               │
│   3:30    School Closes                │
│   4:00    Leave for Home               │
│                                        │
└──────────────────────────────────────┘
```

How Can Allocated Time Be Determined?

Upon closer examination of the sample schedule, it is possible to see that the teacher can be even more specific regarding how the amount of time during the school day is spent. For example, it may be possible to write in the times that the bell rings and the time in between classes. It is also possible to be more specific than simply writing first, second, third, period. Teachers can write in Reading, Math, Science, History, or Art next to the period number. Once that task is done teachers have a complete record of their allocated time during each school day.

How Can Engaged Time Be Calculated?

It has been observed, however, that the amount of allocated time for instruction varies greatly from the amount of time that students spend engaged in academic activities. A simple way of calculating the amount of engaged academic time in classes is to tape record an entire day, or begin with one class period at a time. When reviewing the tape recording of the day, it is possible to calculate the number of minutes that have been spent with students engaged or actively working on the academic tasks. It is also possible to calculate the amount of time that the class was not engaged in academic activities. This time is sometimes referred to as transition time. Transition times may occur prior, during, or after instructional time. Examples of transitions include: wait time, interruptions, managing inappropriate behavior, distributing and collecting materials, unnecessary digressions on the part of students and teachers, sharpening pencils, obtaining drinks of water or restroom breaks. Although some of these transition times are necessary, often these times can be shortened or rearranged to specific time periods so they do not interfere with engaged academic time. It may be surprising, but many teachers have found extra time that can be used for additional practice activities for mainstreamed students during unnecessary transition times. For example, some teachers routinely review previously covered content while students are standing in lines waiting. Additional ways of increasing engaged time are listed next.

Strategies for Increasing Engaged Time

- Decrease unnecessary wait time
- Decrease inappropriate behavior
- Decrease transition time
- Have students come prepared to class
- Have scheduled restroom and water fountain breaks
- Use before school time
- Use after school time

What Other Resources Are Available?

Many resources exist in schools and local communities that are not used as widely as possible. Each resource that is available is described separately next.

How Can the Special Education Teacher Help?

Special education teachers can be a valuable resource to the general education science teacher. First, they often have been working with your mainstreamed student in small group settings and they have been working on the objectives contained on the student's IEP. They are usually very familiar with the student's current level of functioning. They will usually have insight into setting the appropriate expectations for academic and social tasks in the mainstreamed science class. This knowledge can be used to help set realistic goals for the student in the mainstreamed science class. Special educators can help obtain specialized adaptive equipment and materials that may be necessary during mainstreamed science classes.

Regular meetings with the special education teacher can be beneficial. During those meetings, the science teacher can share the types of activities the student is doing and ask for clarifications regarding any particular adaptations that might be beneficial. For example, it may be helpful to ask for assistance from the special education teacher in areas such as: assessing the mainstreamed student's performance, giving tests on an individual basis, providing additional practice on activities in the resource setting, prefamiliarizing the student with language and vocabulary for upcoming science lessons, teaching study strategies, or teaching the appropriate preskills in academic and social areas. Some special educators will even team teach with the regular education teacher and be in the room during science classes to co-teach and to help monitor the instruction.

Resources From the Special Education Teacher

- Provide current level of functioning
- Insight into setting expectations for mainstream setting
- Provide additional practice in resource setting
- Assist with assessing performance and maintaining portfolios
- Assist with prefamiliarization activities
- Teach study strategies
- Help with prerequisite skills
- Team teach
- Help obtain adaptive equipment and materials

How Can Same Grade Level Regular Teachers Help?

Same grade level teachers are a greatly under-utilized resource. For example, most same grade level teachers are using the same curriculum and have the same types of students in their classes. When considering the types of modifications and adaptations that might help facilitate mainstreaming in science for special education students, teachers can collaborate and share ideas, work, and materials. For example, if all mainstreamed students would benefit from the development of additional illustrations and memory-enhancing strategies, same grade level teachers can split the amount of work by the number of teachers, and then share materials that each developed independently. This will reduce greatly the amount of work for individual teachers, while simultaneously increasing the amount of developed adapted materials. If preplanning is undertaken, then teachers can decide to teach units at different times throughout the year. Materials developed for units can be shared when they are taught. This includes making audiotapes of written materials, development of illustrations, development of three-dimensional models, descriptive videos, or any other curricular modifications. Often teachers may have a particular specialty area in science. During that activity teachers may even switch classes, so their class is given the opportunity to study with an expert on the topic!

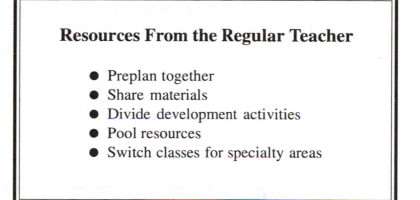

Resources From the Regular Teacher

- Preplan together
- Share materials
- Divide development activities
- Pool resources
- Switch classes for specialty areas

What Additional Resources Are Available in the School?

Schools usually have a media specialist and often have science specialists available who can consult with general education teachers. These specialists may be able to obtain very specialized materials for classroom use that can assist with mainstreaming the special education student. Media and library specialists may be able to offer special instruction on using the library and media equipment. Many schools have also arranged buddy systems in which older students act as tutors or buddies for younger students.

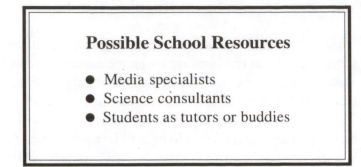

Possible School Resources

- Media specialists
- Science consultants
- Students as tutors or buddies

What Are Resources From the University?

Universities and colleges can provide valuable resources to schools. Often specialized materials can be borrowed from faculty, labs, or libraries at the university. Faculty may have access to a larger variety of materials. Faculty and students may be interested in collaborating on school related projects. Many undergraduate and graduate students would love to be able to volunteer in a classroom during science classes. A volunteer opportunity gives students the chance to determine whether or not they would like to pursue a career in education. Many university special and regular education classes have required practicum components. These practica are usually early field experiences for students. Although these students have not had the class work of more advanced student teachers, they can be very helpful in assisting during science class, and in making adaptive materials. It might be that these students would love the opportunity to develop illustrations or models to accompany science units. Finally, student teachers and graduate level interns can be very helpful in assisting with instruction and development of materials necessary for modifying mainstream science instruction.

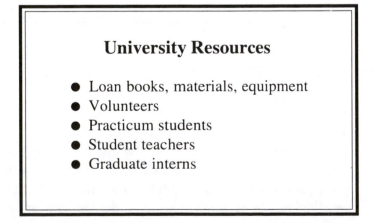

University Resources

- Loan books, materials, equipment
- Volunteers
- Practicum students
- Student teachers
- Graduate interns

What Are Other Community Resources?

Many parents would welcome the chance to help with the development of materials or to assist in the classroom. Also, senior citizens usually welcome advances made from schools regarding the opportunity to help out in schools. These volunteers can make audio recordings of written materials, develop illustrations, or any number of other helpful activities.

Possible Community Resources

- Parents
- Senior Citizens

Maybe elves (or other volunteers) will come into your classroom and help you with your work !

10

Effective Instruction

What Are the Components of Effective Instruction?

This section briefly reviews general information related to effective instruction that is typically associated with success for students with disabilities. These variables are not intended to dictate the approach to science teaching that you may wish to use, or to alter the objectives you may have for students. They do attempt to make your instruction more **focused**, more **systematic**, and more **intensive**. If implemented appropriately, effective instruction should make learning easier for all students. A general model for delivery of effective instruction is presented.

Daily Review

It is generally a good idea to begin each lesson with a review of information from previous lessons. This review will help students with disabilities by providing additional opportunities to practice previously learned information. For example, providing review on ways for dealing effectively with social behavior problems during cooperative learning might be a good review prior to a science lesson that was going to use cooperative learning. Additionally, information relevant to the previous activities that had been completed in science but relevant to the ones that are going to be presented in the new lesson would also be appropriate.

Present New Information

After the daily review teachers can present the new information. The new information should reflect the lesson's objectives. It usually helps students to be directly informed of the purpose of the lesson. For example, in a lesson on estimation and measurement a teacher might say: *"Today we are going to practice using our estimation and measurement abilities."* Discussion could then proceed according to any new information that is necessary, or information that students might need prior to breaking into their cooperative groups. During this time teachers can provide relevant information and involve students in a discussion of relevant information. This is the opportunity for the teacher to ensure students' understanding. Teachers do not want students to practice new information incorrectly, whether individually or in cooperative groups.

When presenting new information, teachers should attend to the "SCREAM" variables, as described in the table on next page.

How to Present New Information: "SCREAM"

Structure. Provide overview and review new information as you proceed. Follow your objective carefully and be sure students understand the sequence and purpose of your presentation.

Clarity. Avoid unnecessary digressions. Use clearly stated examples. Provide instances and non-instances of new concepts. Use simple, direct, clear language. Avoid vague references (e.g., *"a thing like this," "and so on," "you know"*).

Redundancy. Students usually need to hear, see, and/or experience new concepts several times before they understand it well. Repetition allows new vocabulary or terminology to become more familiar, reinforces new learning as it proceeds, and allows students to practice and test their understanding by predicting what you will say when you are reinforcing previously mentioned concepts.

Enthusiasm. Students pay more attention, show more interest, apply themselves better, and learn more when the teacher is enthusiastic. The heightened stimulus arouses their curiosity more, and they begin to model your attitude toward the subject. Enthusiasm is described in detail in the section on "Strategies for Improving Motivation and Affect."

Appropriate pace. Monitor students' understanding so that you proceed neither too swiftly nor too slowly through the content. If you move too slowly, you will bore them. Too fast, and you will lose them.

Maximize engagement. Students learn best when they are directly engaged with the teacher, rather than passively listening. Ask lots of questions directly related to the lesson you are teaching. Ask direct questions about your presentation (e.g., *"What did we say was the major difference between monerans and protists?"*), ask application questions to test comprehension (e.g., *"Give me an example of an insulator that you can see in the classroom"*), and prompt reasoning to promote active thinking (e.g., *"We said that some dinosaurs had twenty rows of teeth. What might that tell us about those dinosaurs?"*). When students answer questions, acknowledge the correctness of response or quality of the thought, give corrective feedback on any part of the response that needs correction, and ask the question again later. Use student responses to guide your instructional delivery.

Guided Practice

Following the presentation of information, teachers should provide guided practice. Guided practice is an opportunity for students to practice new information, but simultaneously receive corrective feedback. As many of the students as possible should be actively involved during this instruction. It is important that teachers provide students time to think through newly presented information. Guided practice can take place in a large group format, during which time teachers can call on students randomly. If students are responding incorrectly, it is a message that perhaps additional instruction is needed. If, however, the majority of students have caught on, the teacher can re-teach the information to those who did not appear to catch on. Guided practice is also possible during small group, cooperative learning formats. During the small group activities, all students would be afforded time to practice learning the new information. Teachers can circulate around the room and provide corrective feedback as necessary. Additionally, if teachers notice that many students in several groups are experiencing difficulties, teachers can re-instruct and provide clarifications and additional information to several small groups simultaneously.

Independent Practice

Independent practice is an opportunity for students to continue to practice newly learned information accurately. Following guided practice, activities can be distributed that are directly relevant to the lesson's objectives and also provide students practice to firm-up responding and knowledge of the lesson's objectives. This can occur within a large group format or within cooperative learning groups.

Formative Evaluation

At least twice a week, if possible, teachers should acquire a product of student responding. Such information is valuable in determining the level of understanding of the course content, and provides important feedback on the pace and quality of your instruction. Formative evaluation can include brief quizzes, completed science activities, or class projects. These evaluation products should reflect acquisition of new content being introduced, and should also reflect consistent progress over time of such long-range science objectives as observing, classifying and predicting. Additional information on formative evaluation is included in the "Evaluation" section in Part II.

11

Cooperative Learning

What Is Cooperative Learning?

Cooperative learning has become a popular way to arrange instructional formats during selected activities in schools. It is sometimes referred to as collaborative learning, working in small groups, and cooperative learning. Cooperative learning refers to organizational situations in school in which students are working in small groups on their academic tasks. It is thought that these cooperative learning situations remove aspects of competition from learning environments, foster cooperation, and increase learning. It is therefore thought by many that cooperative learning situations may be especially conducive for creating successful mainstreaming experiences for students with disabilities. Sometimes students are grouped heterogeneously, such that one special education student is placed in a group with normally achieving peers who are of varying abilities. Although the groups can be arranged any way teachers desire. Several models of cooperative learning have been proposed and implemented in classrooms. Each model may take a variety of forms depending upon how classroom teachers implement the model. There are, however, typically some common features that most models share.

How Is Cooperative Learning Implemented?

This section describes some of the most widely used models, discusses the common features, and presents some illustrative examples of how the various formats could help facilitate the instruction of science for mainstreamed special education students. Additionally, this section addresses specific implementation procedures when cooperative learning techniques are intended for mainstreaming students into science classes that use textbook approaches and those that use activities-oriented approaches. Finally, guidelines are presented for adapting cooperative learning techniques with primary, middle, and junior high school aged populations.

Full Option Science System (FOSS) (Britannica, 1991) is a recently published activities-oriented science curriculum that advocates the use of collaborative groups comprised of four students each during all science instruction. The major emphasis of this approach is a hands-on activities-oriented approach. Most activities require having a variety of manipulative materials, making observations and predictions, recording data, and cleaning-up. The basic components of the FOSS model for collaborative learning are briefly described below.

Cooperative Learning: The FOSS Model
A Model for Activities-Oriented Approaches

- Four students work together and take turns with different roles to complete particular science activities.

- One student is the **Reader**. The **Reader** reads all print instructions, ensures that all students in the group understand the task, and summarizes the activity for the group.

- One student is the **Recorder**. The **Recorder** is responsible for recording all the data, including observations, predictions, and estimations. This would involve using pens, pencils, and the appropriate chart and graph paper.

- One student is the **Getter**. The **Getter** is responsible for getting all of the necessary materials and for returning all of the materials at the conclusion of the activity. This would involve walking and carrying equipment, such as trays, microscopes, water, slides, pans, and eye droppers.

- One student is the **Starter**. The **Starter** begins the manipulations of the materials, supervises the assembly of materials, and ensures that all group members have equal opportunity at using the hands-on materials.

The FOSS model provides teachers with a collaborative learning model that is a potentially successful procedure for having students work cooperatively on science activities. This model can be implemented with mainstreamed special education students by carefully assigning special education students to groups comprised of three general education students. For example, one visually impaired, hearing impaired, physically disabled, or learning disabled student could be placed with three students who have no learning difficulties. By assigning one exceptional student per group, disabled and nondisabled students are provided with opportunities to interact during the science activity. It should be noted, however, that many science educators who are proponents of collaborative group work, would argue that groups comprised of two or three students would have higher success rates.

What Are Issues Surrounding the Implementation of Cooperative Learning?

Two major issues, however, need to be considered when implementing the proposed cooperative learning model. These concern areas include (a) behavior management issues, and (b) individual accountability issues. Each issue is discussed separately below.

Behavior Management Issues

First, appropriate behavior of all students is a necessary prerequisite for the model to work effectively. Students need to know what behavioral expectations are associated with all four roles and how to execute their particular roles appropriately. If students cannot exhibit appropriate behavior, then teachers' time will be devoted more to correcting inappropriate behavior than monitoring the science activities. Acting-out and noncompliant behavior not only can be disruptive, but also can cause safety problems during science lessons in which manipulative materials are being used. It is important to note that "passive" students, who select not to actively participate and who are overly assertive or 'dominant' students also present problematic behavior that needs to be considered during cooperative learning.

What Are Recommendations for Decreasing Behavior Problems?

1. Provide initial practice with the roles and the associated behavioral expectations for all roles prior to implementing the cooperative learning during a science activity. Allow students opportunities to role-play scenarios that encourage appropriate social skills and behavior. For example, discuss how the starter can appropriately ensure all students in a group have equal chances at manipulating the materials, discuss ways to resolve conflicts appropriately, and practice effective group processing skills. Have one group role-play all four roles for the entire class. Discuss instances of appropriate behavior. Provide alternative solutions for instances of inappropriate behavior. Plan very simple science activities initially in order to give students a chance to practice their cooperative group skills.

   Use a T-chart to display class rules. Pick a rule and say *"what will we see if this rule is followed"* and *"what will we hear if this rule is followed?"* For example, if the rule is *"Every one does his or her job",* then:

Looks like	Sounds like
Only a few people moving around the room	Low voices from students in the groups

---

Sample Lesson on the FOSS Roles

Lesson Objective: Students will role play scenarios of getter, reader, recorder, and starter using role-play scenarios. Each student will have an opportunity to try-out all four roles.

Teacher: *Today we are going to learn about different parts we can play during our science classes. In science classes beginning tomorrow, we will be working together in groups of four in order to complete our scientific experiments. Each person in the group will be assigned a different name. These names refer to the jobs each person will be responsible for during science. The names of the jobs are: reader, recorder, getter, and starter. On the chart, I have listed the most important part of each job.* ....[Continues to present critical information, then provides a role-play scenario] *Let's pretend that we are having science today. If our lesson involved using our microscopes to look at onion cells, everyone think for a moment and write down what the getter's job would be.* .... [Evaluate student performance and provide corrective feedback. Discuss problematic areas and provide alternative ways of responding that are more socially appropriate. Additional practice might be necessary on successful ways to resolve conflicts. Repeat practice until you feel the class will be successful at implementing cooperative learning.]

---

2. Structure the chairs and desks in the room so that movement into and out of groups is easy and transition time is minimized. Transition times that are lengthy can often lead to inappropriate behavior. Teacher might "time" transition times and provide directions like: "*You have one minute to get into groups, starting now.*"

3. Pre-organize all the necessary instructional materials. For example, have all the necessary manipulative materials arranged on trays, with one tray per group. Also have the main distribution center for the trays in an easily accessible place, so that students are able to move freely while carrying materials to and from their work stations.

4. Match the assignment of roles with students who have the necessary prerequisite skills and necessary capabilities. For example, do not assign a learning disabled student who has difficulty reading to the Reader role. When students lack necessary prerequisite skills for assigned roles, they may tend to behave inappropriately. Conversely, assign roles freely to exceptional students if they have the necessary prerequisite skills. For example, do not be afraid to assign physically disabled students to the getter role, if such students can easily execute the demands of the task.

5. Set up class rules for cooperative learning time, post them in the classroom, and allow opportunities for practicing appropriate execution of them. For example: teacher assigns roles and groups, move quickly and quietly into groups, stay with your groups, talk quietly and politely, be good listeners, and encourage group members. Most students look forward to participating in science activities. Such participation can be viewed as the reward for good behavior. Students could sign a "safety contract," in which they agree to have appropriate behavior in order to obtain the privilege for participating in science activity time.

Science Safety Contract

I understand that when we have science class we must follow special rules. I agree to:

     1. follow directions
     2. walk
     3. talk quietly
     4. stay with my group
     5. share materials
     6. cooperate with my group members

Frank R. 5/94   *Lori Jones 5/94*

Signature of Student/ Date   Signature of Teacher/Date

---

6. Assign "passive" students to roles essential for the groups' success. This will facilitate active participation for these students. For example, assign a passive student to the role of reader, as that person ensures the group understands the activity and summarizes it for the group. Individually consult with the passive student and provide instruction and consultation on the desired behaviors.

7. Provide instruction on necessary academic and social preskills. For example, many special education students may require practice recording and graphing data prior to being assigned that role, or practice at "sharing" materials appropriately. Similarly, many students may need instruction and practice at "effective group processing" skills in order to work effectively as a group member. Arrange times with Resource teachers for students to obtain those preskills so that they may eventually be able to be the Recorder or Starter for the group.

8. Modify the group size and roles if necessary. The groups might need to be smaller or larger depending upon the size of your class, the age of the students, the number of manipulative materials available, the type of science activity being implemented, and the numbers and types of exceptional students being mainstreamed.

When working with primary students, groups of four may not be feasible. Perhaps a group of two might work better in some learning situations. In circumstances like this, modify the roles for students in the group as well. Assign one or two students as the getters for the entire class. In other situations an exceptional student may need a constant peer helper. If this is the case, assign five students to the group, with the fifth student being the helper for the disabled classmate. In some cases students learning and behavioral difficulties are so minor that no adaptations or modifications are necessary.

9. Provide overly aggressive students with feedback individually before breaking into the cooperative learning groups. An individual contract could be written with the teacher and this student that describes his/her role and how to act in non-dominant fashions. Individual feedback might be preferable to highlighting the feedback in front of the entire class. (See the behavior management section for suggestions regarding the design of contracts.)

10. Rearrange the composition of the groups periodically and vary the assignment of roles across students. This will allow all students opportunities for interacting with mainstreamed students and vice versa. This allows all students practice at all roles and may eliminate assigning blame to any individual student for a group's problems.

Individual Accountability Issues

In some models, individual students are not held accountable for any aspect of learning. In FOSS the reader is assigned the role to ensure student understanding, and although in some cases peers may be able to accurately assess understanding, in many cases, teachers need to arrange individual accountability systems and check for student understanding. This is particularly important for mainstreamed special education students. When these students are asked by peers if they "understand", they may be more likely to reply positively than to admit that they do not understand the activity.

What Are Recommendations for Increasing Individual Accountability During Cooperative Learning?

1. Design procedures for assuring individual accountability. This may be accomplished in a variety of ways, including individual "check-out" times with teachers, or presentations of summaries of learned information in written or oral formats.

Sample Science Class Check-Out					
Student	**Activity**	**Role**	**Date**	**Verbal/Written**	**Check**
Rwey-Lin	ant farm	recorder	1/27/92	verbal	OK
Jeff	ant farm	getter	1/27/92	verbal	OK
Kelly	ant farm	starter	1/27/92	verbal	OK
Shanna	ant farm	reader	1/27/92	verbal	recheck
Ann	ant farm	recorder	1/27/92	verbal	OK
Renee	ant farm	getter	1/27/92	verbal	OK

2. Include formative evaluation procedures to ensure that all students, but particularly special education students have mastered the lesson's objectives. These ongoing assessment procedures could parallel the types of activities that have been occurring during science classes.

3. Include performance-based assessment procedures such that students are assessed using the materials they have practiced with during science activities. Set-up laboratory exams during which time students are required to execute actual experiments similar to those conducted during classes.

4. Arrange additional practice time for special education students to complete activities two or three times if necessary. Special education students may be more successful at catching on or mastering manipulative procedures, if they are allowed sufficient opportunities for practice. When teachers check for individuals' understanding they will know whether or not students need additional opportunities for completing the activities. Additional practice times would also enable students to try-out new "roles." Consult with the special education teacher and determine whether additional practice could be completed in the resource room.

Sample Sign-Up for Extra Session Work

Sign up below for assignment to groups for an additional time working with the electricity units. Groups and roles will be posted prior to the activity. Groups will meet in room 24 at 2:30.

Names: 1. Donna
2. Juan
3. Tomas
4. Leona

---

5. Arrange a reward structure that rewards individual accountability within groups. Students could be assigned bonus points for successfully completing their responsibilities within the group. For example, teachers may want to provide extra incentives for appropriate behavior during cooperative learning time, and students who meet that objective could be allowed a special treat such as assisting with the set-up of the next science activity.

Class Sign-Up Sheet for Group Progress

Group Name	Individuals in Group	Task	Date Checked
Boilers	Shanna, Rosa, Ricco, CJ	sound unit	11/27,11/28,11/29,11/30
Hoosiers	Roy, Jake, Marty, MJ	sound unit	11/27,11/28,12/01,12/04

---

6. Establish a system in which all group members must sign the group's "data" collection sheet, or report, or final product, indicating that they understand the activity.

Data Collection Sheet for Group # 5

We agree that the data on the attached sheet represents the observations we made as members of group # 5. By signing this sheet we agree that we each understand the activity we completed.

_____
Recorder Signature

_____
Getter Signature

_____
Reader Signature

_____
Starter Signature

---

7. Establish a system where all students keep individual lab-booklets, lab-tapes (audio or visual), or journals that allow them to record group and individual observations surrounding the activity.

Are There Any Other Models of Cooperative Learning?

Various other models of cooperative learning also exist. Johnson and Johnson (e.g., 1991), and Slavin (e.g., 1988) have contributed significantly to the development of the various models. The models share similarities with the collaborative learning model advocated by FOSS. However, since these models were not initially designed for a science activities-oriented approach to instruction, they also have some distinct characteristics. Major components of those models are listed below.

Cooperative Learning: Various Models

- Two or more students work together and are rewarded based upon the performance of all group members.

- Two or more students work together and are rewarded based upon individual student performance.

- Two or more students work together and are rewarded based upon the performance both of individuals as well as all group members.

- Two or more students work together for a short-term task and rewards are not provided.

- Jigsaw procedures are employed during the cooperative learning. (Each group member is assigned a different, but necessary component of the group task.)

How Are the Other Models Different?

Major characteristics of these models that vary from FOSS are listed next.

Variations in group size (2 and up). It may be necessary to use a smaller or larger group size than recommended by FOSS. This may be especially true when working with students in the early primary grades, or when mainstreaming a student with many exceptional needs. Occasionally, teachers may even want to have a group of "one."

Variations in reward structures (within group, individual, competition across groups). Establishing reward structures can help ensure individual accountability of tasks. Rewards may be established such that the group reward is based upon all of the individuals within that group successfully mastering objectives. Competitive reward structures have also been established. In these cases, groups that "finish" first and meet the prespecified accuracy requirements are rewarded.

Jigsaw components. Jigsaw components have been designed to allow individuals within groups to have responsibilities for different components of the entire group's task. In some cases, once individuals are assigned their independent tasks, members from all groups within the class who have the same topic meet together in expert sub-groups. These expert sub-groups meet and complete their component of the group task. Then, original groups reconvene and each person is responsible for "teaching" the rest of the group the information learned as part of the expert sub-group. When using the jigsaw component it is important to note that each component stands alone and that each student actually completes only their own component.

Variations in tasks (e.g. text-based approaches employed). Cooperative learning has been used with text-book approaches to content area instruction. If science is a textbook approach, then cooperative learning might also be helpful for allowing students to complete reading assignments, writing activities, learning terminology and unfamiliar vocabulary, and writing reports by using variations of the models described.

Can Cooperative Learning Be Used With Textbook and Activities-Oriented Approaches to Teaching Science?

Cooperative learning examples for science textbook approaches and activities-oriented approaches could actually be quite similar in some ways. For example, the cooperative learning grouping procedures would follow identical procedures. All of the recommendations mentioned earlier would need to be considered for either approach to science instruction. Additionally, the assignment of roles would also adhere to the same guidelines, such that students with disabilities should not be assigned roles incompatible with their strengths. The major difference would be in the type of actual activities completed by the groups. Textbook approaches would most likely emphasize reading, writing, and oral reports of scientific phenomena, as major tasks and activities for members of the groups during the cooperative learning process. Whereas activities-oriented approaches would emphasize the manipulation and execution of scientific experiments as the major activities completed during cooperative learning. Consider the following assignment:

Cooperative Group Assignment:
Research on the Effects of Salt on Growing Plants

Textbook Approach: Assign group members various aspects of the project to research in the library. Employ a jigsaw technique, such that each member has a critical, but unique component of the research to conduct. One student might be assigned the task of describing salt in general. Another student might be assigned to research information regarding variations in salinity. Other students might be assigned to research normal plant growth, while a final student assigned to examine factors that inhibit normal plant growth. The group as a whole could be asked to summarize and synthesize their results. Final results would then be presented to the entire class.

Activities-Oriented Approach: Assign group member roles similar to those described by FOSS. Then, actually conduct an experiment following the scientific method using various solutions of salt on plants. Make group predictions and record them, along with the daily observations based upon plant growth. The group as a whole could be asked to summarize and synthesize their results. Final results would then be presented to the entire class.

What Is the Teacher's Role in Cooperative Learning?

Teachers play important roles during cooperative learning, too. If teachers carefully plan and assume responsibilities prior to implementing cooperative learning, success is more likely. A summary of the responsibilities of teachers is provided on the next page.

The Teacher's Role in Cooperative Learning

- Specify academic objectives

- Specify collaborative objectives

- Decide on group size

- Assign students to groups

- Assign individuals to roles

- Arrange room

- Plan and obtain all necessary materials

- Explain rules, specify expected behavior

- Explain tasks (academic & collaborative)

- Structure individual accountability

- Explain criteria for success

- Teach collaborative skills

- Teach nondisabled students how to interact appropriately with mainstreamed disabled students and vice versa

- Monitor students' behavior and learning during tasks

- Intervene whenever necessary for academic support and for collaborative behavior support

- Evaluate students' science learning

- Evaluate students' collaborative skills on individual and group levels

- Provide summary to class

- Evaluate entire process and make modifications and adjustments as necessary

What Are the Advantages and Disadvantages of Cooperative Learning?

Advantages and disadvantages exist surrounding the use of cooperative learning in science with mainstreamed special education students. Advantages in some cases have corollary disadvantages. Teachers need to carefully consider both advantages and disadvantages when selecting cooperative learning procedures to be implemented with mainstreamed special education students.

Reported advantages include increased positive social behavior and acceptance for handicapped students, higher achievement, increased positive attitudes and increased self-esteem (e.g., Johnson, Johnson, & Holubec, 1988; Slavin, 1990). Additional advantages of cooperative learning approaches during activities-oriented science instruction include the need for fewer manipulative materials for each class (e.g., not every student has to have a microscope in order to participate in the activity), and the assigning of students to roles where they can be successful during a science task (e.g., a mentally retarded student or a student with communication disabilities might be excellent Getters). Even during textbook approaches, however, there appear to be certain advantages for cooperative learning procedures. Students who have difficulty reading or writing can be paired with students who are readers or secretaries, and therefore be more successful at learning desired content. Students with sensory and physical impairments can be included in activities and assume responsibilities within their abilities. Students can also be provided with additional practice activities at learning key concepts and terms by seeing and trying the strategies that normally achieving students employ to study.

As with any teaching procedure, certain **disadvantages also exist**. Limitations that have been mentioned about cooperative learning include increased teacher preparation time, increased transition time, increased allocated time for lessons, and anxieties on the part of both disabled and nondisabled students regarding working together and teaching one another (e.g., especially during jigsaw activities). It has also been reported that dominant students may monopolize groups, passive students may become lost, assignments may not be at the appropriate levels for all students, class-wide behavior management problems may appear, higher noise levels in classrooms will appear, and learning may not occur for all students unless individual accountability systems are in place. It is particularly important to verify that students with disabilities are mastering the desired objective during science.

These limitations may be addressed by examining the listing of recommendation made under the FOSS model. Those recommendations can be applied to the variations of other cooperative learning models. If teachers consider all of the general guidelines recommended for each particular special needs' student and the next listing of considerations during initial planning for cooperative learning, there can be a great deal of success in science. Moreover, as with any instructional activity, teachers must constantly evaluate how well cooperative learning is "working" in their classrooms.

Potential Advantages and Disadvantages

Advantages

● Students with disabilities can be successfully integrated into science classes. Students with visual, hearing, communication, physical, learning, and behavioral disabilities can be allowed to participate with their peers during science activities and during science textbook approaches to instruction.

● Normally achieving peers can be trained to be peer assistants and help facilitate the integration of students with disabilities into mainstream science instruction.

Disadvantages

● Students with disabilities may not be sufficiently prepared with the preskills in social and academic areas for success and may experience failure.

● Regular education students and teachers may lack sufficient prerequisite knowledge on how to interact appropriately with students with disabilities.

What Do I Need to Consider When Mainstreaming a Special Education Student During My Cooperative Learning Science Class?

Prior to implementing cooperative learning during science classes containing mainstreamed special education students, success is more likely to occur if teachers first consider the following questions and continuously consult with the special education teacher. Consideration of specific needs of the disabled student with those questions will help ensure initial adequate preparation.

Mainstreaming Consideration

Does the student have .....?

- Academic preskills necessary for the assigned role

- Social behavior preskills necessary for active participation

- Knowledge of role responsibilities (e.g., Reader, Recorder, Getter, Starter)

- Knowledge of class rules during cooperative learning

Does the teacher have ....?

- Behavior management structure

- Rewards system

- Individual accountability system

- Formative evaluation procedures

Has the teacher considered ..... ?

- Type of instructional approach: Activity or Text

- Age of Class: Primary, Intermediate, Middle, Junior High

- Adequate preparation regarding positive interaction of nondisabled and disabled students

If students lack necessary preskills, specific individualized instruction in deficient areas may be beneficial.

Peer Assistance
and Peer Tutoring

Peer Assistance

Peer mediation strategies refer to strategies that involve having students help one another during instructional and practice activities. General education teachers can arrange peer mediation strategies to facilitate mainstreaming of exceptional students during science classes. These strategies involve using peers as assistants, buddies, or tutors to facilitate mainstreaming activities in science classes. First, issues and procedures involved in using peer assistance strategies are discussed. Second, a discussion involving peer tutoring is provided.

What Is Peer Assistance?

Peer assistance is a system of pairing peers with the goal of having one peer available to assist another student as necessary. This procedure may be especially beneficial when mainstreaming students with disabilities. Some exceptional students may require additional assistance during science activities and tasks. This type of buddy system can be very effective for providing initial assistance, or for soliciting extra help from teachers when buddies require assistance. This does not mean that exceptional students should not be encouraged to participate as much as possible in science activities. Contrary to that, exceptional students should be encouraged to participate to the fullest possible extent in science class and activities. For example, most visually impaired students can complete science activities right along with their peers. However, there are certain circumstances that arise which may mandate some special assistance. It is under these situations that peer assistance from a buddy can prove especially beneficial.

What Do I Need to Do to Implement Peer Assistance Programs?

Most teachers have students in their classrooms that they think are particularly reliable, nice, and bright. These students often are the general education students who can be identified as peer assistants or buddies. Sometimes, the less obvious students who are shy and quiet, or who are even minor behavior problems can be excellent peer assistants. Teachers can provide these students with some general training procedures for buddies. Information could emphasize proper social interaction skills and ways of providing positive and encouraging feedback. Teachers can then match buddies with particular exceptional students. At that point teachers may want to inform buddies of any particular and unique needs their exceptional student buddy might have. This might include information concerning when the student might require assistance from the buddy. For example, teachers might inform general education buddies about the typical times a visually impaired student might require some assistance from their buddy, or also how to properly assist a visually impaired student. This information might be presented by the special education teacher to the general education teachers and buddies. Both types of students (general and exceptional) may require some explicit instruction in effective social interaction skills. Neither group may have had much opportunity for interacting with one another prior to this time period. General education teachers could rely upon assistance from special education teachers with this training. Following this, teachers should arrange time for the buddies to get together, and explain the purpose of the peer assistance program. Opportunities should be arranged to allow buddies to observe in the special education settings. It should be emphasized that at times both partners will probably end up assisting one another.

Then, buddies can be asked to assist mainstreamed students with any particular tasks that might be too difficult or dangerous for the mainstreamed student. It is important that the peer assistance does not interfere with disabled students' ability to perform tasks that in fact are within their capabilities. Exceptional students should be encouraged to complete as many as possible of the regularly assigned tasks. It is important that the buddy be informed that exceptional students may be able to complete tasks, but the rate at which they proceed may be quite a bit slower. However, occasionally, some activities may require assistance for safety precautionary reasons or in order to modify or adapt some of the regularly assigned materials. This may be particularly true for students with physical or sensory disabilities. Teachers should then continue to monitor the progress of the peer assistance program and make any needed modifications. For example, if two students do not appear to get along, then perhaps a new buddy can be assigned. Or, if the buddy is attempting to do too much for the exceptional student, feedback should be provided as well. Guidelines for consideration are summarized next.

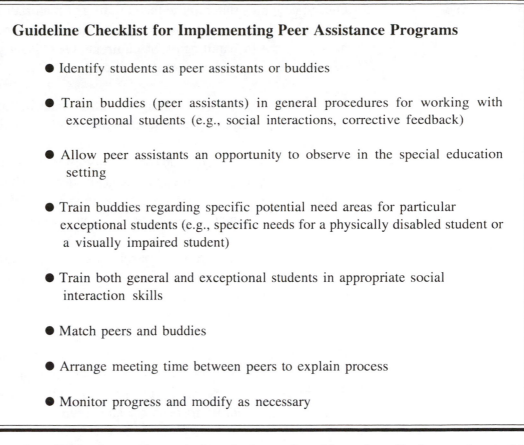

Guideline Checklist for Implementing Peer Assistance Programs

● Identify students as peer assistants or buddies

● Train buddies (peer assistants) in general procedures for working with exceptional students (e.g., social interactions, corrective feedback)

● Allow peer assistants an opportunity to observe in the special education setting

● Train buddies regarding specific potential need areas for particular exceptional students (e.g., specific needs for a physically disabled student or a visually impaired student)

● Train both general and exceptional students in appropriate social interaction skills

● Match peers and buddies

● Arrange meeting time between peers to explain process

● Monitor progress and modify as necessary

Samples of tasks that students can be asked to assist with are described next, along with the types of disability areas that may require special assistance from peers. One example for all categories of special populations includes having a peer assistant be responsible for alerting the disabled student of emergency procedures such as fire drills and tornado drills. These assistants and their back-up assistants can help ensure that students with disabilities are helped during emergency procedures. (See general guidelines section). (Be sure to check your school's liability procedures.)

What Are Some Examples of how Peer Assistance Can Be Beneficial to Students With Disabilities?

Students With Visual Impairments may Benefit From Peer Assistance

1. During activities that require moving the classroom desks and chairs around so that the overall classroom organization becomes unfamiliar to the student, peer assistants can provide verbal descriptions of where objects are now in the way, or provide assistance with guiding the visually impaired student around the room. This example may be true during the first several times the class is organized into cooperative learning groups and the desks and chairs have been rearranged.

2. During activities that require the handling of materials that are potentially harmful or dangerous in anyway, peer assistants can perform some of the manipulations or handling of the equipment for visually impaired students (e.g. burners, certain chemical solutions).

3. During tasks that require reading of textual material that is unavailable in braille or oral formats, peer assistants may read orally to visually impaired students. These peer assistants may even read ahead and tape record important textual information for visually impaired students. This may be especially important during science activities in which common 'trade' books from the library are used as reading materials, or when teachers update reading materials with current newspaper and magazine articles.

4. During science field trips to museums or other unfamiliar places, peer assistants can be helpful in orienting visually impaired students, and assisting them with finding their way to important locations, including exits, restrooms, and the like.

5. During the viewing of videos or movies that do not include 'descriptive' video components, peers could elaborate and provide more detailed descriptions of the events on the screens. These descriptions could be transferred into braille formats for later review.

Students With Hearing Impairments May Benefit From Peer Assistance

1. During activities that require extensive verbal descriptions from teachers, from principals over the school's intercommunication system, peer assistants can provide physical prompts or written summaries of major points covered during the verbal information. An example may include interruptions of important information during a science class. Hearing impaired students could be alerted by peer assistants that the loud speaker is on, and peer assistants could summarize major points in writing for them.

2. During activities that require the handling of materials that are potentially harmful or dangerous in anyway, peer assistants can perform first as models of appropriate behaviors for handling such equipment for hearing impaired students. Hearing impaired students can then 'copy' the procedures implemented by the peer assistant.

3. During tasks that require extensive listening components, peer assistants may take notes for the hearing impaired students. These peer assistants can use carbon paper or NCR copy paper so that they are essentially providing a copy of the notes they have taken for themselves.

4. During tasks that require extensive writing or speaking, peer assistants can perform the role of secretary or speaker for students with hearing disabilities. This can help when oral communication is difficult and when the student's stamina may be insufficient for some oral presentations.

5. During science field trips to museums or other unfamiliar places, peer assistants can be helpful in providing physical prompts or written directions for orienting hearing impaired students, and assisting them with finding out important information.

6. During the viewing of videos or movies that do not include 'closed caption' components, peers could elaborate and provide more detailed descriptions of the events on the screens by writing descriptions of key events or by providing physical prompts.

Students With Physical Impairments May Benefit From Peer Assistance

1. During activities that require moving the classroom desks and chairs around so that the overall classroom organization becomes difficult for mobility, peer assistants can provide physical assistance for improving mobility by either moving obstructions or bringing important materials to physically disabled students who have difficulties with mobility. This may be especially important during the first several times the class is organized into cooperative learning groups, and the physically disabled student's group is difficult to maneuver to. **Try to arrange the room with the needs of the physically disabled student in mind and many problems will be avoided.**

2. During activities that require the handling of materials that are potentially harmful or dangerous in anyway, peer assistants can perform some of the manipulations or handling of the equipment for physically disabled students who have difficulties using their hands (e.g. burners, certain chemical solutions).

3. During tasks that require extensive manipulations of objects that are difficult for some students with physical disabilities, peer assistants may manipulate the materials and orally describe each step to physically disabled students. This may be especially important during science activities in which many fine motor skills are prerequisite skills for successful completion of tasks. Often, manipulatives can be modified with some initial planning.

4. During tasks that require extensive writing or speaking, peer assistants can perform the role of secretary or speaker for students with physical disabilities. This can help when oral communication is difficult and when the student's stamina may be insufficient for some oral presentations.

5. During science field trips to museums or other unfamiliar places, peer assistants can be helpful in orienting physically disabled students, and assisting them to important locations, including exits, restrooms, and the like.

6. During extensive library research or experimentation that requires mobility of both fine motor and gross motor skills, peer assistants can potentially complete some of the leg and arm work for physically disabled students. However, allow the students to complete the tasks if they can do them.

Students With Learning Disabilities, Communication Disorders, Mental Disabilities, and Emotional Disorders May Benefit From Peer Assistance

1. During tasks that require reading of textual material that is above the reading abilities of these students, peer assistants may read orally to disabled students. These peer assistants may even read ahead and tape record important textual information. This may be especially important during science activities in which common 'trade' books from the library are used as reading materials, or when teachers update reading materials with current newspaper and magazine articles.

2. During tasks that require extensive writing or written research reports that may be beyond the levels of some students with disabilities, peer assistants can perform the role of secretaries. Disabled students can dictate their ideas into tape recorders for later write-ups by peers, or peer secretaries can write as students talk.

3. During tasks that require extensive speaking or oral communication, such as oral research reports that may be beyond the levels of some students with disabilities, peer assistants can perform the role of speaker. Disabled students can dictate their ideas into tape recorders for later write-ups by peers, or peer secretaries can read disabled students' work.

4. During lengthy oral presentations, peer assistants can take notes using NCR paper or carbon paper and supply copies of the notes to students who may experience difficulties with such tasks.

5. During tasks requiring additional practice, peer assistants can provide opportunities for additional practice with either the specific activities or with terminology from textbooks. Many students with disabilities will benefit from additional time on task with the manipulative materials and with content covered in reading materials.

6. During science field trips to museums or other unfamiliar places, peer assistants can be helpful in orienting disabled students, and assisting them with finding their way to important locations, including exits, restrooms, and the like.

Are There any Special Considerations for Using Peer Assistance?

It may be necessary to implement some prerequisite training with both general education students and exceptional students prior to mainstreaming and prior to the implementation of special peer assistance. For example, general education students may be totally unfamiliar with how to interact socially with students with varying disabilities. It may prove beneficial to have the special education personnel in your school complete a training program in which the specific disability areas are described and discussed. This would allow general education students opportunities to ask relevant questions regarding the disabilities. Additionally, it could provide an opportunity for them to become familiar with the types of tasks with which they may be able to provide assistance. Specific instructions and practice on social skills may be appropriate. This can be done by modeling and role-playing scenarios prior to initial mainstreaming.

Students with disabilities may be unfamiliar with appropriate ways of interacting with general education students. Teachers may need to watch to ensure that the special education student does not begin to become a pest to the peer tutor. If this happens, the special education student should be told when it's appropriate to interact with the peer tutor or assistant. These students may also need to be explicitly taught how to interact appropriately. Additionally, these students may need to be encouraged to speak up and tell general education students not to do too much for them. **It has often been observed that general education students can take on too many tasks for disabled students**. Sometimes general education students may want to do everything for disabled students, or may become impatient as tasks take disabled students longer to complete.

Carefully select peer assistants. It may be such that many students volunteer to assist. It is especially important to select only those individuals who want to assist. **Never make a general education student be a peer assistant if they do not want to**. This could result in a potentially volatile situation.

Sample Social Skills Lesson

Objective: Students with and without disabilities will role play scenarios on requesting assistance.

Teacher: *Today we are going to practice ways of asking for help. There are many different ways we ask for help. Can anyone tell me one way? ... Yes, that is correct, Gloria. One way is to raise your hand and wait until someone calls on you. What is another way of requesting help? ... Yes, if you have your buddy close by, you can ask the buddy for assistance. Good answer Ramon. What are the important things we need to think about when we ask for help? .. We need to be polite, we need to speak clearly and directly. Do we ever just poke our neighbor for help? No, that is not the correct way to ask for help. ...[Continue with practice. Have several students role play asking for help. Have class identify correct and incorrect features of the examples. Then divide class into pairs and provide several sample scenarios for students to practice. Provide corrective feedback as necessary.]*

What Do I Need to Consider When Implementing Peer Assistance During My Science Class?

Considerations for Peer Assistance Programs

- Academic preskills necessary for the assigned role?

- Social behavior preskills necessary for active participation?

- Knowledge of role responsibilities?

- Knowledge of class rules and procedures?

- Adequate preparation regarding positive interaction of nondisabled and disabled students?

- Types and severity levels of students with disabilities?

- Age of class, primary, intermediate, middle, junior high?

Teachers may decide that kindergarten students are too young to serve as effective peer assistants; or, conversely, that they are quite capable of being peer assistants for students with mild disabilities, but that they are not capable of assisting students with more severe disabilities. Teachers need to carefully consider the age levels of students along with the severity levels of disabilities when using peer assistance programs. It is recommended that if these procedures are implemented that teachers monitor the progress and modify aspects of the program as necessary. These procedures could be employed during both textbook and activities-oriented science instruction. As noted in the above examples, buddies can assist with tasks related to both types of instructional formats. If teachers attend to this set of guidelines when implementing peer assistance, successful mainstreaming of exceptional populations into science classes is more likely to occur.

Peer Tutoring

What Is Peer Tutoring?

Peer tutoring is another popular way to arrange instructional formats during selected activities in schools. Peer tutoring refers to an organizational scheme in school in which students work in pairs on their academic tasks. Various configurations of peer tutoring have been described and implemented. The roles are referred to as tutors and tutees, where tutors hold the instructional responsibilities for the tutees. Often one student is always assigned the tutor role and one student assigned the tutee role. Occasionally, students switch roles during peer tutoring and therefore become tutors part of the time and tutees the remaining time. There have also been a variety of ways in which the ages of students have been divided across tutor and tutee roles. Often peer tutoring is completed within one class, so that the tutors and tutees are all approximately the same age. Other times older students become the tutors for younger students, while sometimes, younger students become tutors for older students.

A variety of tutoring arrangements have also been tested with special education students. Configurations include having special education students tutor special and general education students, and general education students serving as tutors for special education students. It is thought that peer tutoring can assist students with tasks in which they require additional practice, and therefore may be facilitative for successful mainstreaming experiences.

What Are the Major Tutoring Arrangements?

- Students of the same age are tutors and tutees

- Older students tutor younger tutees

- Younger students tutor older tutees

- Students are tutors and tutees at any of the above age configurations

---

Are General Education Students Always Tutors?

Many research programs have demonstrated that students with disabilities can function well as either tutor or tutee in all of tutoring arrangements listed above. During mainstream science instruction, however, it is necessary to determine the purpose of the tutoring activity prior to implementing the procedure. If for example, students with disabilities require additional assistance in mastering science content, then most likely students with disabilities will be placed in the role of tutees, and students with appropriate knowledge will be placed in the role of tutors.

Teachers must decide when tutoring will take place. If tutoring is a supplement to the regular science instruction, where will the additional time for tutoring come from? Will it be before or after school, or during study hall periods? After time decisions have been made and the time has been allocated, it is necessary to prepare for the tutoring sessions.

What Are the Necessary Components for Establishing an Effective Peer Tutoring Program?

Research has indicated that students of all ages and abilities are capable of tutoring effectively. The most effective components that teachers must consider when implementing a tutoring program are listed next.

Peer Tutoring Program

- Clearly specified objectives

- Training procedures for tutors

- Formative evaluation procedures for assessing performance

- Good, clear tutoring materials

- Good personality matches between tutors and tutees

- Monitor the entire tutoring process

- Modify the tutoring process as needed

- Ability and Objective Match

What Are the Components of a Tutor Training Program?

Tutor Training Program

- Introduction to the purpose of tutoring

- Description of the roles: tutor and tutee

- Description of the responsibilities for each role

- Description of the tasks to be used during tutoring

- Practice with the specific materials and procedures to-be-implemented

- Demonstration of how the tutee should be taught to respond

- Demonstration of how tutors should provide corrective feedback

- Demonstration of what effective interpersonal skills should be employed

---

Sample Training in Tutor and Tutee Roles

Objective: All students will demonstrate the role of a tutor and a tutee. When provided a role play scenario, students will demonstrate appropriate tutor and tutee behavior.

Ms. Weagle, the Teacher: *Tutors are like teachers, but usually work individually with one student or tutee.*

Tutees are like students, and answer the questions that tutors ask.

Tutors and tutees need to be polite, speak in a pleasant, moderate tone of voice.

It is very important that tutors encourage their tutees to try hard and that they provide positive corrective feedback.

It is very important that tutees try hard, be positive, and polite with tutors.

[Model example of a positive tutoring situation and have students identify critical components.]

[Model an example of a negative tutoring scenario (e.g., poor corrective feedback) and have students identify what is incorrect and how to correct it.]

[Break group into tutoring pairs and provide practice with types of materials to be implemented at a later date.]

Following practice with the appropriate roles, students will be ready to try out the tutoring with the actual materials. Teachers may desire that students use precise procedures while tutoring. If this is the case, then, explicit instruction and practice with those procedures is recommended. A commonly employed instructional format for tutoring is now described.

Drill and practice formats are fairly easy to teach students. In drill and practice formats, students are using materials that have been previously introduced by teachers. During this type of tutoring the goal is to have students become more fluent at responding with correct answers. An example is having students become more fluent at knowing the definitions of various scientific terms. In this type of tutoring, the scientific terms could be written on one side of a flash card, and the corresponding definition on the reverse side. Tutors could be taught to show the terminology side and say: *"What does _____ mean?"* Tutees should be taught to respond with the appropriate definition. If tutees supply an incorrect response, tutors can be taught to provide appropriate corrective feedback. For example, a tutor might say, *"Not quite, can you think of anything else?"* or, *"No, _____ means _____. We'll try that one again in a few minutes."* or, *"Nice work, _____ does mean _____.* Simultaneously, the tutor could place correct responses in one pile and incorrect responses in another pile. Tutors could be instructed to write down or graph the correct and incorrect responses at the end of the tutoring session. Tutees could then be encouraged to take the stack of missed terms and study them independently. They might be told to try to come up with an elaborative strategy for assisting with remembering the definitions (see memory section for additional information).

Drill and Practice Format

- Prepare tutoring materials on flash cards

- Teach correct responding and feedback

- Separate correct and incorrect answers

- Practice incorrect items again

- Chart progress

Can Tutoring Be Implemented With Any Age Students?

Tutoring can be implemented with students of most ages. However, since there are certain social skills that are necessary prerequisites, students that are very young, may not possess the maturity necessary to make the tutoring situation a beneficial experience. It is necessary that teachers determine whether students can interact well during tutoring situations. Teachers can carefully monitor the effectiveness of the tutoring, and provide corrective feedback as necessary, which will ensure the program's success.

It is possible that most students can function well as tutors. Maturity level seems to be more important than age level in tutoring sessions. If students can handle the responsibilities of being tutors, the particular age level becomes less important. It is also important to consider having special education students function as tutors if they have appropriate preskills, knowledge, and maturity level. It has been reported that tutoring raises self-confidence. Whatever age level students are tutoring, it is recommended that teachers carefully monitor such tutoring situations carefully. Additionally, teachers should not force students to be tutors.

Can Tutoring Be Implemented With Textbook and Activities-Oriented Approaches to Science Instruction?

Tutoring programs can be implemented to assist with textbook and activities-oriented instructional approaches. Any aspect of instruction that appears to be more difficult for some students could potentially become the content for the tutoring program. Frequent tutoring programs have been used to teach basic skills in reading, math, and spelling. However, it is easy to envision a tutoring program designed to increase the learning and understanding of scientific terminology, a large component of textbook approaches to science instruction. Conversely, it is also easy to envision a tutoring program designed to facilitate the manipulation of various scientific apparatus during activities-oriented approaches to science instruction. Illustrations of each are provided in next two pages.

Sample Tutoring Program: Textbook Approach

Objective: Students will demonstrate knowledge of scientific terminology presented in textbook

Prerequisite social skills: Both tutors and tutees have demonstrated appropriate social interaction skills, including, appropriate tone of voice, eye contact, and corrective feedback procedures

Prerequisite academic skills: It is unnecessary that either tutor or tutee have mastered terminology. This type of task lends itself to a switching roles type of tutoring because one student can ask what does the term "electron" mean (or ___ is the definition for what term?), while the other student checks the answer with the textbook or the back of the flashcard. Roles can then be interchanged so both students have the opportunity to ask and answer questions.

Arranging Space: Tutors and tutees will need to sit either next to one another or directly across from one another.

Arranging Sessions: Schedule tutoring for ten minutes, five minutes students serve as tutors or tutees and then switch roles.

Tutoring Format: This type of tutoring lends itself to the drill and practice format described earlier. Tutors say: *"What does ____ mean?"* and *"____ is the definition for what term?"* And tutees respond. Corrective feedback is provided as needed. Include a record keeping system in which students record their progress.

Sample Tutoring Program: Activities-Oriented Approach

Objectives: Extra practice on learning how to build open and closed circuits

Prerequisite Social Skills: Appropriate knowledge of social skills, content, corrective feedback procedures, and evaluation procedures

Prerequisite Content Skills: Tutors have demonstrated the ability to put together open and closed circuits

Arranging space: Sufficient space will need to be designated for the set-up of necessary materials for the execution of the task. This might be at the back of the classroom, or a general work station area if space is available. The tutor and the tutee could share the responsibilities for getting the materials set-up and for cleaning up at the end of the session.

Arranging Sessions: Schedule tutoring for a sufficient amount of time to complete the activity. This may vary depending upon the activity. Include a record keeping system in which students record their progress.

Tutoring Format: In this type of tutoring, the tutor would provide prompts to the tutee throughout the task. For example, the tutor might say: *"Use these materials and build a closed circuit."* As the tutee puts the various apparatus together, the tutor could provide corrective feedback, like: *"Good, the wires are placed in the ___."* Corrective feedback might also be necessary. For example, a tutor might say: *"Not quite, the first wire is properly connected, but look at the second connection you've made. How could it be different?"*

In these two examples, it can be seen that tutors and tutees can switch roles under some circumstances, but not others. In the activity example provided, tutors clearly have more expert knowledge on the topic than tutees. However, it is also possible to envision a tutoring scenario during activities-oriented science in which tutors and tutees have similar levels of knowledge and assist one another. A major consideration in arranging tutoring scenarios involves close monitoring on the part of teachers to ensure that objectives are being met, and that appropriate behavior is being exhibited.

13

Evaluation

What Is Meant by Evaluation and Why Is Evaluation in Science Important?

The purpose of evaluation is to document progress and performance. In special education, evaluation refers to collecting ongoing information of student progress in order to make adjustments in their programs so that Individual Educational Programs (IEP) goals can be met. Evaluation procedures are a continuous component of the special education process. All students receiving special education services have IEPs. These IEPs are legal documents which include mandatory evaluation components. Every year each student's IEP is reviewed to determine the amount of progress made toward the objectives listed on his or her respective IEP.

This section provides some suggested procedures for enabling teachers to evaluate students' progress and performance in science classes. The mainstreamed student's performance during science class can contribute significantly to the evaluation of the student's overall program. First, various types of evaluation are described in relationship to science instruction and mainstreamed students. Applications and adaptations of these techniques are discussed in relationship to both activity-oriented and textbook approaches to science instruction. Finally, guidelines for selecting appropriate evaluation procedures for science classes are provided.

What Are the Types of Evaluation Procedures in Science?

Evaluation procedures for assessing mainstreamed students' performance in science classes can be viewed along a continuum. This ranges from anecdotal teacher comments, to more systematic documentation of student performance on tests and class projects, to performance on standardized tests. In between are various systematic procedures for collecting information on how the mainstreamed student is performing during mainstream science instruction. Many of these procedures have been referred to by researchers by names such as formative evaluation, summative evaluation, curriculum-based-measurement, performance based assessment, and portfolio assessment. Several of these procedures overlap in definition and purpose and all can provide insight into how the mainstreamed student is performing in science classes. Each is described next.

Types of Evaluation

- **FORMATIVE EVALUATION:**   ongoing, continuous assessment

- **SUMMATIVE EVALUATION:**   end of term, semester, or end of year assessment

- **CURRICULUM-BASED-MEASUREMENT:**   assessment directly linked to the curriculum being taught, typically completed continuously throughout the year

- **PERFORMANCE-BASED-ASSESSMENT:**   measurement directly linked to execution of tasks similar to those taught during instruction (implies hands-on assessment procedures)

- **PORTFOLIO ASSESSMENT:**   Collection of student products throughout a specified time period (e.g., semester, year)

Formative Evaluation

Formative evaluation refers to an ongoing assessment process. This means that student performance in science is evaluated continuously, throughout the instructional period, rather than simply at the end of the term. Formative evaluation measures can be any form. They can be paper-pencil quizzes, oral-verbal quizzes, or performance-based measures. Examples of formative evaluation measures are weekly or biweekly quizzes that cover samples of what has been learned during science. The quizzes could require students to write responses, to respond orally, or to execute procedures using manipulative materials that were used during the week.

Formative evaluation provides teachers with ongoing information on how well they are teaching and how well students are learning science information. This information can then be used to help teachers modify and adjust their instruction based upon both teacher's and students' performance. For example, if during an activities-oriented approach or a textbook approach to science instruction, teachers employ formative evaluation procedures, they will know whether or not mainstreamed students (and general education students) are meeting the objectives of the lessons. If, for example, visually impaired students were unable to describe accurately what had been covered during science classes, teachers would know that those students might need additional practice and instructional time with those same activities before introducing new content and concepts. Teachers may also know that the teaching strategies need to be modified. Some examples of formative evaluation measures are now provided.

Formative Evaluation Examples

- **Written Quizzes:** Content covered during the weekly science classes (terminology, concepts). May be multiple choice, short answer, open-ended, or essay formats.

- **Oral Quizzes:** Content covered during the weekly science classes (terminology, concepts, oral descriptions of application activities). May be multiple choice, short answer, open-ended, or essay formats.

- **Applications:** Demonstrations of content covered during the weekly science classes using actual manipulative materials, making predictions, observations, and recording and interpreting data.

It is recommended that **formative** evaluation procedures be implemented with mainstreamed students in science classes. This process provides immediate feedback on whether the mainstreamed students are meeting the desired science objectives.

Summative Evaluation

Summative evaluation refers to an end of the term, semester, or year assessment. Examples of summative evaluation in science include a final exam at the end of the marking term, or a standardized test covering science content. Summative evaluation measures are typically paper-pencil tests, consisting of multiple-choice, short answer, and essay items. However, it is possible to envision teachers designing and administering a summative evaluation test that is performance-based. That is, teachers could design a summative measure that required students to manipulate materials, conduct experiments, solve problems, make predictions, and record and interpret data. Summative evaluation measures provide teachers with information on how much information students learned and retained over extended time periods.

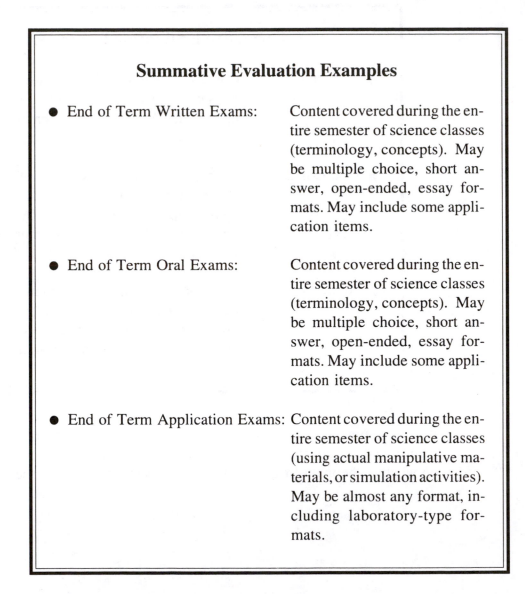

Summative Evaluation Examples

- **End of Term Written Exams:** Content covered during the entire semester of science classes (terminology, concepts). May be multiple choice, short answer, open-ended, essay formats. May include some application items.

- **End of Term Oral Exams:** Content covered during the entire semester of science classes (terminology, concepts). May be multiple choice, short answer, open-ended, essay formats. May include some application items.

- **End of Term Application Exams:** Content covered during the entire semester of science classes (using actual manipulative materials, or simulation activities). May be almost any format, including laboratory-type formats.

Summative evaluation procedures can also provide valuable information to teachers, but if information is only obtained at the end of the term, it may be too late to help special education students. It is important to obtain more immediate feedback on mainstreamed students' progress in science. When more immediate information is obtained, teachers can use that information to determine whether, for example, any additional modifications in science instruction could help facilitate the performance of special needs' students. Special education teachers can be helpful at not only designing short, formative evaluation measures, but also at recording students' performance on those measures.

Curriculum-Based-Measurement

Curriculum-based-measurement (CBM) shares many similarities with formative evaluation. CBM assesses students' progress along the curriculum being implemented, and it is recommended that those measures be taken continuously throughout teaching. For example, when using an activities-oriented approach to science like FOSS, CBM would continuously evaluate students performance and progress in the FOSS curriculum. Similarly, when implementing a textbook approach to science instruction, CBM measures would correspond to the particular curriculum covered in the adopted text series.

CBM procedures have been frequently implemented in the basic skill areas of reading, spelling, and arithmetic. During the implementation of these procedures in the basic skill areas, students are continuously assessed on measures designed to assess their performance toward the long-term or yearly objectives. Items are selected randomly from long term objectives, and student progress is monitored two or three times a week. Suggested procedures for designing and implementing a CBM program in science are listed on the next page.

> ## Guidelines for Developing and Implementing CBM in Science
>
> - Select the curriculum approach (activities-oriented, textbook, or combinded)
>
> - Select the level and materials (e.g., National Science Resources Center, *Science and Technology for Children* series, *Magnets and Motors* unit)
>
> - Select the types of activities to be used for assessment (e.g., performance-based, paper-pencil, pre-post tests)
>
> - Develop the actual assessment measures
>
> - Develop a record keeping procedure
>
> - Arrange assessment schedule
>
> - Develop instructional decision-making guidelines
>
> - Implement procedures
>
> - Monitor and adjust CBM program as needed

Performance-Based Assessment

Performance based assessment refers to assessment procedures that reflect the activities students have been completing during science classes. Performance based assessment procedures emphasize a hands-on approach to testing. The goals are to assess students' abilities to complete experiments, make observations and hypotheses, and collect, record, and interpret data. For example, teachers use materials and procedures for assessment that parallel those employed during teaching. If teachers are implementing an activities-based curriculum in science, then assessment procedures should involve the use of activities. For example, when an electricity unit has been taught using the manipulatives and students have actually constructed open and closed circuits and experimented with collecting data and making inferences, then parallel procedures are employed in assessing whether they have mastered those concepts. These procedures assess application and generalization of concepts and allow opportunities for students to show what they know, rather than relying on paper-pencil, multiple choice format tests.

Portfolio Assessment

Portfolio assessment refers to the process of collecting a portfolio of information on students throughout a specified time period. A portfolio in this sense is similar to a portfolio that artists might keep in order to show prospective employers the types of artwork they have completed in the past. In science this could mean many things. For example, mainstreamed special education students' portfolios might contain some of the following items.

Sample Portfolio Items

- Audiotape of oral reading from science materials collected and added to periodically throughout the year

- Samples of written work completed throughout the year

- Samples of laboratory booklets and notes kept throughout the year

- Samples of formative evaluation measures completed

- Summaries of performance-based assessments throughout the year

- Copies of summative evaluation measures (end of term exams)

- Teacher observations and anecdotal records regarding performance during mainstream science class, updated periodically

- Videotapes taken at various times throughout the year of the mainstreamed student during science classes

---

This type of assessment procedure can provide valuable insight into mainstreamed students performance in science classes. All of the evaluation procedures described could become components of a mainstreamed student's portfolio. This information could facilitate important instructional decision-making in relationship to student performance and progress. Additionally, this information could be used by teachers to determine which instructional procedures were most successful at promoting student learning in science.

Adaptations and Applications of Evaluation Procedures

Numerous advantages exist for implementing systematic, continuous evaluations programs for mainstream special education students. When using the above procedures, it is possible to adapt them sufficiently to meet the needs of students with disabilities. If teachers are going to be able to evaluate whether or not mainstream science placements are optimal placements for students with disabilities, it is critical to conduct some type of evaluation procedures. Recommended procedures are now listed.

Evaluation Applications for Students With Disabilities

- Collect pretest information before beginning units

- Collect posttest information at unit completion

- Collect continuous information throughout unit

Samples of Continuous Measures

- Collect samples of student work (e.g., products developed such as motors, worksheets, quizzes)

- Allow opportunities for students to participate in presentations

- Encourage use of student logs (e.g., notebooks, audio journals)

- Provide guidelines for students for maintaining logs (e.g., date each entry, draw pictures, write explanations, pose questions)

- Maintain teacher log on student progress and performance (e.g., write observations regarding how well the mainstreamed student is interacting socially, discuss adaptations or modifications that were successful or unsuccessful, academic progress)

The major goal of evaluating students is to determine what students with disabilities have learned in science and how they are performing in the mainstream science class. It may, therefore, be necessary to modify and adapt evaluation procedures for students with disabilities, as teachers do not want another assessment of the students' disabilities, but rather want an accurate assessment of their science learning. Examples of these modifications are now provided.

Familiarize Students With Test Formats.

Many special students have difficulty transferring something they learned in one context to another context. Unless "transfer across formats" is something you are testing, give students an opportunity to become familiar with novel test formats, when your test does not exactly parallel previous learning activities. For example, if you intend to give a multiple-choice test, give students a chance to practice responding on this type of test, perhaps as a practice activity, prior to actual test administration.

Alter Written Formats for Students With Writing Difficulties.

Students with visual impairments, learning disabilities, fine motor disabilities, and written communication disabilities will be better able to show what they know if the response formats allow them to verbally describe information or demonstrate procedures using manipulative materials.

Alter the Allocated Time for Testing Periods.

Students with disabilities may be unable to complete tests during the regularly assigned time periods. Many students with disabilities work at much slower paces and teachers will have a better measure of what students know if they allow sufficient time for responding.

Vary the Response Formats.

Students with disabilities may be better able to demonstrate their science knowledge using formats not typically employed in general education classrooms. Allow students with disabilities a variety of options, including use of computers, tape recordings, use of secretaries, oral reports, and options of performance-based measures where they either demonstrate the tasks or tell another student to manipulate the materials appropriately. Remember students with various disabilities may have different ways of demonstrating their knowledge.

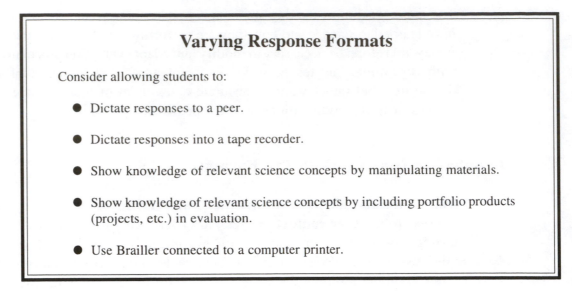

Varying Response Formats

Consider allowing students to:

- Dictate responses to a peer.

- Dictate responses into a tape recorder.

- Show knowledge of relevant science concepts by manipulating materials.

- Show knowledge of relevant science concepts by including portfolio products (projects, etc.) in evaluation.

- Use Brailler connected to a computer printer.

Modify the Presentation Format of the Test.

Students with disabilities may encounter difficulties understanding test directions. Students with hearing impairments, visual impairments, learning disabilities, and communication disabilities may need further explanation on how to respond the test.

Promote Good "Test-Taking Skills".

Some students with disabilities may not be good "test-takers." Apply test-taking skills principles described elsewhere in this manual, under "Improving Note-Taking, Study Skills, and Test-Taking Skills."

Modify the Scoring Procedures.

This should be considered when spelling, grammar, and neatness are considered part of the grade on a test. Some students with disabilities may lack sufficient preskills in those areas, but still be able to demonstrate their knowledge gains in science. Teachers may also consider giving partial credit to items that have been partially answered adequately by students with disabilities.

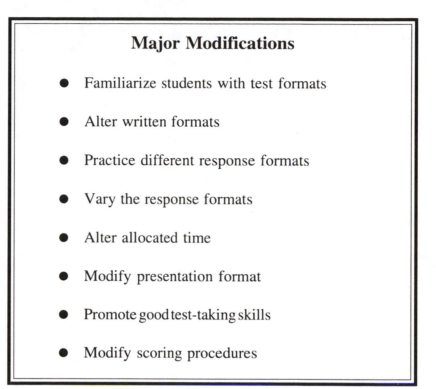

Major Modifications

- Familiarize students with test formats

- Alter written formats

- Practice different response formats

- Vary the response formats

- Alter allocated time

- Modify presentation format

- Promote good test-taking skills

- Modify scoring procedures

The above adaptations can take place in the general education classroom, or special education teachers, or peer assistants can help with the implementation of the adaptations. Finally, there are some specific recommendations for assessment for students with specific disabilities. Turn to the relevant disability area in this manual for these recommendations.

14

Strategies for Managing Classroom Behavior

What Are Behavior Management Strategies?

Effective behavior management strategies help ensure that **mainstream science classes are fun, successful, and safe.** As reported earlier in the cooperative learning section, there may be a potential for inappropriate behavior when students begin to work in more collaborative groups. This section presents some behavior management strategies that teachers can implement to help eliminate inappropriate behavior of mainstreamed special education students, as well as general education students. This section is divided into strategies for teachers to implement, ranging from simple to more complex strategies. The simple strategies include classroom environmental arrangements and teacher behaviors. The more complex strategies rely upon working directly with the student with behavior problems and with peers.

What Are Classroom Environmental Factors?

Many strategies exist that teachers can implement to help control behavior problems. When behavior problems occur during science classes, teachers should first carefully evaluate the classroom environment and analyze the activities occurring just prior to and immediately following the inappropriate behavior. This analysis can help identify the cause of the inappropriate behavior, which in turn helps identify an appropriate intervention for remediation. Brief descriptions of classroom environmental factors to consider are described on the next page.

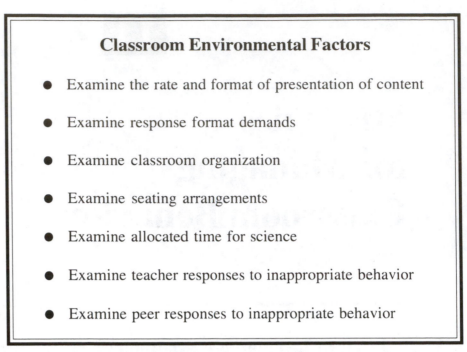

Classroom Environmental Factors

● Examine the rate and format of presentation of content

● Examine response format demands

● Examine classroom organization

● Examine seating arrangements

● Examine allocated time for science

● Examine teacher responses to inappropriate behavior

● Examine peer responses to inappropriate behavior

Examine the Rate and Format of Presentation of Content.

Is the format of presentation of content compatible with students learning needs? Can all students hear, see, or manipulate necessary materials? Have modifications been made for students with hearing problems? ... with visual problems? ... with cognitive problems? ... with physical problems? Is the content being covered at a pace that is compatible with all students? Do some students need additional time for practice and review activities?

Examine Response Format Demands.

Can all students adequately meet the demands of the required response formats? Is reading necessary? Is writing necessary? Is speaking necessary? Can modifications be made to assess student performance using an alternative format?

Examine Classroom Organization and Seating Arrangements.

Are the chairs and desks organized to maximize students' vision? ... hearing? ... active participation? ... appropriate behavior? Do I have students situated appropriately for assisting one another? .... for behaving appropriately? ... for easy and safe exiting for emergency situations? ... Do I have the room organized so a work space is available to clean up messes? Is everything in the room accessible for students with physical disabilities? (e.g., chairs, desks, lab equipment, computers, exhibit tables) .. Is scientific equipment stabilized?

Examine Allocated Time for Science.

How much time do I have allocated for science? Is there sufficient time for preparation and clean-up activities? Do I have the necessary materials? Am I adequately prepared for the lesson? Do students have unnecessarily long transition times? Do some students finish the activities early and have nothing to do? Do some students appear to need additional instructional and practice time?

Examine Teacher Responses to Inappropriate Behavior.

Do I actually reinforce inappropriate behavior by drawing too much attention to it? Can I ignore some things and speak independently with the student? Do I accidently set off behavior problems by requiring students with disabilities to complete tasks that are beyond their potential? Am I sincere, positive, and consistent with my behavior management system? Instead of pointing out a student's inappropriate behavior, praise another student out loud for exhibiting the appropriate behavior.

Examine Peer Responses to Inappropriate Behavior.

Do peers set-off the inappropriate behavior by laughing and making that student the center of class attention? Can peers be cued to ignore inappropriate behavior? Can peers be used to model appropriate behavior?

Once careful consideration of these environmental factors has occurred, teachers may simply alter one of them slightly and the inappropriate behavior may be remediated. For example, inappropriate behavior is likely to occur if a hearing impaired student cannot see and hear during the science class. However, moving the student's seat to a more appropriate spot in the class, will usually result in more appropriate behavior. Similarly, if extensive writing demands are required of students and learning disabled students, behaviorally disordered students, or students with mental retardation are in the class, they may act inappropriately, simply to distract attention from the fact that they lack the necessary preskills to complete the task. Simply altering the response formats of the task to be within the capabilities of the mainstreamed students may modify the behavior sufficiently.

What Are Simple Behavior Management Strategies?

Several strategies exist that require little teacher time and are simple to implement. Often consistent implementation of these strategies is sufficient to increase appropriate behavior of mainstreamed students during science classes.

Establish Rules for Science Classes.

Rules should be simple, direct, positive, and to the point. The number of rules should be kept to a minimum. Rules should be carefully explained and posted openly in the classroom. Careful, safe use of scientific equipment and materials should be emphasized. Teachers may establish special rules for cooperative learning and science periods, as during those activities students will be interacting more than when they work independently. Teachers should ensure that mainstreamed students are informed of the class rules prior to attending a mainstreamed science class. The resource teacher could be asked to review these rules with mainstreamed students. Additionally, realistic consequences should be described for rule infractions.

Consistently Enforce Rules.

Teachers should always consistently enforce the rules. When rules are inconsistently applied, students will tend to behave more inappropriately. The consistent application of consequences when rules are broken is important. Teachers may want to use language like *"You need to..."* instead of saying *"Would you...."*

Direct Appeal.

Often a teacher can speak directly with a student who is having a behavior problem and directly ask that student to alter the inappropriate behavior. This can be done by speaking privately to a student and saying something like: *"Juanita, I know you like science class and I know you know how to handle the lab equipment correctly because I have seen you do it the right way. Yesterday, I noticed you had a hard time during science class. Today, I'd like to see you try extra hard to handle everything appropriately... I know that you can handle the equipment appropriately. Let's see you try extra hard to do it the right way today!"*

Teachers can work out a personal code or signal with a student after discussing the behavior problem. For example, if a student consistently has difficulty attending to task, the teacher can explain to the student that when the teacher uses a particular signal or hand gesture, it is a reminder to get the student back on task.

Proximity.

Many times if a teacher moves physically toward the student who is behaving inappropriately, the physical presence of the teacher is enough to cease the inappropriate behavior. The teacher's presence acts as a reminder of the behavioral expectations.

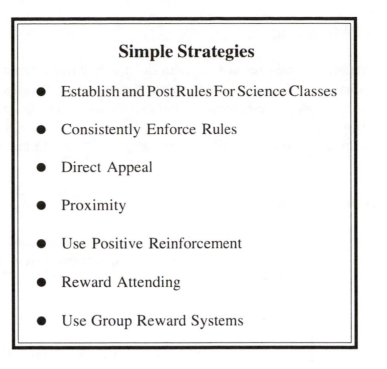

Simple Strategies

- Establish and Post Rules For Science Classes

- Consistently Enforce Rules

- Direct Appeal

- Proximity

- Use Positive Reinforcement

- Reward Attending

- Use Group Reward Systems

Use Positive Reinforcement.

Positive reinforcement is under-utilized in many classrooms. Teachers can often impact behavior change by using additional **verbal praise** during instruction. For example, a teacher might say: *"Jeffrey, Sharon, Ramon, and Shanna from group 2 are working especially well today on the rocks and minerals lesson."* After a statement like that, often other groups will start to work harder so that they can be publicly acknowledged, too.

Set up activities that virtually guarantee success and that can be expected to improve motivation. Then, praise the small steps during projects that involve many separate activities.

Public posting of good student behavior can also help shape appropriate class behavior. A chart including all student names and spaces for writing their individual accomplishments can be displayed prominently in the class. Prior to each science class, teachers can review who had outstanding accomplishments, including "working hard" during science yesterday. Some teachers post group rules and pass out rewards if students are following a particular rule. The rewards are then displayed in the room with the students' names on them. Teachers can even name an award, such as **scientist of the day** or week and have a ceremony distributing the award to deserving students.

Some special education students may be very anxious when they are initially placed in a mainstream science class. This anxiety may cause them to act inappropriately. Teachers can help these students relax in science class by using positive reinforcement. If teachers use positive comments and encourage these mainstreamed students they may tend to relax and try to actively participate in class activities.

Reward Attending.

Statements that reward attending can also be beneficial for increasing appropriate behavior. When it is clear that positive attention to tasks is important and rewarded, often appropriate behavior occurs simultaneously. Comments like: *"I like the way Ann is carefully watching Renee while she records the data from the experiment!"* can help show others students the rewards for attending are public praise.

Use Group Reward Systems.

Group reward systems can be implemented to help maintain appropriate behavior of an entire class. Many variations of group reward systems exist. One simple variation is now described.

Sample Group Reward System

Explain to the class that good behavior during science classes is very important. And, that during the next week every time "good behavior" is exhibited by students, a marble will be placed in the jar on the teacher's desk. Conversely, every time inappropriate behavior is noticed, a marble will be removed. On Fridays, if the marbles fill the jar, popcorn will be distributed to everyone in the class. Provide examples of good behavior and inappropriate behavior for everyone.

In the above example, marbles were removed when inappropriate behavior was exhibited. However, many teachers prefer to leave marbles in the jar when inappropriate behavior is exhibited by one student. These teachers attempt to respond to the inappropriate behavior separately from the group reward management system. An attempt should also be made to shift to intrinsic rewards whenever possible.

Another Group Reward System

At the end of the week one student's name is drawn from the "hat" (containing all names). If that student has not been "checked" for a behavior problem during the week, the class gets a reward.

What Are More Complex Behavior Management Strategies?

There are many strategies that are more complex than those just described that may be necessary to facilitate appropriate behavior. They are listed next.

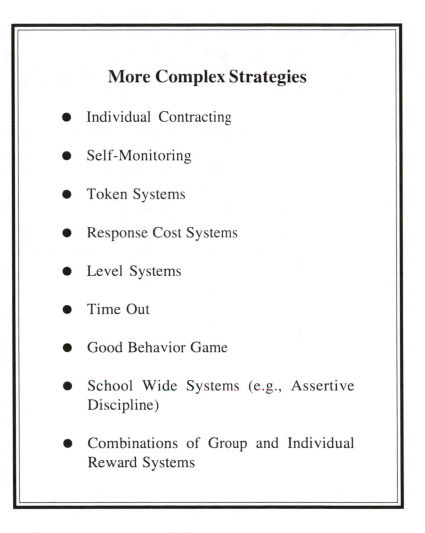

More Complex Strategies

- Individual Contracting

- Self-Monitoring

- Token Systems

- Response Cost Systems

- Level Systems

- Time Out

- Good Behavior Game

- School Wide Systems (e.g., Assertive Discipline)

- Combinations of Group and Individual Reward Systems

This chapter concludes with a discussion of each of the listed strategies together with examples of each.

Individual Contracting

Individual contracting is a behavior management system that has proven highly effective. Contracts influence student behavior by involving the student in writing a document that specifies contingencies for appropriate behavior. Doing this, students are involved in setting goals for more appropriate behavior. This allows students to see that privileges accompany appropriate behavior and consequences accompany inappropriate behavior and that teachers are not merely "picking" on them. The key components include: (a) meeting with the individual with the inappropriate behavior and selecting an obtainable behavioral goal; (b) specifying the circumstances under which the behavioral goal must be exhibited; (c) specifying the conditions that will be employed to evaluate the behavior; (d) specifying the rewards and consequences for the behavioral goal.

Key Components for Contracting

- Meet with student

- Select obtainable behavioral goal

- Specify reward for meeting objective

- Specify circumstances for meeting behavioral goal

- Specify times for evaluating status of contract

- Write-up, sign, and date contract

Special education teachers can be helpful in designing the specific behavioral contracts with mainstreamed students and general education science teachers. These contracts can be written to change almost any behavior including: (a) increasing on task behavior, (b) decreasing inappropriate behaviors, (c) increasing science performance, and (d) increasing appropriate behavior. Before writing a contract with a student it is important to carefully determine the precise behaviors to be included and to be sure that students can actually execute the behaviors in the contract. It would be detrimental to the student to include a behavior that was beyond the control of the student at the present time, as then the student would be less likely to try. A sample contract is presented on the next page.

Individual Behavioral Contract

Goal: Sharlene will follow the class rules in science classes. This means that she will participate actively with her cooperative group during all science activities. She will carry-out the responsibilities associated with her assigned roles, even if the role requires hard work. She will ask for help from the teacher when necessary.

Reward: If Sharlene meets the behavioral goal, she will be allowed to select the next activity from a listing and select her role for next week's science classes.

Start Date: September 10th.

Review Date: Every Friday, fourth period.

Student Name & Signature: *Sharlene Gomez*
Sharlene Gomez

Teacher Signature: *Terry Milham*
Ms. Milham

Witness: *Jeffry P. Ball*
Mr. Bakken,
the resource teacher

Goals can be numbered on a contract, rather than written as in the above example. Additionally, the rewards can also be more clearly specified. For example, a listing of activities from three categories could be appended to the above sample contract. Finally, all parties signing the contract should receive copies.

Contracts appear to be most successful when teachers involve students in the design, development, and evaluation process. Teachers may even want to involve the parents in the design of a contract. Often parents may reward the child at home for successful completion of the contract's goals. Additionally, it is imperative to determine a schedule for reviewing progress on the contract.

Self-Monitoring

Self-monitoring procedures are widely used with special education students and have been very successful at modifying inappropriate behavior. Self-monitoring procedures are sometimes referred to as self-recording, self-management, self-control, self-evaluation, and self-instruction. All procedures are intended to actively involve students in the process of taking control over their own inappropriate behaviors and changing them to more appropriate, acceptable behaviors. These procedures have been successfully implemented to increase attention to task and to increase academic and social behavior performance. The first key element to include in teaching students to implement self-monitoring procedures is an awareness of the purpose of self-monitoring and an awareness of the behavior that needs to be modified. Dialogue for a sample self-monitoring session for increasing attention during science instruction is presented on the next page.

Self-Monitoring Instruction:
Increasing Attention During Science

Sr. Sharon,
the teacher: *Jeff, we know that you have had a hard time paying attention during science classes. Many times during class you seem to be thinking about something other than science. For example, yesterday, you were playing with your trucks in your desk while you were supposed to be reading your science materials. The day before yesterday you were wandering around the room disturbing other students, when you were supposed to be completing the minerals activities. Do you agree?*

Jeff: *Well, yes, it's sometimes hard to pay attention.*

Sr. Sharon: *We are going to try something new to help us see if you can learn to pay attention better during science. OK?*

Jeff: *Yes.*

Sr. Sharon: *First, we need to agree on what we mean by **pay attention**. What do you think I mean by pay attention?*

Jeff: *Well, I should be working on science things.*

Sr. Sharon: *Yes, you should be working on science activities during science class. But let's be more specific about what we mean. Since we do lots of different activities during science, we need to be more precise about defining paying attention. I mean some of the following: listening to directions, following directions, working well with partners in your cooperative group, completing all reading, writing, and science activities. Jeff can you think of any other examples of what I mean by paying attention?*

Jeff: *Sitting at my desk and not poking Rick.*

Sr. Sharon: *Exactly right. You've given me an example and a nonexample of paying attention. Paying attention also does **not** mean: doing things other than science during science, playing with toys in your desk or your pocket, being out of your seat unless you are the getter for group. Now I'm going to show you a self-monitoring sheet with some examples of paying attention and examples of not paying attention. Every time you hear this beeper* (press beeper on watch) *I want you to record whether or not you were paying attention. If you were paying attention, place a check under that column, if you weren't, place a check under that column. Understand?*

Jeff: *Yes, I think so.*

Sr. Sharon: *Good, let's practice this procedure.* (Provide examples and nonexamples and practice checking off when the timer beeps. It is important to ensure that the student knows what is expected and how to do it prior to implementing the procedure during instruction.) *Good work. I think you understand how to do this. Any questions?*

Jeff: *I think I get it.*

Sr. Sharon: *Now I want you to keep this self monitoring sheet on your desk during science class. Every time you hear the beep, place a check mark in the correct column.* (Teacher has a prerecorded tape with beeps occurring at random intervals)

Self-Monitoring systems like the example can be implemented across a wide variety of tasks. Most importantly, the targeted tasks need to be task analyzed and all necessary steps identified for the student. This might be as simple as: Getting out the pencil, sitting with feet on the floor, keeping hands to myself, etc. Effects have proven to be robust across disability areas and across types of tasks. Students have also been taught to use these procedures in conjunction with specific learning strategies to increase academic performance (see strategies for reading). Success at self-monitoring procedures helps create independence in students. Eventually, the beep tape would be removed, followed by removal of the self-monitoring sheet itself. Students who are using the beep tape could also use head phones so that the beep does not disturb anyone else in the room. A sample self-monitoring sheet is now presented.

Sample Self-Monitoring Sheet

Renee's Science Class Monitoring Sheet

Week of February 10 - 14

Place a + every time the beeper rings and you are on task. Place a 0 every time the beeper rings and you are off task

Monday	Tuesday	Wednesday	Thursday	Friday
++++	00++			
++++	0+++			
0000	++++			

Monday	Tuesday
8, +s	9, +s
4, 0s	3, 0s

Another Sample Self-Monitoring Sheet

Token Systems

Token systems are designed to increase appropriate behaviors such as task completion and on task behavior. Tokens, such as chips, points, or tickets are given to students for appropriate behavior and are exchanged later for a privilege or reward. The target behavior must be carefully identified as in the previous examples, and the schedule for awarding tokens should be explained to students. The schedule could be similar to the beep tape example used in the self-monitoring example. In this case, every time the beep sounds, the teacher distributes tokens or points **only** to students who are exhibiting the targeted behaviors. Additionally, the teacher needs to specify when the allocated time period for exchanging tokens for other privileges will occur. As with all reward systems it is imperative that teachers identify "what are rewards" for their students. If, for example, a teacher assumed that all students would like a popcorn party as a reward, and later found out that half the class did not like popcorn, then popcorn would not be considered a reward for the half of the class that did not like it. Teachers can administer surveys requesting student likes and dislikes and use that information in designing any reinforcement system.

Keys to Token Systems

● Discuss what tokens represent

● Discuss when tokens will be distributed

● Discuss when tokens can be exchanged

● Discuss any response cost components

Response Cost Systems

Response cost systems refer to the loss of reinforcers when students exhibit inappropriate behavior. Teachers often implement this type of system when they keep students in from recess or do not allow them to participate in fun activities. It can, however, be systematically implemented alone, or in conjunction with any of the other positive reward systems. For example, in designing a token system, teachers state that students automatically lose a token for arguing with a teacher. However, once all rewards are lost, the system has nothing positive to offer the student.

Level Systems

Level systems have been implemented with a great deal of success in increasing appropriate student behavior by simultaneously increasing student responsibilities. Students earn rights and responsibilities according to a system of levels. The lowest levels usually have little to no privileges associated with them. However, in the upper levels students take more control of their own behavior and earning more privileges. The relationship between responsibilities and rights is emphasized, and students earn more rights as they demonstrate they can handle more responsibilities. This type of system has worked well in special education settings and can work well in mainstreaming special education students. One of the highest levels in the level system can be to go to science class in the mainstream. In this way the general education science class is seen as a privilege and the student must adhere to certain behavioral responsibilities in order to maintain the right to attend class. A sample level system is now described.

Sample Level System

Note that each level contains **rules** and **privileges**.

Level 1 **Rule:** Be prepared for class, sit in desk at all times, no talking, raise hand for assistance.
Privilege: If all assignments are accurately completed students can independently read a book at their desk.

Level 2 **Rule:** Be prepared for class, self-monitor on-task behavior in accordance with beep tape, raise hand before speaking.
Privileges: Getting out of seat to get drink of water or going to pencil sharpener when work is completed; cooperating in group science activities with peer or teacher supervision.

Level 3 **Rule:** Be prepared for class, self-monitor on-task behavior in fifteen minute intervals, raise hand before speaking.
Privileges: Getting out of seat to get drink of water or going to pencil sharpener when work is completed, going to the back of the room to the science activities exhibit when work is completed, cooperating independently in group science activities.

Level systems are most effective when the rules are clearly described and when regular review procedures are established. That way, students know when their weekly performance will be reviewed and they can help in determining whether or not their level should be increased, decreased, or remain the same.

Time Out

Time out decreases student inappropriate behavior by removing the student from access to the environment with the reinforcers, in this case, the science classroom. In the mildest form of time out, teachers may simply remove the student from participation in class activities, although the student can continue to observe the classroom. At another level, the student may be required to face the wall. At a more severe level, it may mean that the student is removed from class to a **supervised room** away from the science class. Many variations of time out exist and teachers should ask their school administrators for their school policies regarding time out prior to implementing it. Generally, time out is most effective when (a) the behaviors that result in time out are made very clear to students, (b) time out is relatively brief in duration, and (c) students are given a personal "debriefing," by the teacher, before being returned to the classroom, as shown in the table.

Debriefing for Time Out

Before you return to the classroom you must answer these questions to your teacher's satisfaction:

1. What did I do that got me into trouble?

2. What could I have done to have stayed out of trouble?

3. What will I do the next time to stay out of trouble?

Good Behavior Game

The "good behavior game" is used to promote cooperative group behavior management. Assign students to groups (this can be done when working in groups, or even when students are working individually) and prespecify the target behaviors (talking out, out of seat, arguing, etc.). When a group member exhibits one of the behaviors, the entire group is given one mark on the blackboard. At the end of the activity, post the name of the winning group, or provide a reward. To avoid too much competition, prespecify a target number of acceptable marks (e.g., three) for groups, and reward each group that meets the standard with, for example, posting the group name, free time, or a desired activity.

School-Wide Systems

Many schools have implemented school wide behavior management systems. Systems such as Assertive Discipline have been successfully implemented across the nation. It is recommended that teachers question whether or not their school has any system-wide policy, and be consistent in implementing school wide policies within their own classroom settings. The system may be simple ranging from a common set of rules, to a more complex system such as Assertive Discipline.

Combinations of Group and Individual Reward Systems

Some behavior plan systems can combine individual and group contingencies to optimize student behavior. Often teachers may need to implement a variety of behavior management systems. This can include combinations of the various strategies described.

Strategies for Improving Attention

What Are the Sources of Attention Problems?

Attention problems are common in classrooms, and range from mild, occasional problems (such as daydreaming) to severe, in which the attention problem is chronic and involves hyperactivity. Although some students have genuine difficulties sustaining attention in any environment, it is wise to first examine the student's environment for contributing factors. Often, students do not pay attention because they cannot **read** the assigned text, they do not **understand** the concepts being taught, or because they lack **motivation** to try hard, or are distracted because of **personal problems**. In other cases, students may not pay attention because they have difficulty **seeing or hearing** the presentations, or because physical impairments hinder their ability to **interact** with the curriculum materials. If any of these problems seem to be operating, consider some of the suggestions for dealing with these problems described elsewhere in the text. If you can rule out these problems, or if you have addressed them and still find the student inattentive, consider the following.

What Are Strategies for Increasing Attention?

Direct Appeal

Sometimes students may begin to pay less and less attention, simply because they do not think it matters to the teacher. You may see this behavior with students who are used to small special education classes and now feel insignificant or unimportant in a large regular education class. Try simply speaking to the student alone, and pointing out that you are concerned about his or her learning. Emphasize the importance of paying attention in class. Although this may seem a very simple intervention, it may be surprisingly effective. To be effective for an extended period of time, however, you may have to speak to the student at regular intervals, or interact with the student during class in such a way that he or she realizes that you are concerned.

Proximity

In some cases, standing nearer the inattentive student (or moving the student nearer you) and increasing the rate of questioning can increase attending. Some students may be much more likely to attend to you if they feel that you are attending to them. Encouraging questions and comments from the student with positive feedback can also be an important strategy in promoting attention.

Allow Movement

Some students are naturally more active than others. In some cases, allowing a student to get out of his or her seat and move around the class for some particular purpose (e.g., collect worksheets or distribute materials) may allow the student the movement he or she needs.

Intensify Instruction

Is there some way of making your presentation more engaging? Using more enthusiasm, humor, and variety in your teaching can serve to increase interest on the part of the students (see the section on "Strategies for Improving Motivation and Affect"). Use demonstrations and examples to make the content more real. Use a variety of media in your presentations, including color transparancies on the overhead projector, slides, films, and audiotapes. Find ways to increase student participation. Whenever possible, move your class model away from lectures and individual workbook activities and toward active student interaction with you and with scientific materials and phenomena.

Teach **enthusiastically**: Make positive and emphatic physical gestures and facial expressions; vary your tone of voice to express interest and excitement; move about the classroom and make eye contact with all students; express acceptance and interest in student ideas and other contributions.

Use **visual aids**: Color transparancies on the overhead projector, slides and films, interesting demonstrations.

Provide **more student activities**: Give students things to do, rather than just look and listen; involve them in experiments; prompt them to make predictions about experiment outcomes, and compare the results to their predictions; break students into groups which compete to finish first, or complete most correct answers. Ask one rotating student from each group a question from the present unit -- the student can listen to suggestions from other group members, but must decide on the answer him or herself. One point is awarded to the group for each correct answer.

Use classroom peers. Position reliable classroom peers to watch for lapses in attending and point out these lapses to the student. Tell the peer to be subtle in the feedback (e.g., lightly touch the student's back), and don't point out inattending to you unless the student fails to benefit from the feedback. Make sure all students involved understand that you are all working to help the student do better in school. When using cooperative learning groups, enlist all students in the group to prompt attention in the student.

Reinforce attending. Set an egg timer, alarm clock, or tape recorder to sound at random intervals (e.g., every 5-15 minutes, but also set some surprise intervals of only a minute or so). If the student in question is attending when the sound occurs, give him or her some type of positive feedback. (Pre-record the beeps onto a tape and have the student wear earphones so the beeps will not disturb the rest of the class). This can include verbal praise, points on a check sheet, or tokens which the student can save and exchange later for desired objects, privileges, or desired activities. For example, if the student earns 90% of possible points or tokens in a two week period, he or she is given additional time to work on a desired science activity. If such an approach seems likely to promote jealousy or resentment among mainstream students (e.g., that the student is able to work for rewards that are unavailable to others), consider making the reward a class privilege, such as additional recess time, or a favored activity. This may help the class feel they are all invested in the target student's improved attending, and share responsibility for the student's success or failure.

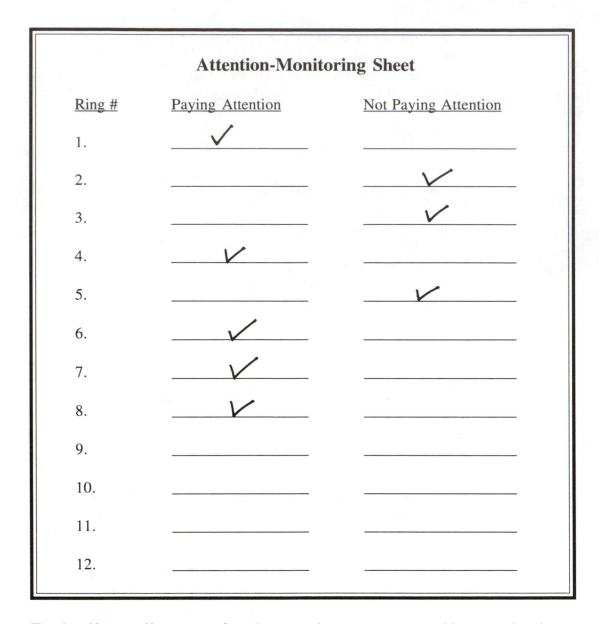

Attention-Monitoring Sheet

Ring #	Paying Attention	Not Paying Attention
1.	✓	
2.		✓
3.		✓
4.	✓	
5.		✓
6.	✓	
7.	✓	
8.	✓	
9.		
10.		
11.		
12.		

Teach self-recording strategies. Some students may not attend because they have not learned how to monitor and evaluate their attending. In this case, self-recording training may be helpful. First, discuss the attending problem with the student, prompt the student to acknowledge that attending is a problem (provide evidence if necessary), and to agree that it would be in his or her own interest to improve attending skills. Then, show the student how to evaluate and record whether he or she is paying attention during class. Provide the student with tape-recorded "beeps" which occur at random intervals, or a kitchen timer which you set for random intervals. Typically, the cuing interval has been from about one to about five minutes, depending on the needs of target students.

When the student, or students, (this procedure can work for more than one student at a time) hears the cue sounding, he or she should record, with, for instance a "+" or "-", whether or not he or she was paying attention. At first, record for yourself whether the student was attending, and compare records at the end of the period. The student can be reinforced (with praise, privileges, tokens, or other rewards) for recording at all appropriate times, or for approximating the results of your recording of their attending. Calculate the percent of cues during which the student was attending and make a chart of progress. You may not have to reinforce the student for improving attending -- in many cases, directing the student's attention to attention can increase academic engagement and achievement.

When the student becomes accurate and automatic, and attending improves sufficiently, you can fade out the cues (i.e., fewer and fewer "beeps" or "rings" each period). However, you should continue to advise the student of the importance of paying attention, and continue to provide the student with feedback on his or her level of attending.

Self-recording strategies can be used for attending to teacher presentations, attending to group activities, or attending to individual work activities. Self-recording can also be used for management of classroom behavior, as described in the section on behavior management.

Frequently, special education teachers teach self-recording strategies in their own classrooms. These strategies do not always generalize to the regular classroom, but generalization is more likely to happen if it is also directly prompted and monitored by regular classroom teachers. With systematic communication between regular and special educators, attentional problems can be improved.

Self-Monitoring of Attention

- Come to an understanding with the student about the nature of the problem and why it needs to improve.

- Set up a self-recording sheet and a cuing system.

- Reinforce the student for matching your assessments of attention.

- As goals are met, fade the explicit self-recording system.

- Continue to provide feedback.

- Reinstate self-recording when needed.

Strategies for Improving Memory

What Are the Causes of Memory Problems in School?

As all teachers know, many students (not just students with disabilities), have difficulty remembering important information. In this section are listed some strategies for improving memory for science content.

Before attending to these specific strategies, be certain that the problem is primarily a memory problem, and not the consequence of some other consideration. For instance, students may not remember because they have particular difficulties with remembering school content. However, they can also fail to remember because they do not pay attention, lack study skills, can not read the text, do not comprehend the content, or because they lack motivation. If some of these factors may also contribute to the "memory" problem, they should be considered, in addition to the following.

What Are Recommendations for Improving Memory?

1. Increase attention. Many students do not remember because they were not paying attention, or only partly paying attention, in the first place. To increase attention, consider the recommendations in the section, "Strategies for Improving Attention."

2. Promote use of external memory. External memory refers to devices outside of the student's own mind intended to enhance memory. This includes writing things down (in notebooks, appointment books, or language cards) placing things to be remembered (books, notes, laboratory equipment) in prominent places where they will be seen, and physical prompts (e.g., tying a string around the finger) to remember things. External memory systems for tests ("crib sheets") are generally inappropriate, and students should be made to realize this.

3. Enhance meaningfulness. Meaningful things are more easily remembered than nonmeaningful things. New science content can be made more meaningful by relating it in some fashion to the things that are already known. For example, when discussing levers, use see-saws as examples. When discussing the characteristics of amphibians, use examples of amphibians the student already knows.

4. Use pictures or imagery. Science content is more easily remembered when it is pictured. The picture makes the concept more concrete, and more concrete things are easily remembered. Additionally, pictures can be stored and retrieved as mental images, which adds another dimension to the memory process. Verbally presented concepts are not generally stored as images, and are more difficult to remember. Pictures shown on the overhead projector can produce particularly strong images. When pictures are not possible, describe the phenomenon very clearly, and encourage students to make a picture in their mind. Have students draw their images. If they produce a clear and detailed mental image, this also will enhance memory.

5. Minimize interfering information. Emphasize the most important aspects of the content, and avoid unnecessary digressions. Provide only highly relevant examples.

6. Promote active manipulation. Science concepts are better remembered if students actively manipulate examples of these concepts, with particular respect to their critical features. For example, if students create closed and open circuits, they are more likely to remember relevant concepts than if they simply read about them.

7. Promote active learning. Encourage students to actively reason through new content (e.g., "Why do you think the beaver's front teeth never stop growing?"). Encourage them to create new examples of the concept being taught (e.g., "Who can give me another example of a second-class lever?"). Promote active rehearsal (practice) of newly presented information (e.g., with pairs of students with flash cards), and review frequently.

8. Increase practice. Find additional time periods, however brief, in which, students can review and practice important science content. They can review individually, drill each other with flash cards, or ask questions out of the book, or review orally with the teacher as a whole class activity. Although finding additional time may be a difficult proposition, it may be possible, for example, to find an extra ten minutes a day by rewarding students for coming back from recess or lunch promptly and undertaking ten minutes' intensive drill of science content before starting the next activity. Perhaps they could be assigned randomly to "teams" who compete with each other for "Best Scientists" status (see also the chapter in this section on cooperative learning). Teachers can also use time while students are waiting in lines or doing other trivial activities to provide brief review sessions.

9. Use mnemonic techniques. Mnemonics are procedures designed to increase memory. They were first applied by the ancient Greeks, who had limited access to written implements or written material, and therefore had to store more information in their minds. The same can be said for many students with limited reading ability, who can rely less on printed material, as well as for students who simply have difficulty remembering things. **Mnemonics are intended to supplement, rather than replace, other teaching methods, and are intended to be used at times when vocabulary or other factual learning needs to be facilitated.***

Mnemonics, appropriately adapted to student needs, can be effectively applied with most students with disabilities. However, the utility of mnemonics, or any verbal elaboration technique, with students with hearing impairments is uncertain. Different mnemonic techniques are described separately in the sections which follow.

How Can Mnemonic Strategies Be Used?

Some General Examples

There are several general types of mnemonics that you are probably already familiar with. They all involve using the sounds of words to remind you of a particular usage of a word, as with strategies to help you discriminate between the aspects of concepts. For example, many people think that *stalactites* must hang on "tight" to remember that they hang down from the ceiling of a cave, while stalagmites grow up from the floor (When there are only two potentially confusing words, you only need to learn a mnemonic for one). To remember the distinction between *concave* and *convex*, remember that concave "goes in," like a cave; therefore, the other word, convex, must mean, "goes out." Teachers have often heard mnemonics similar to this. More systematic applications of mnemonic techniques include the keyword method, the pegword method and letter strategies. Each is described separately below.

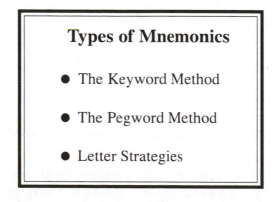

Types of Mnemonics

- The Keyword Method

- The Pegword Method

- Letter Strategies

*Although mnemonics do not necessarily inhibit comprehension, they do not guarantee that remembered information will be comprehended. Mnemonics are best used to promote recall of facts and terminology when the underlying concepts are thoroughly understood, ideally through active manipulation and exploration.

The Keyword Method

This versatile mnemonic technique is particularly effective when applied to new **facts, concepts, vocabulary or terminology**. For example, consider the vocabulary word *erode*, meaning "wear away by wind or rain." First think of a word that students know, that is easily pictured, that sounds like erode. One word you could choose is "road." Road sounds like erode, it is easy to picture, and it is familiar to students. In this case, road is the keyword. Next, you must picture the keyword, road, *interacting with* (not nearly next to) the new word to be learned. In this case, you could picture a road being "eroded" by wind and rain, as in the accompanying picture. Example teacher dialogue could be the following:

> Erode means "wear away by wind or rain." The keyword for erode is "road." What's the keyword for erode, Billy? Correct, road. Now [shows picture on overhead projector], remember this picture of a *road eroding* by wind and rain. When I ask you what erode means, remember the keyword, road, think back to the picture of the road, and remember that it was wearing away from wind and rain. Now, you try it: Mary, what's the keyword for erode? Good. And what does erode mean? Good! Tell the class how you remembered that...

Keywords can also be used to **interact** with one another. For example, to teach that a *parasite* is an organism that lives off a *host*, first create keywords for parasite and host. A good keyword for parasite is "pear," because it sounds like parasite and is easily pictured, and a good keyword for host is "ghost," because it sounds like host and is easily pictured. To show a parasite living off a host, you can picture a pear living off a ghost, as in the accompanying picture. More realistic examples of parasites and hosts can ensure the concepts are clearly understood.

Sometimes the only keyword you can think of is difficult to picture. When this happens, some **dialogue** in the picture may be helpful. For example, "trick" seems like a good keyword for *trichina*, the parasitic roundworm that is found in uncooked pork and causes trichinosis. However, "trick" is abstract and therefore, difficult to draw, so we created the following dialogue as shown in the picture: A trichina appearing from pork, saying, "I have a trick, I'll make you sick!" This dialogue ties the picture to the keyword, and ties it to the idea of illness.

For another example, the keyword "stink" could be created for the vocabulary word *extinct*, and shown interacting with dead dinosaurs, in the dialogue, "These extinct dinosaurs sure stink!" Discussion can ensure that students understand that the mnemonic picture is intended to help them remember the word, and that 'extinct' does mean the same as 'dead.'

Keywords can also be used for **word parts**, which can then be combined to enhance comprehension and memory of complex words. For example, to teach that *ptero-* means "wing," use the keyword "tire," and show a tire with wings, as shown in the picture. To teach that *saurus* means "lizard", use the keyword "saw," and show a lizard using a saw, as in the picture. Students who have learned these two word parts can infer the meaning of pterosaurus ("winged lizard"), and will also know components of other related words, such as *sauropod* and *archeopterix*.

Keywords can also **build on one another**. For example, you can teach relevant information about three parts of the earth, *core*, *mantle*, and *crust*, using keywords, as shown in the pictures. The core of the earth, made of iron and nickel, can be represented as an "apple core" (keyword for core), made of "irons" and "nickels." The mantle, composed of rock, can be represented as a "man" (keyword for mantle), made of solid rock. The crust, the upper part of the earth containing mountain ranges and ocean floor, can be shown as crusts of bread (keywords for crust), on mountains and oceans on the surface of the earth. These three pictures can then be combined, to demonstrate the relative position of these three parts, as shown in the picture.

Keywords can be employed to illustrate **attributes** of scientific phenomena. For example, you may wish your students to remember important attributes all **mammals** have in common: hair or fur, young drink milk, warm-blooded. This can all be accomplished in one integrated picture using the keyword "camel" for mammal, as shown. Riding on the camel are examples of mammals, drinking milk, on a warm, sunny day. The warm day is a symbol for warm blooded, and students should be familiarized with this.

Finally, keywords can be used to learn and remember **abstract concepts**. This is usually done by picturing a single instance of the concept. For example, the term *radial symmetry* is used to describe organisms that are symmetrical from the center outward, such as starfish. To picture this, a keyword can be created for radial symmetry: radio cemetery. The radio cemetery is drawn in the shape of a starfish, with headstones made of radios on each arm, as shown in the picture. Additional examples of radial symmetry can ensure complete comprehension of the concept.

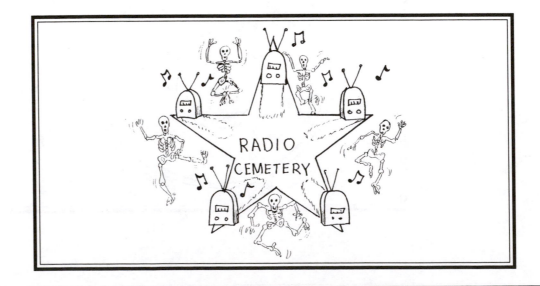

Most mnemonic pictures need **additional explanation** to enhance comprehension. Many of the concepts pictured mnemonically necessarily represent only one instance of the concept being learned, and are sometimes oversimplified for the purpose of the mnemonic. This should not be a problem, if you take the time to remind students that the mnemonic picture is to help them remember the name of the fact, concept, or vocabulary word, and that the actual meaning may be a little different. Mnemonics are generally intended to support, rather than replace, other types of instruction.

The Pegword Method

The pegword method is similar to the keyword method, but is used for remembering numbered or ordered information. Pegwords are rhyming words for numbers, as shown in the table.

Pegwords

One is *bun* (or *sun* or *gun*)

Two is *shoe*

Three is *tree* (or *tea*)

Four is *door* (or *floor* or *store*)

Five is *hive*

Six is *sticks*

Seven is *heaven*

Eight is *gate*

Nine is *vine*

Ten is *hen*

Pegwords can be used whenever information is associated with numbers. For example, in physical science, students may need to remember *first-class*, *second-class*, and *third-class levers*. First-class levers can be represented by oars in a rowboat, second-class levers by a wheelbarrow, and third-class levers by a rake. To tie these effectively to their numbered designations, a *bun* (one, or first-class) can be shown holding an oar in place, a *shoe* (two, or second-class) holding a wheelbarrow, and a *tree* (three, or third-class) holding the end of a rake. Each pegword can be placed at the fulcrum of the lever, to reinforce the critical attribute, as shown in the pictures.

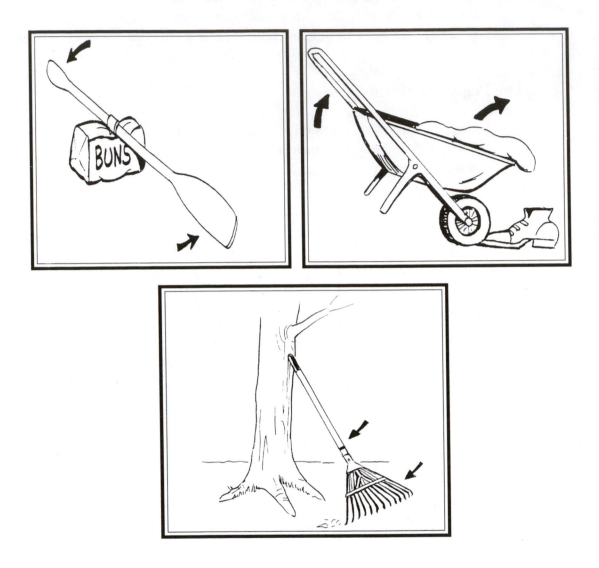

Pegwords can also be used with *ordered* information, such as explanations or causes of scientific phenomena, such as dinosaur extinction or the origin of the universe. Such reasons can be ordered for plausibility or level of acceptance by the scientific community. For example, it has been suggested that dinosaurs died out because small mammals destroyed their eggs. If this reason was assigned plausibility #4, a picture could be shown of small mammals destroying dinosaur eggs in a *store* (pegword for four), as shown in the picture.

Other ordered information, such as Newton's laws, could be shown in a similar way. To show, for example, Newton's first law of motion, that an object at rest tends to stay at rest, a *bun* could be pictured "staying at rest."

Pegwords can also be combined with keywords, when the names of unfamiliar things are ordered. For example, the hardness levels, according to the Mohs scale, of various minerals, could be pictured mnemonically. To remember that the mineral *crocoite* is #2 on the hardness scale, picture a *crocodile* (keyword for crocoite) wearing *shoes* (pegword for two). Some other examples are given in the accompanying table.

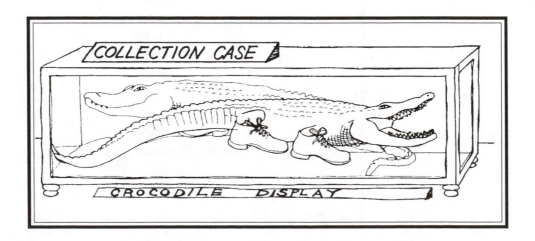

Strategies for Mineral Hardness Levels

Talc (tail) is one (bun): An animal with a *bun* on its *tail*.

Gypsum (gypsy) is two (shoe): A *gypsy* wearing tennis *shoes*.

Calcite (cow) is three (tree): A *cow* in a *tree*.

Wolframite (wolf) is four (door): A *wolf* at the *door*.

Apatite (ape) is five (hive): An *ape* poking a *hive*.

Pyrite (pie) is six (sticks): A *pie* on *sticks*.

Quartz (quarter) is seven (heaven): A *quarter* in *heaven*.

Beryl (barrel) is eight (gate): A *barrel* at a *gate*.

Corundum (car) is nine (vine): A *car* caught in *vines*.

Diamond (diamond) is ten (hen): A *diamond* worn by a *hen*.

Notice in the table that the keyword for diamond is *diamond*. When the word is already familiar and easy to picture, there is no need to change it.

There are also pegwords for numbers 11-19. These are given in the accompanying table.

Pegwords 11-19

Eleven = a lever

Twelve = elf

Thirteen = thirsting (e.g., a glass of water)

Fourteen = forking

Fifteen = fixing (e.g., a wrench)

Sixteen = sitting (e.g., a chair)

Seventeen = severing (cutting with a knife or scissors)

Eighteen = aiding (e.g., an ambulance)

Nineteen = knighting

It is less likely that you will need to go higher than ten or twenty, but if you do, there are pegwords also for the 10s. They are given in the table.

Higher Pegwords

Twenty = twin-ty (e.g., twenty-one, *twin buns*)

Thirty = dirty (e.g., thirty-two, *dirty shoe*)

Forty = warty (e.g., forty-three, *warty tree*)

Fifty = "gifty" (i.e., gift-wrapped)(e.g., fifty-four, *gifty door*)

Sixty = witchy (e.g., sixty-five, *witchy hive*)

Seventy = heavenly (e.g., seventy-six, *heavenly sticks*)

Letter Strategies

Acronyms. First letter strategies are among the most commonly known mnemonics. A well known example is the acronym HOMES, which letters stand for the first letter in each of the Great Lakes: Huron, Ontario, Michigan, Erie, Superior. Even in this strategy, it is important to remember that this type of strategy will work only if the names the letters represent (e.g., Ontario) are well known to the students. If not, students will need to spend additional time practicing the names of the lakes.

Another common example is ROY G. BIV, a fictional name representing the colors of the prism: Red, Orange, Yellow, Green, Blue, Indigo, Violet. An advantage of this particular strategy is that the colors can be remembered in order. A disadvantage is that the name Roy G. Biv, does not represent anyone in particular, and can therefore be easily forgotten, if additional practice on the name is not provided.

An acronym that has been shown to be useful for remembering five classes of vertebrates is FARM-B. The letters stand for Fish, Amphibian, Reptile, Mammal, Bird, as shown in the accompanying picture.

Acrostics. Acrostics make use of whole words, the first letter or letters of which are meant to indicate something. They are infrequently used in spelling, where a sentence represents individual first letters (e.g., GEOGRAPHY = George's Elderly Old Grandfather Rode A Pig Home Yesterday). Extensions of this method can be used to remember the classifications, in order, as shown in the table.

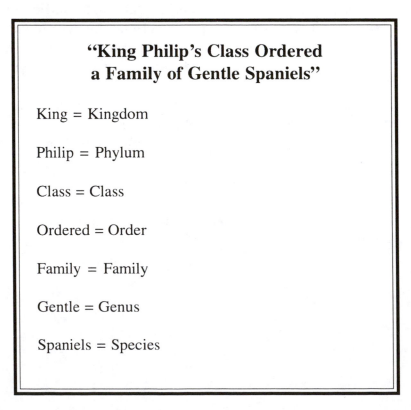

"King Philip's Class Ordered a Family of Gentle Spaniels"

King = Kingdom

Philip = Phylum

Class = Class

Ordered = Order

Family = Family

Gentle = Genus

Spaniels = Species

Another popular acrostic that has been used to teach the planets in the solar system is: <u>M</u>y <u>V</u>ery <u>E</u>ducated <u>M</u>other <u>J</u>ust <u>S</u>erved <u>U</u>s <u>N</u>ine <u>P</u>izzas. In this example the first letter of each word represents the first letters of each planet: Mercury, Venus, Earth, Mars, Jupiter, Saturn, Uranus, Neptune and Pluto.

Another example, for learning the constellations of the zodiac, in order (provided by H.A. Rey) is shown in the table. This rhyme can be very helpful in remembering the order of constellations of the zodiac; however, students will still need practice applying these strategies to actual identification of constellations in the sky.

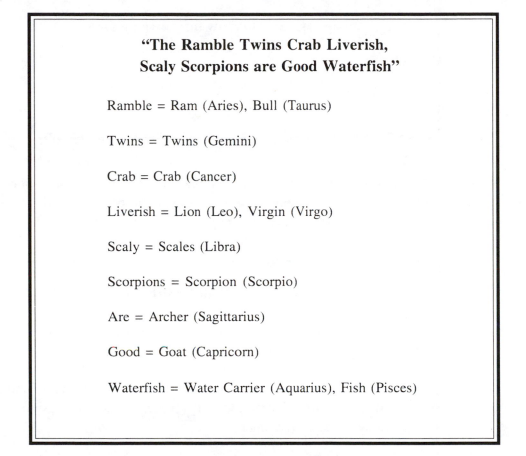

**"The Ramble Twins Crab Liverish,
Scaly Scorpions are Good Waterfish"**

Ramble = Ram (Aries), Bull (Taurus)

Twins = Twins (Gemini)

Crab = Crab (Cancer)

Liverish = Lion (Leo), Virgin (Virgo)

Scaly = Scales (Libra)

Scorpions = Scorpion (Scorpio)

Are = Archer (Sagittarius)

Good = Goat (Capricorn)

Waterfish = Water Carrier (Aquarius), Fish (Pisces)

Many teachers appreciate the value of mnemonic techniques, but do not feel that they can draw well enough to provide the necessary pictures. In the accompanying table, we have listed alternatives to teacher-drawn mnemonic pictures.

Alternatives to Teacher-Drawn Pictures

- Instead of high-quality drawings, use simple stick figures. Quality of the drawing is not particularly important.

- Use cut-out pictures from magazines.

- Ask an artistically talented student to draw the pictures.

- Encourage students to draw their own pictures.

- Promote the creation of mental images in the students. (Note: if you do this, be sure to insist they carefully create a detailed image in their mind and are able to describe details).

Another concern teachers have expressed with mnemonics such as the keyword method is that the strategies are time-consuming to develop. Suggestions for saving time on strategy development are given in the accompanying table.

Suggestions for Saving Time on Strategy Creation

- Collect just a few strategies at first, for the most difficult-to-remember information. You can add to these strategies in later years.

- Do not belabor particular words that you are having difficulty creating strategies for. Think about it seriously, then put it aside. The answer may come to you later.

- Ask your class to help you come up with strategies throughout each unit. Save the best for future incorporation.

Remember, you only have to think of good strategies once. Once developed, good mnemonics can be used for years and years.

Mainstreaming Students With Reading Difficulties

What Are Strategies for Students With Reading Difficulties?

Many students who are mainstreamed in science have difficulties with reading. These difficulties range from mild to severe and can influence performance in science. Adaptations which involve listening to rather than reading text can be very helpful for most students with reading problems. Students with hearing impairments who also have reading problems, however, will probably not benefit from such adaptations. Various strategies are described that can facilitate reading problems during mainstream science instruction. The first section describes guidelines for altering the presentation format of text materials, while the second section presents strategies for enhancing reading comprehension of textual material.

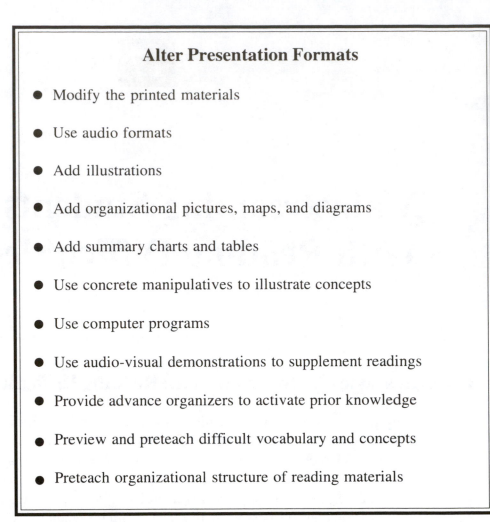

Alter Presentation Formats

- Modify the printed materials

- Use audio formats

- Add illustrations

- Add organizational pictures, maps, and diagrams

- Add summary charts and tables

- Use concrete manipulatives to illustrate concepts

- Use computer programs

- Use audio-visual demonstrations to supplement readings

- Provide advance organizers to activate prior knowledge

- Preview and preteach difficult vocabulary and concepts

- Preteach organizational structure of reading materials

What Are Presentation Formats That Can Be Altered?

Modify the Printed Materials.

Braille is often used to replace reading from traditional texts. Braille letters consist of 1 to 6 raised dots, and students read these by feeling the dots with their fingertips. Braille can be written with a Perkins Brailler, or with a slate and stylus. State departments, schools for the blind, the American Printing House for the Blind, and the Library of Congress, can help you obtain reading material in Braille. However, Braille is very difficult to learn to read, and braille text consumes a great deal of space. Only about 15% of the blind population use Braille for their primary means of reading.

Braille-like symbols can be used to shorten the length of braille materials. A typical braille version of a printed text can become 12 to 15 volumes in length, due to the size and translation constraints. The use of braille symbols can significantly reduce the volume and size of materials.

Large-print books can be used with students who have some eyesight. The most popular size of type is 18-point type, although larger types can be used. Large print (e.g., 18 point or greater) on yellow paper can be very helpful for some students with visual impairments.

18-point type looks like this.

American Printing House for the Blind can help you locate relevant books in large print; however, the numbers of books available are limited.

Magnifying devices can also be helpful in making books easier to read. Glasses, magnifying lamps, and magnifying glasses are available. Closed circuit television (CCTV) scanners can reproduce the pages of a book on a television screen, or on an extra large monitor and enhance reading for many students.

Technological aids, such as the **Opticon**, and the **Kurzweil Reading Machine**, when available, can be very helpful. (See also the computer-assisted instruction section in this manual).

Reading materials that cover the same information and concepts but that are written at **lower readability levels** can be substituted for too difficult material. Be cautious that the student with disabilities is not a target of ridicule for having lower level materials. Some districts (e.g. Mesa, Arizona) have developed student laboratory booklets that contain various reading level materials within one grade level booklet. This way all students have the same booklet, and can be called on to read orally because there are some passages written at their readability level.

Some **science reading materials have very controlled vocabulary and syntax** throughout the series. Materials such as these can be substituted as necessary for mainstreamed students with reading difficulties.

High interest, low vocabulary reading materials that cover the same content can be substituted for regularly assigned texts. This includes the many **trade** books that are available in science that provide excellent coverage of specific topics and that are written on a variety of reading levels. (See Children's Press, Phoenix Learning Resources, and Steck Vaughn publications for examples.)

Peer assistants can write shortened summaries of textual information. These shortened summaries can be distributed to students with reading difficulties. For example, a hearing impaired student and a normal hearing student can be paired and asked to create a smaller booklet version of the reading materials. The booklet can contain overhead transparencies and the students can present their booklet to the class. This strategy would also work well with any student with reading difficulties.

Provide **adaptive devices for students with physical disabilities who may have difficulties turning pages**. Devices are available which enable such individuals to turn pages more easily.

Make **book marks** available for students to use while reading independently. Many students with reading difficulties find that using book marks makes reading easier. Window book marks can be made available for students with visual tracking difficulties. Cut a slit the size of one line of text in a large index card. Students can then see only one line at a time through the window.

Use Audio Formats.

Tape recordings of readings may be very helpful for many students with reading difficulties, including those with visual impairments. If appropriate tapes are not available, you could read parts of the text into a tape recorder for the visually impaired student to listen to. Once recorded, the tape can be copied for other students who have difficulty reading. If you do not have enough time, ask another student to read into the tape, as he or she studies. Students could take turns reading different sections, and cover a large amount of text. Be sure to highlight headings, and describe pictures and figures. Summary statements are also very helpful. The visually impaired student must have good listening skills.

Audio taped descriptions of all visual presentations including lessons and laboratory experiments can be made. For example, clear, verbal descriptions can be made to accompany any printed materials, including organizational illustrations, charts, and diagrams.

Variable speed cassettes can be made available so students with reading problems can regulate the speed of the tape that contains the reading materials. This modification helps speed up the process of listening, typically more time-consuming than reading text silently, at a normal rate of speed. Students can either speed up the presentations or slow them down depending upon individual need. These cassettes also allow students to regulate the pitch of the tape, so that faster playing speeds do not result in inappropriately high pitched voices (e.g., "chipmunk" speech).

"Compressed speech" devices are also available. Rather than speeding up the speech, these devices remove speech sounds that are less necessary for comprehension, allowing listeners to proceed through the text at a rate approximating silent reading.

Services are available to transfer text materials to audio formats for visually impaired students. Teachers may also want to establish a peer assistant system where good readers make audiotapes of textual material. These tapes may prove beneficial for students with learning disabilities, communication difficulties, mental retardation, and hearing impairments, in addition to those with visual impairments.

Set-up a listening center in the classroom. Have the audiotapes available at the listening center for students to use and reuse as needed. Encourage them to review the tapes frequently.

During oral reading activities include **pauses and summaries** of important features. This would include discussions of tables and diagrams and new terminology and concepts.

Add Illustrations.

Illustrations can help all students with reading difficulties, but can be particularly helpful for students with hearing impairments who also have reading difficulty. Since this population is less likely to benefit from audio presentations, the **use of many pictures, combined with real examples, pantomime, and modeling**, may be the optimal way to present important content from textual material. Illustrations can be made of almost all vocabulary included in science textbooks.

Illustrations that depict relevant concepts can accompany reading materials. Although some illustrations are used as decoration to motivate students, illustrations can pictorially represent difficult-to-read content. For example, illustrations of the parts of the cell, parts of plants, and animals can be drawn. Illustrations such as these can assist students with reading difficulties comprehend important content.

Illustrations can be placed on **transparencies and displayed on overhead projectors, or photocopies of them could be inserted into booklets for students with reading difficulties**. Illustrations of words known to be difficult to read can also be placed within regular text. This is also known as **"rebus" writing**, and can be helpful for students with a variety of reading problems.

Booklets that contain mostly illustrations that summarize important information contained in text materials can be made. These booklets can be enlarged and put on overhead transparencies or on bulletin boards.

Three-dimensional illustrations can be developed to help facilitate the learning of visually impaired students. Such illustrations can be made using a variety of textured materials and modeling clay. A three-dimensional model of the parts of the cell could be made and each different part of the cell can be represented by a different texture. Some three-dimensional models are available commercially.

Enlarge all examples of illustrations. This will ensure that students pay attention to them and that students with low vision can adequately view them. **Glue** can be used to draw simple pictures. When the glue dries there is a raised line picture.

Special paper is available that produces a raised line when written on with a water-based marker. If drawn appropriately, these raised-line pictures can be read tactually by students with visual impairments. Illustrations can be traced from views seen by projection microscopes onto this special paper to provide visually impaired students opportunities at learning.

Braille descriptions of illustrations can be made and will help facilitate the understanding of information presented pictorially for students with visual impairments. Braille label makers can be used to label illustrations.

Audio taped descriptions of illustrations can also be made to help facilitate the understanding of information presented pictorially for students with reading and visual difficulties.

Add Organizational Pictures, Maps, and Diagrams.

Organizational illustrations, including maps and diagrams, can integrate information presented in texts. These types of pictures integrate concepts and information presented via print and therefore facilitate comprehension, especially for students with reading difficulties. Some examples of these types of illustrations include: open and closed circuits, the food chain, a life cycle of a butterfly, or diagrams of how the blood flows through the body. These pictures can be displayed on overhead projectors and copied into student booklets.

Colors can be used in organizational illustrations. Different parts of the organizational pictures can be represented by different colors. This is commonly done with geographic maps, but can also be added to many other types of diagrams. For example, the route electricity travels in a closed circuit can be a different color from other components in the illustration.

Enlarge all examples of organizational pictures, maps, and diagrams. This will ensure that students pay attention to them and that students with low vision can adequately see them.

Three dimensional organizational pictures, maps, and diagrams can be made to assist with comprehension with students with visual impairments. Again, the use of textured materials (e.g., sand, glue, string) and the use of special paper that produces raised lines can be used to add the three-dimensional aspects to figures. Some three-dimensional models of scientific phenomena are available commercially.

Braille descriptions of organizational pictures, maps, and diagrams can be made and will help facilitate the understanding of information presented pictorially for students with visual impairments.

Audio-taped descriptions of organizational pictures, maps, and diagrams can be made and will help facilitate the understanding of information presented pictorially for students with visual impairments.

Add Summary Charts and Tables.

Summary charts and tables can be used to synthesize important concepts covered in textual material while simultaneously decreasing the need for reading skills. Large print summary charts and tables could be posted on bulletin boards or placed on overhead transparencies, or photocopied into student laboratory booklets.

Summary charts can contain pictures of information presented in the text. For example, pictures of the types of small machines discussed in textbooks can be placed on the chart. Critical attributes associated with each type of machine can be represented pictorially. Students can be asked to complete their own versions of the class summary charts to help reinforce major ideas from reading materials.

Enlarge all summary charts and tables to ensure adequate visibility for all students.

Braille descriptions of summary charts and tables can be made and will help facilitate the understanding of summary information presented pictorially for students with visual impairments.

Audio-taped descriptions of summary charts and tables can be made and will help facilitate the understanding of summary information presented pictorially for students with visual impairments.

Use Concrete Manipulatives to Illustrate Concepts.

Use actual examples of scientific phenomena whenever possible. Use concrete manipulatives when reading about abstract concepts. For example, bring in samples of open and closed circuits in electricity, make electromagnets, allow students opportunities to see, touch, and explore instances of the concepts covered in reading materials. These examples will facilitate the comprehension of difficult-to-read textual materials for all students with reading difficulties.

Use **adapted science materials and activities** as supplements or major foci of science content when appropriate. Many curricula materials exist that emphasize similar content to text-based materials, and students with reading difficulties are apt to be more successful when using such approaches.

Include exhibits, simulations, demonstrations, and hands-on activities to help reinforce and teach concepts. All students with reading difficulties will benefit from these types of activities. They will be particularly important for students with severe reading difficulties and students with hearing and visual difficulties.

Braille descriptions of concrete manipulatives can be made and will help facilitate the understanding of summary information presented pictorially for students with visual impairments.

Audio-taped descriptions of concrete manipulatives can be made and will help facilitate the understanding of summary information presented pictorially for students with visual impairments.

Use Computer Programs.

Use relevant **computer programs to provide practice** on information presented in texts. Some computer programs provide excellent pictorial representations of information described in textbooks. These illustrations can be used to reinforce content presented in written formats. Some computer programs are written in game-like formats and provide motivation for students to engage in practice.

Obtain large screens as monitors for computers. This will enable students with visual impairments to use the computer and benefit from supplemental programs.

Obtain screen/text reader software to accompany computer programs. Some programs have the capacity to orally present what is visually presented. Depending upon your computer's capabilities, you may need an additional speech output device to run these programs. Additionally, teachers can potentially write some programs that include the speech components in order to make the computer a more adaptable learning environment for students with disabilities. A speech synthesizer or digitizer is necessary for those types of programs.

Obtain braille overlays for keyboards for computers. This will adapt the computer for those students who communicate via braille formats.

Some computer programs help foster **creative writing and science** activities. These types of programs can be beneficial to many students with reading difficulties.

Use Audio-Visual Demonstrations to Supplement Readings.

Supplement reading materials with audio-visual materials such as video, slides, and videodiscs. The quality of some videodisc programs is excellent. These videodiscs can display examples of scientific phenomena that are virtually impossible to present in the classroom. This is beneficial when actual manipulatives cannot be obtained. Some districts have selected to adopt videodisc curriculum over traditional textbook approaches.

Provide "descriptive" descriptions of any video portions of visual displays so students with visual impairments can benefit from the activity. **Descriptive video** is a process of augmenting videos with detailed descriptions of the events occurring on the video, but not included in the dialogue. The descriptive video components do not interfere with the dialogue. Public Television has been completing these components for some of their programs. However, teachers can provide these descriptive components to any visuals used in class. The added description is especially beneficial for visually impaired students, however, these supplemental descriptions will also help students with hearing, learning, and cognitive disabilities focus attention on critical components of the videos.

Have individual stations arranged in classroom so that students can view this information repetitively and independently for extra practice when necessary.

Allow students to **sign-out audio-visual aids** for home viewing for additional practice and review. Often teachers show a film strip or videotape only once as a supplemental activity. Many students with reading difficulties would benefit from multiple viewings of such audio-visual aids. Students can bring these home and view as homework activities.

A student using a hand-held scanner to help him read a textbook.

Provide Advance Organizers to Activate Prior Knowledge.

Advance organizers can be verbal, pictorial, or three-dimensional. Advance organizers are presented to students prior to their independent reading to activate their prior knowledge on the new topic. Teachers can precede reading with instruction using an advance organizer. These organizers help to focus attention and preview up coming readings. Statements or illustrations can be presented to the class with instructions to: Think about this. *"Have you seen/heard anything like it before?"* This will prompt students to activate their prior knowledge on the topic and get them thinking about the new topic.

Preview and Preteach Difficult Vocabulary and Concepts.

Preview and preteach difficult vocabulary and concepts prior to assigning independent reading. Teachers can preteach difficult-to-read vocabulary and concepts. The use of concrete examples and teaching for understanding will help ensure more success on the part of students when they are required to read the information.

Teachers can use any variety of **strategie**s for teaching the vocabulary and concepts. Some of the mnemonic strategies described in the memory section have proven successful with students with reading difficulties.

Have students maintain **dictionary booklets** that are their own personal dictionaries that contain all vocabulary learned. Students can include strategies they used to learn the words and new concepts, as well as descriptions of the activities in which the new words were applied. The booklets can be made with pictures, words, audio-tapes, or in braille formats.

Teachers can use the **teacher effectiveness variables** in presenting new vocabulary and concepts to students. Opportunities for guided practice could be included to check for student understanding.

Teachers can use **cooperative learning and peer tutoring** for helping students acquire new terminology and concepts prior to assigning independent reading.

Preview and Preteach Organizational Structure of Reading Materials.

Prior to assigning reading activities present **information on how the textual material is organized** and presented. Information regarding types of subheadings, summary paragraphs, and types of questions are beneficial to readers if they are alerted to them prior to undertaking independent reading. Special education teachers and aides may be able to preteach some of this information to mainstream students.

For example, some **science texts highlight important vocabulary**, some texts present illustrations that pictorially represent difficult concepts, and some texts insert comprehension questions. Many students with reading difficulties are unaware of how these built-in features actually provide comprehension fostering information for them. Guidance in suggesting ways to read may be especially beneficial to students with reading difficulties.

Teachers can use the **teacher effectiveness variables** when previewing the organizational structure of text materials with students. Opportunities for guided practice could be included to check for student understanding.

Teachers can use **cooperative learning and peer mediation strategies** for teaching students about the organizational structure of the textual materials prior to assigning independent reading. Members of each cooperative group could be asked to explain text structures to other group members.

A table-top scanner can be used to enlarge the text of a textbook onto a television screen for easier viewing.

What Are Strategies for Enhancing Comprehension?

Many comprehension fostering strategies have recently been tested with students with disabilities. These strategies can be reviewed with the student by the general education science teacher. Research has shown that when these strategies are taught to students they typically recall and comprehend more text-related information. It has also been seen repeatedly that students with disabilities do not tend to use such reading comprehension strategies spontaneously and independently. This means it is important for the general education science teacher to remind or prompt mainstreamed students to employ such strategies.

Encourage Self-Questioning Strategies.

Self-questioning shares similarities with almost all of the reading comprehension strategies. It can be an important individual strategy, or it can be coupled with components of many different reading strategies. Students can be taught to continually **stop and question themselves about the content they are reading**. The questions can be very general or very specific. For example, a general question might be, "*What did I just read?*" While a specific question might be, "*What are the components of an electrical circuit?*"

It may be necessary to emphasize that the purpose of reading is to comprehend the material and that the rate at which students read is not as important as the understanding that is obtained from the reading. Sometimes students with disabilities have been taught to read as fast as possible when they are working on decoding skills. If this is the case it is important to teach students that when reading difficult science textual material it may be necessary to read slowly. Students can be taught to stop after every few minutes and self-question: "*Do I understand what I am reading? If not, I'll reread until I do*", or to ask for help if there are too many difficult scientific terms in the text.

Self-questioning strategies can also be very explicit as in teaching students to summarize or predict. Examples of those are discussed under each heading.

Encourage Students to Use Self-Monitoring Procedures.

Self-monitoring procedures can be coupled with almost any instructional strategy, and as such are particularly beneficial when added to reading comprehension strategies, such as the self-questioning strategies. Encourage students with disabilities to use self-monitoring procedures that promote active understanding of text materials. The self-monitoring sheet could list questions like: "*I understand this information; I can summarize this information; I can tell someone about what I just read.*" Students could be asked initially to answer items on their self-monitoring sheets as frequently as after every paragraph initially, and then after every page. If they answer negatively, they should re-read the information until they can successfully respond to the question.

Encourage Students to Identify What They Don't Understand and Why They Don't Understand It.

Encourage students to read and identify information that they do not comprehend. Tell students to **underline, highlight, write into a separate booklet, or audio-tape** any information they don't understand. They will then be in a better position to request assistance for further explanation. Many times they can be taught to identify difficult vocabulary and terminology. Once those terms are explained to them, comprehension can occur.

Encourage Students to Summarize Information.

Teach students how to summarize important information in their own words. Have them read paragraphs and practice summarizing the information. Summarization and paraphrasing demonstrate an understanding of the reading material.

Summarization and paraphrasing activities can be written, oral, or pantomimed. Ensure that the response format is within the abilities of the students with disabilities, when requiring summarization. Many teachers of hearing impaired students have reported that pantomime activities allow hearing impaired students to "act-out" their understanding. Students can be easily taught to write, say or act-out a summary sentence. Feedback can be provided as to the accuracy of the summary. Start with simple paragraphs and ask students to *"tell me what you just read."* Proceed to more complex readings and continually provide corrective feedback.

Add self-monitoring components to summarization procedures. Self-monitoring procedures can be developed to accompany summarization strategies. Booklets can be designed that eventually contain a student's rewritten (or audio-tape) summary of the written textual materials. Within the booklet, students could be required to check-off on self-monitoring forms whether or not they understood the material and whether or not they came up with good summary statements.

Peers can be used to test the quality of summaries. Peer assistants can check for accuracy of students' summaries by checking with the text.

Braille summaries can be written by visually impaired students.

Computer written summaries can be completed by students with writing difficulties. Again, peer assistants or cooperative learning groups can be employed and some students can function as secretaries for students with physical disabilities. Or, special keyboard adaptions can be used by students with physical disabilities, so they can create their own summaries.

Encourage Students to Predict Information.

Teach students how to make predictions. Have them read important information from science materials and **make predictions**. This is the same skill they use when they make predictions during laboratory experiments, so use the analogy and tell students to begin to use prediction skills during reading activities as well. Teachers can model the procedures by reading and talking out loud their thoughts.

When reading science texts, have students stop and ask themselves questions like: *"What is going to happen next? What will the author tell us next? What do I think will be important to know next?"* This will encourage active thinking about the reading materials.

Encourage Highlighting Skills.

Teach students highlighting skills if they are able to write in the text materials. If students are unable to write in their textbooks, parts of the text could be photocopied (with publisher's permission) and highlighting could be practiced on the photocopied versions. In order for highlighting to be effective for students with disabilities, it may be necessary to determine whether they can identify the most important information.

Once they know how to identify the most important information, they can be taught to highlight that information. This information can then be reviewed and studied more easily than the entire text.

Teach students to highlight using audio-tapes, braille formats, or via computer whenever necessary. Students using these alternative formats can be encouraged to keep the tape recorder, computer, or brailler handy so that instead of highlighting important information in the text itself, the information is recorded directly onto the tape recorder, computer, or brailler.

Encourage Outlining Skills.

Teach students how to make outlines and study guides of important information included in science textbooks. These reduced versions of content can then be used to study the most important information. Traditional outlining procedures can be taught, or teachers can use semantic feature analysis procedures. Semantic feature analysis procedures require students to describe relationships among important facts and concepts in science texts.

Outlines can be made in braille or audio-taped formats as well.

Portable scanners can be used for any type of library reading.

Encourage Students to Draw Pictures.

Teach students to keep log booklets and keep notes and pictures of important information as study guides. Often students may be able to pictorially draw mnemonic strategies that can help facilitate their learning of important information. Additionally, with a little practice students can be taught to record pictures of scientific information that they read in textbooks. For example, after reading about the stages of life of a butterfly, students could draw pictures representing the life cycle. This would reinforce the reading and help with retention of the information.

Teachers can provide some basic drawing lessons that will facilitate all students' abilities to reproduce illustrations of scientific materials. Some examples of activities to include in drawing lessons are discussed in the National Science Resource Center materials. Additionally, art teachers could be asked to provide some lessons for science drawings.

Teachers can also have Polaroid cameras available for taking instant photos for students who have difficulty drawing.

Three-dimensional pictures can be completed by visually impaired students to help reinforce scientific concepts. Multi-textured materials such as glue, sand paper, string, beads, and spices can be used.

Photo journals, braille format journals, or audio-taped journals can provide valuable information for evaluating students' comprehension of reading materials.

Encourage Students to Use Graphic Organizers.

Students can be taught not only to interpret graphic organizers, but also to complete their own. Graphic organizers are a type of study guide that can be used to summarize important information from textbooks. These organizers can contain illustrations and visually-spatially displayed related concepts of important science content. For example, to learn the attributes of various minerals, a graphic organizer can be made to contain information about hardness level, color, and common use of minerals. Additionally, mnemonic strategies can be embedded within these organizers to help facilitate learning. Similar graphic organizers can be made to accompany the learning of attributes of any scientific phenomena.

Braille descriptions of graphic organizers can be made to accompany traditional organizers.

Descriptive audio-tapes can be made to accompany any graphic organizer.

Encourage Students to Use Visual Imagery.

Visual imagery can be taught to students as a strategy to foster comprehension of reading materials. Teach students to visualize exactly what types of materials are discussed. Such visual imagery procedures can be coupled with drawing illustrations of the images created to increase comprehension.

Teachers can prompt students to use visual imagery during reading by asking questions like: *"I want you to get a picture in your mind of what the dinosaurs looked liked during the early periods."* Or, *"when I say go, everyone visualize what the minerals look like. What do your minerals look like? Here's an example of what I visualized. Did anyone have trouble visualizing something?"* Teachers can provide actual illustrations to reinforce the use of imagery. And, during questioning for comprehension, teachers can remind students to think back to the pictures they made in their mind while they were reading, before answering any questions.

Encourage Students to Review Textual Materials.

Students with reading difficulties may need to be taught that they can review important reading materials to locate answers to comprehension questions. Often, students with reading difficulties will avoid the text material even though it is available. Teach them to use the text to go back and find appropriate information before answering questions.

Peer assistants can be helpful in assisting students to locate important pieces of information. Guidance on finding where text materials describe specific procedures can be beneficial for all students with reading difficulties. Science textbooks contain a different type of writing from the textbooks used during reading classes, and many students with reading difficulties may have a hard time making the transition to the more technically oriented text.

Encourage Students to Use Study Skills and Test-Taking Skills.

Study skills and test-taking skills are important and can be used to assist students with reading difficulties. The reader is referred to the section "Improving Note-Taking, Study Skills, and Test-Taking Skills."

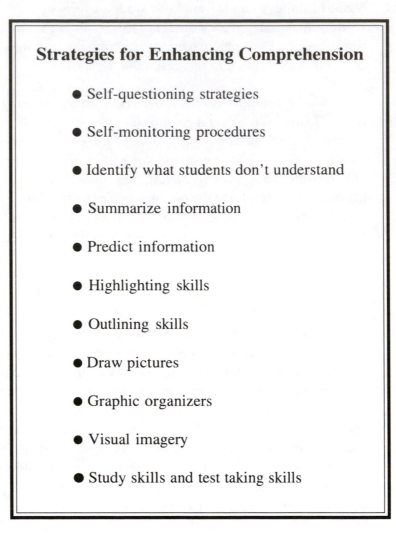

Strategies for Enhancing Comprehension

- Self-questioning strategies

- Self-monitoring procedures

- Identify what students don't understand

- Summarize information

- Predict information

- Highlighting skills

- Outlining skills

- Draw pictures

- Graphic organizers

- Visual imagery

- Study skills and test taking skills

18

Improving Note-Taking, Study Skills, and Test-Taking Skills

Many students with disabilities have difficulties with note-taking and study skills, and do not always take tests efficiently. In this section, we will discuss some ways of facilitating these academic skills.

What Can I Do to Promote Good Note-Taking?

Good study skills begin with good note-taking. Note-taking is commonly considered in the context of teacher lectures or media presentations; however, good note-taking and record keeping are important components of hands-on science activities. Many students with disabilities have spent a great deal of time learning more basic skills, have spent less time in lecture or independent work situations, and may be less prepared than their classmates to take notes effectively (you may have other, nondisabled students who are not good note-takers). Here are some strategies you can implement to improve student note-taking.

1. Provide important organizational information ahead of time. These strategies are similar to the "advance organizers" described in the section on reading skills. There are several ways to do this. The first strategy to consider is to **provide outlines** of the content to be presented. This can be done, in the instance of a media presentation, as shown in the accompanying table.

Providing Outlines for Media Presentations

1. **Preview** the presentation, and, if possible, consult the instructor's guide for the presentation.

2. Develop a **general outline** of the presentation which emphasizes the points you think are important, and de-emphasizes less important information. Include only the main points.

3. Reproduce the outline and **distribute** it to the class before the presentation.

4. **Go over the outline** with the class, so that they are familiar with the overall structure of the presentation before it begins.

5. **Demonstrate** effective note-taking with a transparency of the outline shown on the overhead projector. Specify the level of detail you think students should record. Provide instances and non-instances of what is important.

6. Briefly **review** student notes after the presentation.

This model can also be followed for teacher presentations.

An alternative to the outline is the **listening guide**. A listening guide generally lists the important terms and concepts that will be covered in the presentation, in the order in which they will be presented. Since science presentations often include extensive use of unfamiliar vocabulary and terminology (even in "hands-on" programs), a listening guide may be very helpful.

You can implement the listening guide in a manner similar to the outline. It is helpful to preview the presentation, list the important vocabulary and concepts in order, and distribute and preview them prior to the presentation. After the presentation, you can review the listening guide with the class, and use student products to help determine how well the presentation was comprehended. Alternately, have students review each other's notes, to ensure that the format and content are acceptable.

Note-taking guides for science activities can also be developed, if they are not already part of the curriculum. An example of a note-taking guide for a mineral scratch test activity is given in the accompanying table. If students have difficulty writing, the note-taking guide can be adapted to contain items that need to be circled (see number 1).

Note-Taking Guide for Mineral Activity

1. What are the minerals you are using in the activity?   (*circle*)

calcite	quartz	feldspar
beryl	wolframite	bauxite

2. Briefly describe the scratch test procedure.

3. For each mineral, describe which other minerals it scratched.

4. What did you conclude from the scratch test procedure about the relative hardness of these minerals (that is, which was the hardest mineral, the second hardest, etc.)?

If it is not possible to create and distribute outlines prior to a media presentation, try keeping the videotape or videodisc on "pause", or stopping the film strip momentarily when an important new concept is first mentioned. In your own presentations, list important heading or concept information on an overhead transparency as you proceed. Take time to review the outline or listening guide after the presentation. You can make a similar list, on the overhead projector or blackboard, to promote good note-taking during science activities.

2. **Promote attending to main points**. When you present information, be sure to emphasize information that you feel is particularly important. Pause, and tell students that the next point you are to make is important. Provide feedback to any students who do not record information you have identified as important.

3. **Discuss good note-taking skills**. Different types of presentations require different note-taking skills. It may be worthwhile to discuss with your entire class the different types of note-taking, and occasions for their use. Some of these are given on the following page.

Note-Taking Skills

When deciding on note-taking format, consider the following questions:

1. Does the presentation **differentiate** or **contrast**, or otherwise **classify** scientific information? (Examples of this include discussions of properties of minerals, types of rocks, different theories for the origin of the universe). If so, create a **chart** of the information, in which similarities and differences are spatially recorded.

2. Does the presentation provide **information in sequence**? (Examples include the history of discoveries in the study of electricity; events in geological history; sequence of events in the space program). If so, create a **time-line**, which spatially displays the events along a temporal order.

3. Does the presentation provide **lists** or **steps** in a procedure? (Examples include listing several examples of metamorphic rock, or providing specific steps in a scientific experiment). Then list information **numerically**, under subheadings. Example:

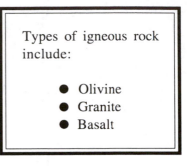

Types of igneous rock include:

- Olivine
- Granite
- Basalt

All these strategies can be used for one presentation, depending on the content being presented. In addition, some general suggestions for notetaking can be provided, as shown in the following table.

It may be helpful to review some of these suggestions with the class and provide feedback on student note-taking after the presentation.

General Rules for Notetaking

- Write notes in your own words.

- Skip lines to indicate transitions.

- Highlight relationship to text, if possible, including page reference or heading (e.g., "See text under 'Lasers'").

- Highlight points teacher has emphasized (with star, circle, arrow, etc.).

- Include examples provided by presentation or demonstration when possible.

- When information is missed, or there is insufficient time to write it down, indicate with a special symbol (e.g., "!"), and confer with teacher or peers as soon as possible to insert this information.

---

4. **Address literacy problems**. Some students have difficulties with note-taking because they lack adequate literacy skills. These students may be able to tape record presentations, or their comments during activities, and listen to or transcribe the tapes at a later date. Otherwise, a peer's notes, ones that are clear and easy to read, can be duplicated.

5. **Provide additional time**. Note-taking may present some special problems for some students with disabilities. In most cases, students can function well if allowed sufficient time to complete note-taking. Some students with low vision may need additional time to view the outlines and write responses. Students with very limited vision may use a stylus to take braille notes. Students with hearing impairments, learning disabilities, physical impairments, and mental retardation will also require additional writing time. If you allow this time by stopping the presentation frequently, reviewing main concepts, and monitoring understanding with the entire class, you may find that you can allow all students the time they need for note-taking, and not lose any instructional time for the rest of the class.

How Can I Promote Good Study Skills?

As a regular classroom teacher, the amount of time you have to devote to study skills training may be limited. However, you may be able to provide general recommendations for students, review them periodically, and provide feedback to students who do not appear to be using good study skills.

What Study Skills Should Be Provided to Students?

1. **Promote good reading comprehension skills**. A description of these skills are given in the section on reading. Previewing, organizing, reviewing, summarizing, and self-questioning techniques can be particularly helpful.

2. **Promote skills for outlining and highlighting text information**. As with note-taking, different types of text in science call for different outlining formats. These are given in the following table.

Outlining Text Information

- Does the passage provide a **main idea**, with supporting evidence or examples (e.g., a generalization about photosynthesis, with examples)? If so, write the main idea and list supporting information.

- Does the passage provide a **list of facts**, one after another (e.g., defines the properties of hardness, cleavage, luster, fracture, and heft in mineral classification)? If so, list the main topics and subtopics.

- Does the passage **describe a connected series of events** or **provide steps in a procedure** (e.g., the steps in the digestive process or the series of events in the formation of planet Earth)? If so, number and list in sequence.

3. **Promote skills for studying illustrations**. Illustrations in texts can facilitate study objectives if carefully attended to. The table lists recommendations for considering text illustrations.

Considering Text Illustrations

Illustrations have been well studied and understood when the following questions can be answered correctly:

- To what section of the text does the illustration refer?

- Does the illustration augment and enhance text information, or simply picture it?

- Is the illustration primarily intended to enhance comprehension or memory?

- Can the relevance of all aspects of the illustration be described?

- Can the student describe the illustration in detail without looking at it?

4. **Promote skills for enhancing memory.** Refer to the skills presented in the section on improving memory.

5. **Promote extensive practice of text material and student notes.** After notes have been taken, and the text outlined and highlighted, students should go over the content several times, monitoring comprehension as they go. After several re-readings (or re-studying) of the content, students should test themselves (or each other) on vocabulary, concepts, and content. Based on their assessment of their performance on self-testing, they should review again, or move on.

What Are Strategies for Preparing Science Projects?

Beyond academic studying, a common task in science classes is to prepare science projects, and present findings to the class. A checklist of procedures is included in the table.

Preparing Science Projects

1. Identify **interest area** through brainstorming, reading, and discussion.

2. Identify specific **scientific question** (e.g., "*What is the effect of salt on plant growth?*") through brainstorming, reading and discussion with teacher or peers.

3. Identify specific plan for using **scientific methods** for addressing the question (e.g., different amounts of salt added to similar plants which are otherwise exposed to the same growth conditions). Gain teacher feedback and approval before proceeding.

4. Obtain relevant **equipment and supplies**. If these are not available, identify a different method or a different question.

5. **Execute** the experiment, and keep careful record of progress (e.g., plant growth charts).

6. **Observe and record** findings.

7. **Summarize** subject area, question, equipment and supplies, method and procedures, results and conclusions.

8. **Organize** summaries to prepare for class presentation. Decide on what **exhibits and charts** to be displayed and prepare these. **Practice** the presentation and get feedback from others. Consider clarity, interest value, and adherence to time limits.

9. **Present** findings to the class.

Students who have intellectual or learning deficits may need assistance from the teacher or peers identifying interest areas and identifying specific research questions and corresponding methods. Students with physical or sensory impairments may need some peer, teacher, or parent assistance obtaining supplies or executing the experiment. Students who have difficulties with literacy or writing mechanics may need assistance or equipment (e.g., tape recorder) in recording, organizing, and summarizing findings. Students with communication difficulties may need peer assistance or other help (e.g., overhead transparencies, tape players) in making the class presentation.

How Can Students Learn to Become Better Test-Takers?

Students with disabilities often fail to demonstrate what they have learned in school because the physical, sensory, or cognitive/intellectual demands of the test format create difficulties which are unrelated to comprehension of the subject matter. Several adaptations of traditional testing procedures are described in the "Evaluation" section. However, students can also be trained to perform more efficiently on achievement tests as well as classroom chapter or unit tests. Following are some general recommendations for improving test-taking skills.

What Are Strategies for Objective Tests?

Objective tests include such traditional test formats as multiple choice, true/false, or matching items. Here are some recommendations for improving student performance on these tests.

1. **Be familiar with test formats**. Some students have more difficulty with novel formats, and require more experience before they can effectively apply their knowledge on them. Provide experience with novel formats before the test, so students will not waste time or lose points because the format was not understandable. For example, if you know students will be tested in a particular type of multiple choice format, incorporate this type of format (not the same items as those on the test, of course) in worksheet activities. If you are giving an achievement test, provide any practice tests that are included with the materials. Give students feedback on how they handled the format.

2. **Respond to the test-maker's intentions**. Words such as "important" (e.g., "Acid is an important product of pyrite: True or False") should be interpreted in terms of what the test maker would consider important. If the test maker is the teacher (you), the student should consider whether you highlighted acid as an important product, or simply one possible product, of which others are more important.

3. **Anticipate the answers**. Students generally do better on tests if they **actively reason** through the test items, rather than passively respond to answer options. Encourage students to read the question, then think about what the answer might be, then read and choose an answer.

4. **Consider all alternatives**. After students have read and thought about the question, they should be encouraged to read all answer choices before selecting one. Sometimes one option may seem attractive at first, but is not the best answer.

5. **Eliminate unlikely alternatives**. Multiple choice formats require only that the student select the most likely item of several options. This can be done either by recognizing the correct answer, or by identifying all other options as incorrect. Even if only one or two choices can be effectively eliminated, based on the knowledge the student does have, the probability of answering can be greatly increased over a random guess.

6. **Use time wisely**. When the test is first passed out, students should examine the entire test, and estimate how fast they should proceed through the test. If there are 20 items of similar difficulty and 30 minutes to take the test, students could choose to attempt to answer all items at the rate of one per minute, and use the final ten minutes to recheck their work. If some items appear more difficult or complicated, additional time should be allocated.

7. **Guess when all else fails**. Multiple choice tests with four items usually provide a 1/4, or .25 probability of guessing correctly (sometimes there is a penalty for incorrect guessing). The probability of correct responding when an item has been left blank is zero. Furthermore, research has indicated that many students who read through such test items have a **higher** probability of answering correctly, even when they think they are guessing. Students often have more knowledge than they think they have, and their guesses are more than purely random selections.

The table provides some questions students should ask themselves when taking objective tests.

Test-Taking Skills: Objective Tests

1. Am I **familiar** with the test format, and understand what is expected (if not, ask the teacher)?

2. Am I considering the **purpose** of the test, and the test maker's **intention**?

3. Am I **anticipating** each answer before I read the options?

4. Did I **consider all alternatives** before I responded?

5. Am I **working fast enough** to complete the test in time to check my answers?

6. Have I **answered every question**, including those I was unsure of?

What Are Strategies for Short Answer and Essay Tests?

Short answer and essay tests are usually thought to be more difficult than objective tests, because students must **produce**, rather than **identify** correct answers. Written tests usually require broader, more general knowledge, rather than the specific information often requested on objective tests. Be certain students have had opportunities to think about the content and produce responses in the way they will be tested. Following are some specific strategies.

1. **Read the question carefully and consider wording**. Answers are not helpful, however accurate, if they do not directly respond to the question. Further, consider carefully "key words" such as *compare*, *contrast*, *discuss*, *list*, and *explain*. These words all express different implications for answering. Further, examine questions for subquestions (e.g., *Why or why not? Give examples*); these must all be addressed in the answer.

2. **Write the expected amount of information**. An answer that is too brief will not receive complete credit; however, an answer that is too long can take time away from answering other questions adequately. Consider cues in the question (e.g., *In the space below, write ...*; *Briefly list ...*) or ask the teacher for information on expected length of answers.

3. **Jot down main points immediately**. Some students find it helpful to jot down the main points to every essay question as soon as they receive the test. Next, they organize these points and write the answer. This strategy is efficient for time use, and is helpful toward the end of the test, when fatigue begins to occur.

4. **Write to the point of the question**. Sometimes students write extended but irrelevant (or only marginally relevant) answers because they know more about that topic than the one being asked. This is rarely an effective strategy. Students' time is better served by focusing attention on the main point of the question.

5. **Answer every question**. As with objective tests, students may know more about a topic than they think. Even if a relevant statement appears trivial to the test-taker, it may seem less so to the teacher. Examiners generally give partial credit for partial information.

6. **Use time efficiently**. As with objective tests, students should estimate how much time they have for answering each question (Teachers could also provide this information). If time runs short, students should list information in outline fashion. Teachers often grade the number of points covered, so these answers may still earn credit.

Test-Taking Skills: Essay or Short Answer Tests

1. Have I **read the question carefully**? Did I consider key words and subquestions?

2. Did I first jot down the **main points**?

3. Did I write the **appropriate amount** of information?

4. Did I **write directly to the point** of each question?

5. Have I **answered every question**?

6. Am I **using time wisely**?

The table above provides some questions students should ask themselves when taking essay or short answer tests.

19

Strategies for Improving Motivation and Affect

What Contributes to Problems With Motivation and Affect?

Many students with disabilities experience difficulties with motivation and positive affect. Most of these students have had problems coping with academic task demands, the attitudes of others, or both. As a result of a history of academic failure or lack of acceptance by others, some students with disabilities may take a "who cares" attitude, a defense mechanism designed to devalue the task, and therefore feign indifference to success or failure. Similarly, students who expect to be unsuccessful may deliberately not try hard, either to provide an excuse for failure *("I didn't care anyway"),* or because personal history has taught the student there is little relation between effort and success *("What difference does it make?").* What is important to remember is that virtually all students want to succeed, no matter how much they wish to convince others that they don't care. There are several things you can do to help turn negative attitudes into positive attitudes, and to increase the motivation of your students.

How Can Motivation and Affect Be Improved?

Here are several suggestions for improving motivation and affect:

Be Positive.

Students work harder to gain rewards than they do to avoid punishment. The more positive you are able to be, the more work you will get from your students.

Teachers often unknowingly get drawn into a negative posture by their students, who, by "testing the limits" too frequently, seem to require negative and critical responses simply to maintain behavior. Their teacher behavior gets more and more negative, and the students ultimately respond with poor affect and motivation. Test yourself for positive vs. negative comments, as shown in the table.

Assessing Your Own Statements

- **Tape record** (or videotape, if possible) some of your science classes.

- Go back and record the number of **positive statements** you made to students (e.g., *"That's a very good answer, Todd! I can tell you're really thinking about this"*). the number of **neutral statements** (e.g., *"I put the week's cafeteria menu on the bulletin board by the door"*), and the number of **negative statements** (e.g., *"If you had been listening, instead of talking, you would have heard what I said"*).

- Don't count the number of neutral statements (although too many of these can be a sign of an uninteresting class). Compare the number of positive comments with the number of negative statements.

- The positive comments, over all, should outnumber the negative comments by **four- or five-to-one**. If you have very young students, you may wish to be even more positive. With older students, you do not wish to be so positive that your manner is interpreted as insincere. However, you may be surprised to see how much students respond to your positive affect.

Being more positive does not mean that you must lower your behavioral expectations. When student behavior is inappropriate, you should correct it; however, express your concern in such a way that conveys your optimistic expectation that the student will improve, as shown in the table. Notice that the language typically employs a statement: *"You need to ...,"* rather than a requesting format: *"Would you ...."*

Positive and Negative Ways of Correcting Behavior

Positive	Negative
1. *"Jamie, you have a lot of really fine qualities, and I know you can do better than that. What do you say?....Good!"*	*"Jamie, I've told you a hundred times not to do that. Now stop it!"*
2. *"Please remember to walk."*	*"Don't run! How many times do I have to tell you?"*
3. *"Shanna, I need you to put the microscope on the shelf now."*	*"Shanna, don't keep playing around with that microscope."*

Use statements that **encourage** students. Statements such as: *"You can be proud of the thinking you showed in that answer!"* or *"This is hard, you really worked well to figure it out!"* Encouraging statements can help students appreciate their own work.

If you find you have to get angry to get the students' attention and cooperation, you will have little choice other than to let your anger and negative affect run the classroom. This is almost certain to be harmful to classroom motivation and affect. If you remain calm and use a comforting voice, your students respond better than when you seem angry or upset. Set a goal for yourself to make a high proportion (e.g., 80% or 90%) of positive statements to students. Take an active interest in them. Act like you sincerely like them. You will find that, in time, your positive affect will be mirrored by your students.

Teach Enthusiastically.

Enthusiastic teaching can lead to improved attitudes, effort, and achievement on the part of students. Teaching is an active process and teachers often walk around the room while teaching. The components of teacher enthusiasm are given in the accompanying table.

Some teachers feel that this type of enthusiastic teaching is simply not their personal style. And, in fact, enthusiastic teaching does take more effort and energy than unenthusiastic teaching. Nevertheless, enthusiastic teaching may result in higher levels of attention and better classroom behavior, and therefore save you energy in the long run. It has also been seen that teachers who are not "naturally" enthusiastic can nevertheless alter these variables in themselves, and improve their teaching when they do. Remember, teachers are in many ways **performers**. The quality of their performance has great influence on how much their students learn, and the amount of energy they put into learning. Science is a fascinating and highly motivating subject; however, it does not sell itself. It is important that teachers show the type of energy, enthusiasm, and excitement that science can generate.

Components of Teacher Enthusiasm

- A rapid **rate of speaking**, varied **inflection**, and uplifting **vocal delivery**.

- Open, animated **eye movements**.

- Frequent **gestures** that demonstrate and emphasize what you are saying.

- **Body movements** that are dramatic, varied, and meaningful.

- Animated, emotive **facial expression**.

- Variety in choice of **words**.

- Open and positive **acceptance of ideas or suggestions** made by students.

- Demonstration of a high general **energy level**.

Include Exciting Demonstrations.

Sometimes motivation and interest can be increased by the use of demonstrations and exhibits designed to arouse student interest. Schedule a touring science demonstration to visit your school, of the sort presented by university science departments or science museum. Meet with the science coordinator, or a high-school science teacher for suggestions about high-interest demonstrations. Some activities that are used to enhance student interest are given in the table. For additional ideas, consult science activities books and *Mr. Wizard* videotapes, for demonstrations that may be particularly interesting for your students.

Activities to Increase Interest in Science

- Activities with **Van de Graff generators**, which can demonstrate principles of electricity by generating large sparks and making students' hair stand on end.

- Activities with **repulsion coils** ("ring jumpers") which can shoot a metal ring high in the air.

- Activities with **liquid nitrogen**, which can shrink or launch balloons, cause racketballs to shatter, or fire a cork out of a tube.

- Activities with **live animals** to create nocturnal habitats.

- Activities with **vacuum chambers**, which can expand and shrink a "marshmallow person," or raise or lower a helium balloon.

- Activities with **strobe lights** or **lasers**, which can be used to produce interesting visual effects.

Many of these activities require careful, **special handling** of the materials. Consult individuals expert in their use before demonstrating in your classroom. Make contact with local companies for possible demonstrations. Many electric companies have materials available for teaching about concepts on electricity.

Include Discrepant Event Activities.

Discrepant event activities are activities in which the result is unexpected. These types of activities enhance student interest and can be used to begin a lesson. The activities can be very simple, such as a balloon that sinks. Mesa (Arizona) Public Schools has designed materials based upon Liem's book, *Invitations to Science Inquiry*, called "Delightfully Discrepant". Student interest is enhanced because what they predict is going to happen doesn't happen.

Choose Topics and Activities That Reflect Student Interest.

Survey students to determine their interest areas, and try to select activities that represent those areas. Allow students to create personal products, and be certain they are allowed to finish these projects. Build as much personal interest into tasks as you can. For example, computer activities are very interesting to many students. Their inclusion in science class can provide motivation for these students.

Set Realistic Expectations.

Some students simply quit trying when they feel that they cannot meet the standards they or others have set for them. Set expectations that are higher than the student's current level of performance, but one that you have reason to believe the student can meet. When the student meets that standard, respond positively and consider setting a higher standard.

Monitor Progress Toward Goals.

Students often do not notice the progress they are making. Save records of student performance, including tape recordings of their reading or discussion, test answer sheets, or science projects, and share them with the student so that he or she can see what progress is being made.

Intensify Rewards.

Some very mature students work hard because it is personally satisfying; however, these students are not always common, and in the primary grades may be rare. Many mainstreamed special education students may work harder when the rewards are more concrete and obvious. For example, we have already mentioned open, positive, enthusiastic feedback from the teacher when students try hard and achieve more than expected. You may also consider writing students' names on the blackboard, posting their names on a bulletin board, giving them stickers, or tokens toward some class privilege. Watch for any real effort on the part of an unmotivated student and reward it very positively -- it will be more likely to occur again than if you ignore it.

Many teachers believe that the student "should" work for personal satisfaction and feel they shouldn't make reinforcement so tangible. This may be a good goal to aim for. But, students may need to learn that their effort is valued highly by others before they can learn to value it themselves.

Teach Positive Attributions.

Many students with disabilities do not appropriately attribute their success to effort and/or choice of an appropriate academic strategy. Rather, when they succeed, they may attribute their success to "luck" or to their teacher "grading easy".

Positive Attributions

Success:

    "I succeeded because I followed directions carefully and tried my hardest."

    "I succeeded because I put a lot of time into this project."

    "I succeeded because I got help from the teacher when I didn't know what to do."

Failure:

    "I didn't succeed because I didn't use the study strategy I learned. Next time I will study the right way."

    "I didn't succeed because I didn't plan enough time to finish the project. Next time I will plan better."

    "I didn't succeed because I didn't understand the directions well enough. Next time I will be sure I understand what to do."

Negative Attributions

Success:

    "I succeeded because I got lucky."

    "I succeeded because the teacher felt sorry for me."

    "I succeeded because it was an easy assignment."

Failure:

    "I failed because the teacher doesn't like me."

    "I failed because I'm too dumb."

    "I failed because the test was too hard."

When they fail, they may attribute the failure to environmental factors beyond their control (e.g., *"the teacher doesn't like me"*) or to internal variables beyond their control (e.g., *"I'm just too stupid"*). These negative attributions shift the blame away from anything the student can do anything about, and encourage lack of effort (e.g., *"What's the use in trying?"*)

Poorly motivated students often use negative attributions for their failure. Negative attributions provide them with a temporary excuse for not working hard, but are not satisfying in the long run. When students succeed at tasks, help them talk through the things they did that resulted in their success. When they do not succeed help them identify the specific things they could have done differently, and encourage them to do those things in the future. Don't accept negative attributions, and positively reward positive attributions.

Find Help for Troubled Students.

Some students who display negative affect or appear unmotivated may be troubled by a personal problem. Sometimes, the student is responding to a particular incident (e.g., the death of a pet), and will recover in time with little assistance. In other cases, the problem is ongoing, and the student may need assistance in learning to cope with it. Encourage the student to meet with relevant school personnel, such as the school psychologist, counselor, social worker, or special education teacher, to discuss the problem. As a classroom teacher, you should encourage the student to seek help with the problem, but to use appropriate attending strategies when in science class, and reward the student for attending to the class, rather than the problem.

20

Instructional Media

What Instructional Media Are Available for Teaching Science?

Instructional media can augment presentations in science. Various types of equipment are available and all can be used to facilitate learning in science for mainstreamed special education students. Although computers are examples of instructional media, they are discussed in a separate section (see "Computer-Assisted Instruction"). This section provides an overview on various instructional media and possible adaptations for mainstreamed students.

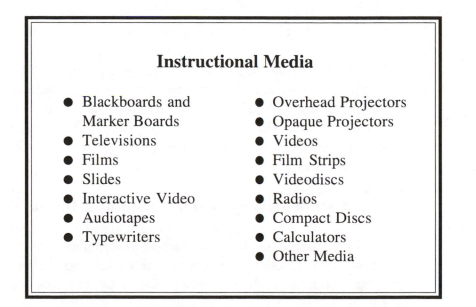

Instructional Media

- Blackboards and Marker Boards
- Televisions
- Films
- Slides
- Interactive Video
- Audiotapes
- Typewriters

- Overhead Projectors
- Opaque Projectors
- Videos
- Film Strips
- Videodiscs
- Radios
- Compact Discs
- Calculators
- Other Media

How Should Teachers Maximize the Use of Instructional Media?

To maximize the use of instructional media for mainstreamed special education students in science classes, major guideline areas can be addressed. The first area concerns accessibility issues and mainstreamed students, the second concerns teacher and student preferences for specific instructional media formats, and the third concerns possible teacher modifications. These areas are described next.

What Are Accessibility Issues?

Most accessibility issues have been discussed in earlier sections of this manual. However, each major area is briefly reviewed.

Can All Students See the Instructional Media?

Most types of instructional media rely upon the visual display of information. Since being able to accurately view instructional media is a necessary prerequisite for learning, teachers may need to consider the following guidelines when using instructional media during science instruction. It may be beneficial to always use the same part of the room for specific media presentations. For example, assignments can always be placed in the same spot on the blackboard, films can always be viewed from the same location, and overhead projectors can be placed in the same spot. This way, teachers can attend to the guidelines on the following pages for modifying instruction for mainstreamed students, and then not have to constantly re-think about the modifications.

Can Students Hear All Instructional Media?

Students must be able to hear adequately all information from instructional media, or there must be sufficient alternative devices available to facilitate understanding of information from the media. Most instructional media rely upon sound as a vehicle for transmitting knowledge. Teachers can attend to the guidelines on the following pages in arranging instructional media in their classrooms. As with the visual recommendations, if teachers consider the guidelines and then consistently designate the same places in the room for media demonstrations, they will not have to re-think about classroom modifications.

Can All Students Access and Manipulate Instructional Media?

Some instructional media require active manipulation on the part of students. For example, some teachers regularly require students to use the overhead projector and present summaries of their science projects. Other teachers arrange learning centers at which students are required to manipulate video players, tape recorders, typewriters, computers, and calculators. Teachers should consider the guidelines on the following pages when using instructional media requiring active use for mainstreamed students in science.

Visual Accessibility Checklist

1. Determine whether **students with low vision** can see instructional media.

   ___ Seating position in room?

   ___ Background lighting and color contrasts?

   ___ Enlarged sufficiently?

   ___ Legibly written?

   ___ Focus attention?

2. Determine whether **students with no vision** have alternative instructional media or aids available.

   ___ Descriptive audio components available?

   ___ Three-dimensional model alternatives?

   ___ Braille alternatives?

   ___ Focus attention?

3. Determine whether instructional media are at an **appropriate height** for viewing for students with physical disabilities.

   ___ Seating position in room?

   ___ Height necessary for viewing compatible with seating?

   ___ Sufficient time allocated for movement to viewing areas?

4. Determine whether **content is comprehensible** for students with hearing, reading, communication, behavior, and intellectual difficulties.

   ___ Familiar vocabulary?

   ___ Use of pictures?

   ___ Adequate teacher explanations?

   ___ Adequate time for questions?

   ___ Focus attention?

Auditory Accessibility Checklist

1. Determine whether **students with low hearing** can hear instructional media.

    ___ Seating position in room?

    ___ Background noise and media sounds?

    ___ Volume sufficiently loud?

    ___ Clear speech?

    ___ Focus attention?

2. Determine whether **students with no hearing** have alternative instructional media or aids available.

    ___ Clear video or pantomime components available?

    ___ Three-dimensional model alternatives?

    ___ Interpreter available?

    ___ Alternative communication system available?

    ___ Focus attention?

3. Determine whether instructional media are **within an appropriate distance** for hearing for students with physical disabilities.

    ___ Seating position in room?

4. Determine whether **content is comprehensible** for students with visual, reading, communication, and intellectual difficulties.

    ___ Familiar vocabulary?

    ___ Use of pictures?

    ___ Adequate teacher explanations?

    ___ Adequate time for questions?

    ___ Focus attention?

Manipulability and Task Performance
Accessibility Checklist

1. Determine whether instructional media are at an **appropriate height** for students with physical disabilities to be able to interact appropriately with materials.

    ____ Seating position in room?

    ____ Mobility issues within room?

    ____ Height necessary for interacting with equipment?

    ____ Materials sufficiently stabilized?

2. Determine whether instructional media have **sufficient adaptive devices available** for students with physical disabilities to be able to interact appropriately with materials.

    ____ Adaptive communication devices?

    ____ Adaptive fine motor devices?

    ____ Adaptive gross motor devices?

    ____ Materials sufficiently stabilized?

    ____ Allocate adequate time for handling materials?

3. Determine whether **content and directions for manipulation are comprehensible** for students with visual, hearing, reading, communication, and intellectual difficulties.

    ____ Clear, specific directions?

    ____ Familiar vocabulary?

    ____ Use of pictures?

    ____ Adequate teacher explanations?

    ____ Adequate time for questions?

    ____ Focus attention?

    ____ Adequate practice time?

Are Some Instructional Media Better Than Others?

The above considerations can help teachers use instructional media more effectively. When analyzing instructional media, teachers may begin to see advantages of one type of instructional media over another. For example, using **overhead projectors** may be better than using **blackboards** in several ways. First, teachers can maintain eye contact with students while writing on the overhead transparency to facilitate on-task behavior for students with behavioral difficulties and to facilitate understanding for students with hearing impairments. Second, transparencies can be enlarged to a greater degree than writing on a blackboard to facilitate viewing for students with visual difficulties. Third, transparencies can be saved and photocopied for students with note-taking problems. Fourth, transparencies allow greater vividness by using more colors.

Advantages may also be seen for the use of **videodiscs** over **videotapes, filmstrips, television, and slides**. Although all formats may present virtually identical information, teachers can search and locate places faster with videodiscs than with videotapes, television, filmstrips, or slides. Additionally, teachers can leave a frame showing indefinitely with a videodisc, or slide, but not with a videotape or film.

Similarly, advantages of various types of audio cassettes may be found. Teachers may find that keeping **variable speed cassettes** at the listening center is much more efficient for most students than regular **audio cassettes**. Variable speed cassettes can decrease the amount of time it takes to listen to a tape recording, while remaining comprehensible for most students.

Teachers may also find that keeping **secretarial centers** with instructional media equipment available for students is beneficial. It may also be seen that some types of computers, software, typewriters, calculators, and tape recorders are easier for most students to use. Adaptations of height, directions, etc. can be made without too much difficulty on most cases.

What Are Some Possible Teacher Modifications?

Teachers can also implement some procedures to help maximize the benefits of instructional media for mainstreamed students during science classes. Most modifications require little additional time and most modifications will benefit not only mainstreamed students, but also some general education students as well. These modifications are described on the next page.

> ## Teacher Modifications of Instructional Media
>
> - Preview instructional media
> - Prepare advance organizers
> - Prepare outlines
> - Prepare descriptive video components
> - Prepare summaries
> - Allocate sufficient practice time
> - Use peers
> - Provide adequate reviews

1. **Preview Instructional Media.** Teachers can preview any instructional media prior to showing the film, video, overhead, audiotape, etc. to the class. During the preview activity, teachers can note any difficult or new concepts, determine the amount of time necessary to adequately present the media, and prepare students for instruction on those areas. Then, teachers can orally present a preview of the media for students prior to presenting it to the class.

2. **Prepare Advance Organizers.** After previewing media materials, teachers can prepare some advance organizers for the class. The advance organizers can be verbal or pictorial, but can provide information to activate students' prior knowledge on the topic. This will help students become actively engaged in thinking about the topic of the upcoming media presentation. For example, in using the *Voyage of the Mimi II* (Bank Street College of Education, 1992), an integrated, multi-media science curriculum, teachers may want to prepare an advance organizer on ships or ancient cultures. The advance organizer would prompt students to think about related information and experiences they have had with the topic. This activity can help activate prior knowledge and motivate students.

3. **Prepare Outlines.** While previewing instructional media, teachers can prepare instructional outlines for students. These outlines can be discussed before and after the instructional media. The outlines can be placed on overhead transparencies and photocopied into student study booklets. Additionally, students can use the outline as a guide for note-taking and reviewing major points of the instructional media.

4. **Prepare Descriptive Video Components.** Either while previewing materials or during the actual showing, teachers can provide descriptive video components. Descriptive video refers to the provision of additional verbal descriptions of information contained on visual displays, but not included in the dialogue. The descriptive components do not interfere with the dialogue on the video, but do provide information for visually impaired students that they would otherwise not be alerted to. Additionally, such descriptive video components would appear to be very beneficial for students with learning, cognitive, communication, and attentional difficulties. The added emphasis on what was happening might help alert students to what they should be seeing in the video.

5. **Prepare Summaries.** Teachers can prepare summaries of instructional media for students. These summaries can highlight important concepts and vocabulary as well as major ideas that are important. Summaries can be verbal, written, or pictorial. Students can be asked to prepare summaries and then compare their summaries with the teacher's.

6. **Allow Sufficient Time For Practice.** Often mainstreamed students may require additional time to practice something presented by instructional media. For example, many students with disabilities would benefit from viewing the *Voyage of the MiMi* tapes two or three times each before proceeding to the next one in the sequence. This would ensure that students have acquired the necessary concepts before advancing in the series. Students with visual disabilities may need to be allowed to hear the audio component several times before they feel comfortable with a video. Students with hearing disabilities may require similar opportunities at seeing videos. Likewise, students with physical disabilities may need additional time to practice using manipulative media. Teachers may want to arrange a media center in the room and allow students opportunities to practice and review all instructional media presentations.

7. **Use Peers.** Establish the use of peer assistants using the peer mediation strategies presented or tutoring procedures described earlier. Using peers can provide opportunities for students with disabilities to obtain the necessary additional practice, while freeing the teacher to complete other necessary tasks. Cooperative learning strategies may also prove beneficial for use with instructional media. Cooperative groups can be asked to provide their own summaries and outlines of information presented via instructional media.

8. **Provide Adequate Reviews.** Teachers can also provide adequate reviews and closure of instructional media activities. Such reviews can re-emphasize important features for students. Teachers can focus students' thoughts to the media and require them to review in their own minds the major purpose and information from the presentations.

Computer-Assisted Instruction

What Computer-Assisted Instruction Devices, Software, and Techniques Are Available for Teaching Science?

Computer-assisted instruction can augment presentations in science. Various types of computers and computer software are available and all can be used to facilitate learning in science for mainstreamed special education students. Computers can be a motivating instructional tool for students with disabilities, as they can provide immediate feedback and present information in game-like formats. Computers can also be used to collect data during scientific experiments and collect evaluation data on individual student performance. There are also many adaptive devices that have been developed to accompany computers. These adaptive devices make computers and computer software available for students with disabilities. This section describes adaptive devices that have been developed to promote computer usage by students with disabilities. Following this, information pertaining to the instructional variables surrounding the use of computer-assisted instruction in science are discussed.

What Are Some Adaptive Devices Developed to Make Computers More Accessible for Students With Disabilities?

Many major companies and professional organizations have been advocating the use of computer-assisted technology to assist with the mainstreaming of students with disabilities. Many advances have been made, and more are likely to follow. Teachers are encouraged to contact major organizations and major computer companies for additional information. For example, IBM maintains a National Support Center for Persons with Disabilities, this and other relevant centers can provide information beyond the scope of the present project (see Appendix for a sample listing of agencies) and many of the suggestions here are adapted from their comprehensive listing. Next some adaptations are presented for major disability areas.

What Are Some Adaptive Devices for Computers to Assist Visually Impaired Students?

Adaptive Devices

- **Enlarged monitors** and touch sensitive screens can be obtained.

- **Magnifying lenses** can be placed over standard monitor screens.

- **Enlarged characters** can be obtained for standard size monitors.

- Monitors with **different colors and resolution** can be obtained.

- Printing can be completed with **larger and darker than standard fonts**.

- **Speech synthesizers and screen readers** and accompanying software allow visually impaired students to hear what is printed on screens.

- **Braille printers** are available to print output. Some braille printers are referred to as braille embossers and create braille output.

- The **braille pocket computer** is available. This portable computer is battery operated and stores about 200 pages of text.

- **Opticon II** is a tactile reading device that can be read by visually impaired students.

- **Adaptive keyboards** are available for typing.

- **Optical reader and character recognition software** are available. These allow printed information to be scanned into the computer which can then be synthesized into speech formats.

- Software, including **word processors with synthesized speech, talking calculators, and talking telephone directories**.

- Special **documentation on computer software** (information explaining how to use the software) on audio cassettes is available.

- Special **braille labeled diskettes** are available.

- Computers can be hooked up to **closed circuit television** systems and enlarge output.

What Are Some Adaptive Devices for Computers to Assist Physically Disabled Students?

1. **Modified keyboards** can be obtained. These include **keyguards, expanded keyboards, miniature keyboards, and membrane keyboards, foot pedals, joysticks, and headpointers**. These adaptive devices can be used with students who have difficulty with the standard keyboard. Keyguards, for example, cover part of the keyboard and allow students to rest hands while using the keyboard for typing.

2. **Software** is available that allows adaptations of keyboards to work. For example, a "sticky" program is available that enables students to have less control with certain keys.

3. **Modified input techniques** are available. Some students with motor difficulties may not be able to use a keyboard to input information. For example, special switches designed to activate with some signal that the individual with the physical disability can execute reliably may be obtained. For example, a program called "Twinkle" by Icom Designs detects eye movement.

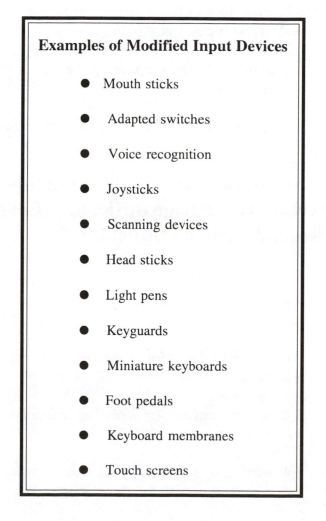

Examples of Modified Input Devices

- Mouth sticks
- Adapted switches
- Voice recognition
- Joysticks
- Scanning devices
- Head sticks
- Light pens
- Keyguards
- Miniature keyboards
- Foot pedals
- Keyboard membranes
- Touch screens

4. **Special software to accompany alternative input devices** are available and can be obtained.

5. **Voice recognition** systems are available for putting information into the computer. These systems operate by recognizing an individual's voice and speech pattern.

6. **Abbreviated expansion and adapted word lists and prediction lists** can be obtained.

7. A **robotic workstation attendant** is available. This robotic device weighs approximately 18 pounds and can be controlled with computers to execute tasks such as retrieving files, turning pages, and handling diskettes.

8. **Touch screen** is available. Touch screen is a plastic overlay for the monitor and when coupled with the correct software enables students to interact with the computer by touching the screen in designated places.

9. **Software that emphasizes pictures for communication** is available.

10. **Adaptive devices** listed under visual disability section may also be helpful for students with physical difficulties.

11. An **Adaptive Firmware Card** makes it possible to use many adaptive devices with regular software.

12. Obtain a **wheelchair accessible computer carrel**.

What Are Some Adaptive Devices for Computers to Assist Students With Speech and Language Difficulties, Learning and Cognitive Disabilities, and Hearing Difficulties?

1. Some of the **same devices** mentioned under the sections **for students with visual and physical disabilities** may also be suitable for students with speech and language difficulties, learning and cognitive disabilities, and hearing difficulties.

2. **Special adaptations for speech reading** may be beneficial for all students with reading difficulties.

3. **Special adaptations for accessing** computers may be beneficial for all students with fine motor controls.

4. **Software** designed to help facilitate learning of science information can be included to work with the above adaptations.

5. **Software for assisting word processing** is available. This software anticipates the words being typed based upon first letters. Students can then select the correct word from a numbered list.

6. **Spellcheck** components are also features of many word processing programs.

What Are Ways to Use Computers During Science to Help Mainstreamed Students?

Computers can be used to **deliver instruction**, to serve as a **supplement to instruction**, to **record data** from scientific experiments, and to act as a **motivator** for science activities. All uses of computers can be valuable and all can be adapted to help the mainstreamed student be more successful in science classes. Guidelines for each use are described next.

How Can Computers Be Used to Deliver Instruction?

Computers can be used as a replacement for teacher delivery of information. Software is available that presents science information and students can work independently at computers to learn new information. For example, in the **Voyage of the Mimi II**, students are taught Mayan math via a computer program. Teachers may want to allow **additional time** for mainstreamed students to work on computer software.

Prioritize instructional objectives and determine whether the new instruction in science as delivered by the computer is essential for the mainstreamed student. Not all science objectives may be necessary for all students.

Peer assistants can be assigned to work with a mainstreamed student during these activities. Peer assistants can monitor mainstreamed students' performance on the computer activity.

Cooperative learning strategies may also be implemented. An entire group may be assigned activities that must be completed on the computer. Teachers should determine the number of available computers and how to best allocate computer time when using cooperative learning techniques.

Additionally, teachers can obtain modems and **electronic mail** systems so that students can communicate with questions and teachers can respond electronically with answers.

Teachers can also encourage students to learn and use **word processing skills**.

Finally, teachers can obtain **adaptive devices** for students who cannot access and communicate with the computer in standard ways. Resource teachers can be helpful in identifying adaptive devices. In cases like this the next set of guidelines may help teachers with mainstreamed special education students.

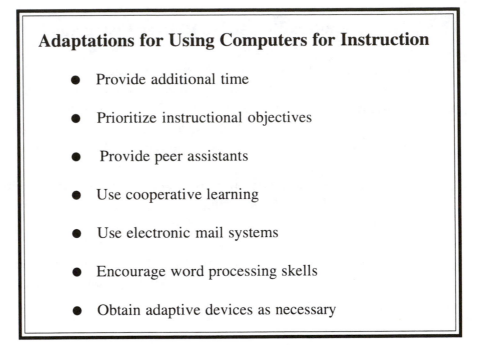

Adaptations for Using Computers for Instruction

- Provide additional time

- Prioritize instructional objectives

- Provide peer assistants

- Use cooperative learning

- Use electronic mail systems

- Encourage word processing skells

- Obtain adaptive devices as necessary

How Can Computers Be Used as Supplements to Instruction?

Computers can also be used to provide **supplements to instruction** in science. Often, software is available that can provide students with additional practice on concepts that teachers have presented in class.

Mainstreamed students benefit from **additional practice** and usually enjoy working with computers. Some types of software are developed in game-like formats and students really enjoy completing them. Some mainstreamed students may need more time than is allocated for the majority of the class to practice using the software.

Peer assistants or tutors can be assigned to work with mainstreamed students on computer practice activities.

Teachers can set up **cooperative learning** activities that involve the use of computers. Often, this will require planning on the numbers of available computers and assigning work based upon available computer time.

Teachers can use **electronic mail** systems so mainstreamed students can send questions and receive responses electronically. At times a good peer assistant might be the person who could send responses to the electronic mail questions.

Most computer programs have a HELP key. Mainstreamed students can be taught how to use the HELP key.

Additionally, teachers can provide time for students to practice their **word processing** skills using computers. Teachers can encourage students to complete science assignments using the computer.

Finally, teachers may acquire **adaptive equipment** for using computers as necessary depending upon the needs of the mainstreamed students. Adaptations that teachers can make for mainstreamed students when using computers as supplements are virtually identical to those recommended when using computers as instruction.

Adaptations for Using Computers as Supplements to Instruction

- Allocate extra time

- Assign peer tutors

- Use cooperative learning

- Employ electronic mail systems

- Acquire adaptive devices when needed

How Can Computers Be Used to Record Data?

During science classes teachers can use computers to record and chart data from scientific experiments. Various data tables, spreadsheets, and graphing programs exist and students can be encouraged to learn and use the programs. Mainstreamed students can be provided additional time at learning relevant software and be encouraged to use the data collection and chart producing procedures.

How Can Computers Be Used as Motivators?

Most mainstreamed special education students view working on computers as fun and motivating. Teachers can use computers as rewards for mainstreamed students who perform well in science. This will help reinforce practice, learning, and provide students with positive reinforcement.

Field Trips and Demonstrations

What Are Important Considerations for Mainstreamed Students During Field Trips and Large Group Demonstrations?

Field trips and large group demonstrations can be wonderful, informative, and fun additions to science instruction. Many school districts include field trips to museums, outdoor facilities, and large group demonstrations in their science curriculum. These supplements contribute significantly to science and can augment mainstreamed students' understanding of science and the world around them. There are several guidelines that if teachers consider prior to making field trips instructional opportunities will be enhanced for mainstreamed students.

What Initial Planning Should Be Done With the Personnel at the Facility?

Take advantage of all special tours, enrichment activities, visiting speakers, outdoor activity centers, and field trips to zoos or museums. These types of activities can make science more concrete and meaningful for mainstreamed special education students. **Visit the facility in advance if you've never been there.** Arrange to bring an aide or a parent volunteer to help out.

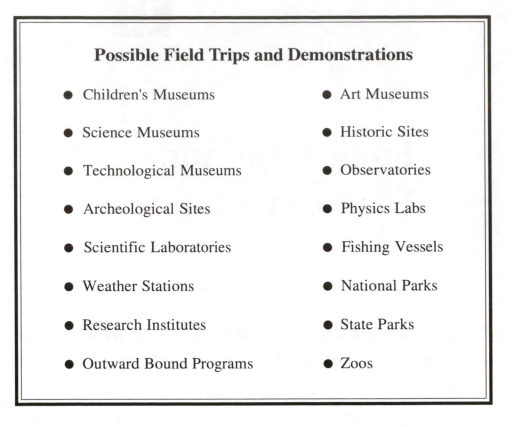

Possible Field Trips and Demonstrations

- Children's Museums
- Science Museums
- Technological Museums
- Archeological Sites
- Scientific Laboratories
- Weather Stations
- Research Institutes
- Outward Bound Programs

- Art Museums
- Historic Sites
- Observatories
- Physics Labs
- Fishing Vessels
- National Parks
- State Parks
- Zoos

Call ahead and inform tour guides, docents, speakers, and curators that you are coming and you have mainstreamed special education students in your group. Tell them about any special needs your students have. Statements that are simple, direct, and to the point will be most beneficial. Information on mobility needs, visual needs, hearing needs, learning needs, medical needs, and behavioral expectations will help tour guides plan any modifications for tours, demonstrations, or participatory activities to accommodate any special needs your students may have. Try to obtain copies of any handouts ahead of time. Tell docents you will accompany students during the tour and be there to assist if necessary. Allow students to drop out of tour early if necessary, but find a supervised place for the student who dropped out to stay for the remaining time.

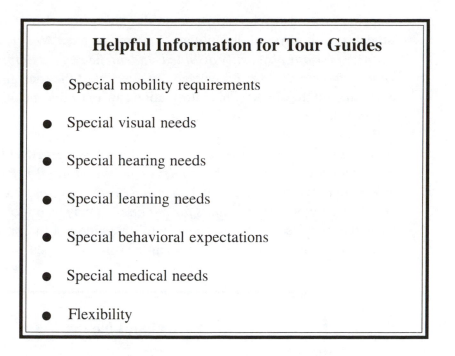

Helpful Information for Tour Guides

- Special mobility requirements

- Special visual needs

- Special hearing needs

- Special learning needs

- Special behavioral expectations

- Special medical needs

- Flexibility

Mobility requirements information can be as simple as statements such as: "*We have two students who use standard size wheelchairs.*" "*We have one student with leg braces, who tires easily (specify amount of walking time).*" "*We have a student who has difficulties with tasks requiring fine motor skills.*" Information pertaining to the viewing level of students in wheelchairs can be helpful to docents. Tour guides can then prepare ahead of time the viewing levels of exhibits for your tour, or select exhibits that meet viewing requirements and eliminate those that don't from the tour. Information related to the extent of time required before students require rests may also be helpful for docents planning long tours. They may be able to arrange the tour with a break near some benches after a specified time period, if they are alerted to the information prior to the arrival date. Teachers could try to borrow a wheelchair for the tour for students with physical disabilities who tire easily.

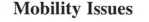

Mobility Issues

- Accessibility Issues

- Viewing Levels

- Preferential Seating

- Rest Periods

- Length of Tour

- Adaptive Devices

Teachers can also relay information they have found useful in working with their students with physical disabilities. Statements like: *"We really do not do anything different for our physically disabled student, he can participate in everything all the other students do."* Or, conversely, you can alert the tour guide to any unique need your student may have. This information can assist docents in selecting specific tours that are accessible for all students.

Visual needs information can be presented with statements like: *"We have a student with very low vision, but this student can read normal print when it is sufficiently magnified. We have a student with visual disabilities who uses a cane while walking, and relies upon braille formats for reading."* It may be important to point out that the visually impaired students "hold-onto" a guide's arm for assistance, rather than having the tour guide hold the student's arm.

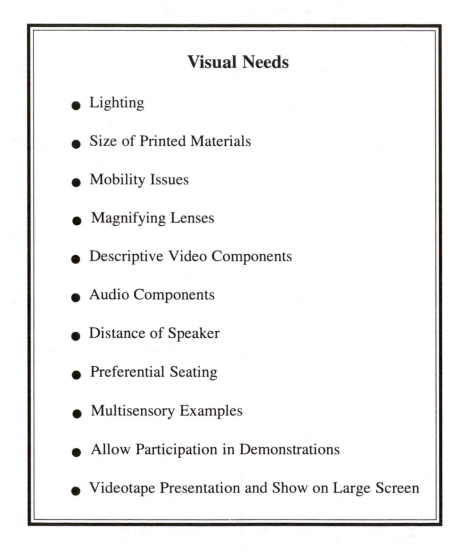

Visual Needs

- Lighting

- Size of Printed Materials

- Mobility Issues

- Magnifying Lenses

- Descriptive Video Components

- Audio Components

- Distance of Speaker

- Preferential Seating

- Multisensory Examples

- Allow Participation in Demonstrations

- Videotape Presentation and Show on Large Screen

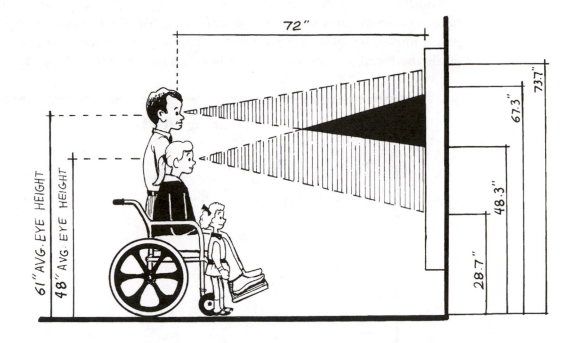

Other relevant information includes techniques that you have found successful in working with the visually impaired student. Statements like: *"I try to use very descriptive language when I present information. And, I try to keep pathways uncluttered, and always be aware of different lighting levels, as low light influences the visibility for my student."* Teachers may ask if during demonstrations students with visual impairments can place their hands over the demonstrator's hands. Teachers can recommend that the lighting be adequate and that demonstrations occur against a contrasting background. Ask specific questions related to the availability of special adapted materials. For example, "descriptive video" components for visual displays may be available. Many museums now have enlarged-type and braille format tour brochures and special adaptive magnifying devices available upon request. Finally, there may be an opportunity to have the demonstration videotaped and played simultaneously on a large screen that visually impaired students can use to view the demonstration from. Provide opportunities for the tour guide to ask specific questions regarding needs of mainstreamed students.

Hearing needs can be identified in similar ways. Statements like: *"We have a hearing impaired student who will be accompanied by an interpreter,"* and, *"We have a hearing impaired student who can hear some voice tones with the assistance of an FM sound system,"* can provide valuable information for tour guides to use in planning for your tour. Relating techniques that you have found successful might be helpful. For example, statements like: *"I have found that if my hearing impaired students sit or stand directly in front of me while I speak and if I can keep the background noise level sufficiently low, my hearing impaired students can comprehend everything quite well."* Or statements like: *"Also, at first it was hard for me to remember to always face my hearing impaired students while I talked. Then, I remembered that the student needed to be able to read my lips in order to understand me."* Or even statements like:

"Initially it was difficult for me to remember that the interpreter had to have sufficient time to communicate information to my hearing impaired student. Now I remember to pause during my oral presentations." These types of statement can reassure tour guides and tend to eliminate fears of having a hearing impaired student in the group.

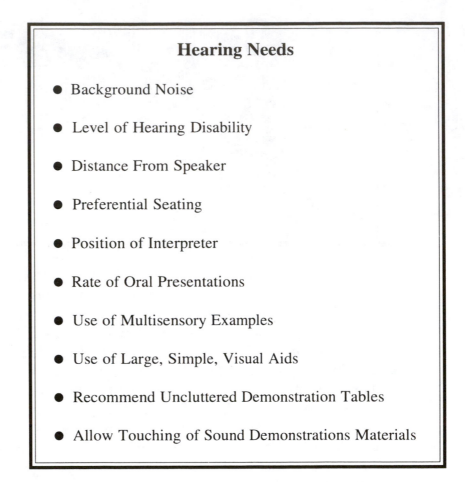

Hearing Needs

- Background Noise
- Level of Hearing Disability
- Distance From Speaker
- Preferential Seating
- Position of Interpreter
- Rate of Oral Presentations
- Use of Multisensory Examples
- Use of Large, Simple, Visual Aids
- Recommend Uncluttered Demonstration Tables
- Allow Touching of Sound Demonstrations Materials

Teachers can also ask specific questions related to the adapted materials that might be available at the museum. For example, many museums have special adapted hearing devices for the hearing impaired, and that equipment can be made available for your students. Finally, teachers can ask if tour guides can include as many visual aids as possible to help facilitate the understanding of hearing impaired students.

Learning needs can be communicated with statements like: *"We have two students with learning disabilities. They learn best when presentations are not longer than (specify approximate amount of time) and include visual and verbal information."* Or, *"We have three students with mild mental disabilities. These students learn best when their attention is focussed and examples are very concrete and familiar."* Information regarding the age levels and academic levels may help tour guides select relevant examples for use during the tours. Often, small practice activities are included in tours, and this type of information can help with the selection of the most appropriate activities for the learning needs of the group.

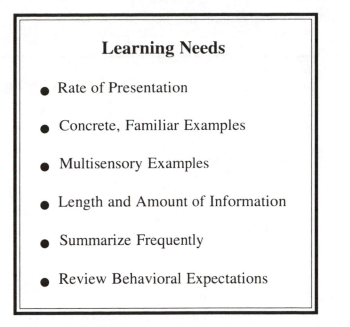

Learning Needs

- Rate of Presentation

- Concrete, Familiar Examples

- Multisensory Examples

- Length and Amount of Information

- Summarize Frequently

- Review Behavioral Expectations

Special transportation needs may need to be arranged. Most students in wheelchairs need a special van or bus with a lift. Since the number of vehicles with lifts is usually limited, arrangements need to be made well in advance.

Medical needs that can be communicated include information pertaining to students who may be prone to seizures. Statements that alert the tour guides, but that do not frighten them will be most beneficial.

When you call ahead, also **determine the accessibility of the facility**. Determine whether mobility requirements are sufficient. Determine where restrooms, water fountains, special exhibit halls, gift shops, and lunchrooms are located. Sometimes it takes more than one person to assist a student with physical disabilities in the restroom. It is important that someone who knows how to assist the student is with the class on the field trip. Determine accessibility of sleeping and bathing facilities for overnight trips. Specific emergency procedures for the facility can be obtained simultaneously and teachers can use that information to prepare students ahead of time.

What Initial Planning Should Be Done With Your Students?

Prepare your students prior to departing. Adequate preparation with your students can also enhance the success of the field trip. Once the information above has been communicated with the personnel at the facility, teachers can complete some preparation activities with their students. Describe the trip and the learning objectives for the trip. Review the behavioral expectations for the trip. Practice any new social skills in role playing scenarios prior to departing. Describe any emergency routines and procedures that may be different from classroom procedures.

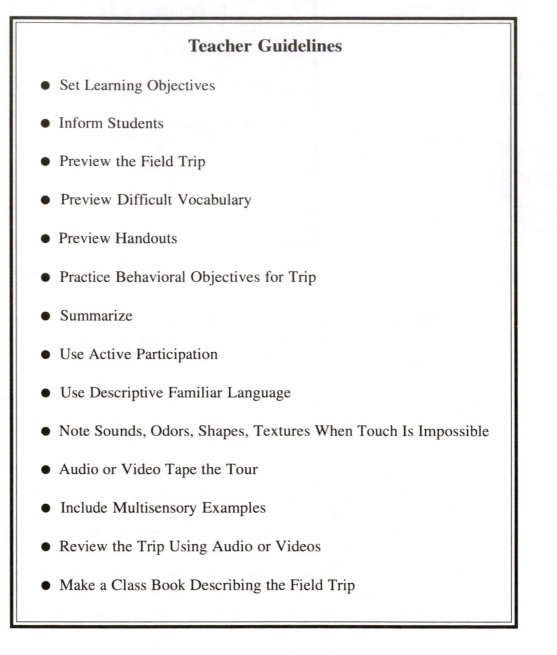

Teacher Guidelines

- Set Learning Objectives

- Inform Students

- Preview the Field Trip

- Preview Difficult Vocabulary

- Preview Handouts

- Practice Behavioral Objectives for Trip

- Summarize

- Use Active Participation

- Use Descriptive Familiar Language

- Note Sounds, Odors, Shapes, Textures When Touch Is Impossible

- Audio or Video Tape the Tour

- Include Multisensory Examples

- Review the Trip Using Audio or Videos

- Make a Class Book Describing the Field Trip

Teachers may also want to ensure that they have previewed the handouts with students and reviewed any difficult vocabulary and concepts. Teachers may be able to think up many good multisensory examples to supplement the activities and to relate them to students' prior knowledge. It is generally a good idea to have either an audiotaped or videotaped version of the trip for later review in class, or for simultaneously viewing on a large screen for visually impaired students. The taping can be completed by students who are assigned the roles of photo-journalists. These students could practice providing "descriptive video" components to the tape. Teachers can point out sounds, shapes, textures, and odors when items cannot be touched. Teachers can encourage the active participation of students.

Class "books of knowledge" can be made describing information learned while on a field trip. The class can brainstorm ideas from the entire field trip or demonstration. Each student can be assigned one of the brainstormed topics and asked to write a one page summary and/or illustrate the topic. All students' summaries can be reproduced and bound into a "class book of knowledge". This type of book contains language students are familiar with and they can share it with their friends and parents.

Are There any Special Considerations for Outdoor Activities?

Essentially the same set of guidelines can be used as a framework for evaluating outdoor facilities as indoor facilities. Accessibility for mobility, and visual and hearing issues are among the most critical considerations for outdoor activities. It is more difficult to control the type of walking surface or the level of the background noise or the amount and type of lighting during outdoor activities. However, essentially the same guidelines recommended above will help facilitate the effective mainstreaming of special education students.

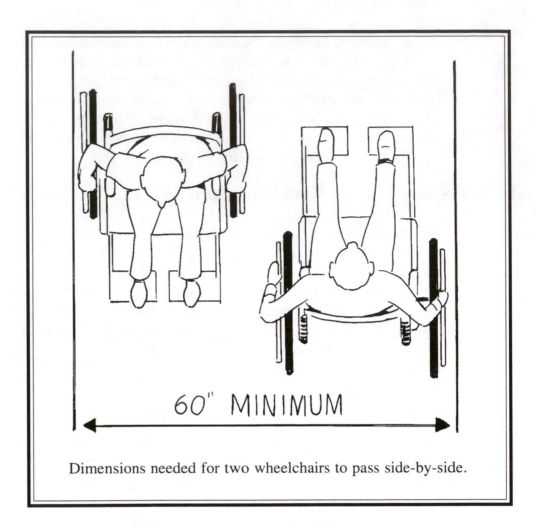

60" MINIMUM

Dimensions needed for two wheelchairs to pass side-by-side.

Part III

Guidelines for Implementing Specific Science Activities in Mainstreaming Settings

23

Introduction to Part III: Recommendations for *All* Activities

In this section, specific recommendations are made for adapting a variety of common science activities to the special needs of individual students. Nevertheless, there are some general guidelines that should be employed when virtually any science activity is employed. Following are some general guidelines.

What Are General Guidelines for Science Activities?

General recommendations for laboratory activities are included at the end of the sections on each disability area. Consult these sections for disability-specific recommendations.

Prioritize your **instructional objectives**. Before conducting each activity, ask yourself, *"What is my major objective for this activity?"* Are your objectives any different for students with disabilities? Are there subobjectives that may not be necessary for all students? In some cases, students are expected to manipulate special equipment (e.g., microscopes) in order to study the phenomena. In such cases, ask, *"Is learning to use a microscope, or is examining cellular structure my major objective?"* If the objective more directly reflects examining cellular structure, perhaps instrumental objectives can be modified. Additionally, some activities may seem less important, overall, than other activities. While some students engage in newer "enrichment" activities, for example, perhaps other students could benefit more from repeating an earlier activity.

Most special education students have difficulties with language, and new **vocabulary or terminology** which can be expected to create difficulties with comprehension, even in activities-oriented curricula. Use the **strategies** in the section "Strategies for Improving Memory" to facilitate acquisition of new vocabulary terms. For students with hearing impairments, use **language cards with pictures**. Use lots of **concrete examples and illustrations**, and **emphasize** the **sound** of the word. Prioritize the importance of learning specific vocabulary words. For all students, provide lots of practice with new vocabulary, until you are certain they have mastered it. Many science educators recommend using real concrete examples with students before introducing the term.

Most students with disabilities learn general concepts better when the **examples are concrete and directly relevant to experience**. If possible, avoid use of "contrived" apparatus, or materials that do not bear obvious relation to the outside world. If unfamiliar phenomena must be used (e.g., student or teacher-made pendulums), make sure the relationship between the demonstration activities and the "real" phenomena is clear.

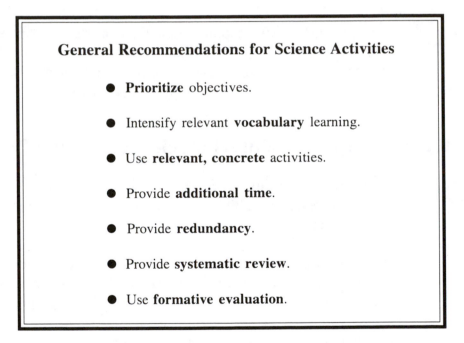

General Recommendations for Science Activities

- **Prioritize** objectives.

- Intensify relevant **vocabulary** learning.

- Use **relevant, concrete** activities.

- Provide **additional time**.

- Provide **redundancy**.

- Provide **systematic review**.

- Use **formative evaluation**.

One variable which has proven repeatedly to be invaluable for students with disabilities is **additional time**. Although time is a precious commodity for most teachers, many students with disabilities can succeed with most tasks if given a sufficient amount of high-quality instructional time. Additional time may be found by **prioritizing activities**, in which students may, for example, have additional time to complete a specific electricity activity rather than participate in the next electricity activity. Additional time may also be found by **replacing** other, less important activities. **Peer tutors or assistants** can help give students with special needs additional time for task completion. Students may be given additional time by coming in **after school**, or enlisting the aid of **parents or guardians**.

Provide **redundancy** in experiential activities. Many students with disabilities will benefit more from activities if they are provided with opportunities to **repeat** them one or even more times. **Redundant activities should vary slightly to enhance the student's understanding of the general concept.** It may not be necessary for the rest of the class to do this. Leave one set of relevant materials out, and provide opportunity for them to be re-examined by students (including some nondisabled students) whom you think would benefit from additional exposure. Assign a student who has exhibited competence with the activity to monitor performance. Students who have limited intellectual, cognitive, sensory, or physical disabilities may need to participate in the activity once simply to learn how to manipulate the materials and otherwise cope with task requirements. The second or third time, the student may be able to really learn the important concepts underlying the activity.

Provide **systematic review** after each activity. What was the purpose? What activities were undertaken? What was concluded? Often, science activities take longer than anticipated, and in the hurry to put materials away in preparation for the next period, valuable instructional time is lost. After students with disabilities (and many other students) have completed an activity, they need to **review and discuss** the activity.

Evaluate progress frequently. The section on evaluation provides several suggestions for conducting frequent evaluation of progress. Generally, the more you evaluate progress, the more likely you will be to step in at important moments and make appropriate modifications. When students do not appear to have learned, ask yourself, *"What went wrong?" "What was the source of the problem?" "What can I do to correct it?"* The special education teacher may be able to provide helpful suggestions.

A teacher using a language card.

Measuring and Pouring

A large number of activities undertaken in science education classes involve measuring and pouring. Students measure a variety of scientific phenomena and pour different liquids (primarily water) into other containers. Measurement itself is a valuable scientific objective. In this section are some recommendations for undertaking these activities with students with disabilities.

In some cases, measurement is studied as independent units that are introduced early in the curriculum. Concepts and skills acquired in these units are applied in subsequent units. Overall, this is a good approach for students with special needs, as it includes prefamiliarization and training, and redundancy in use of materials and methods.

What Are Recommendations for Measuring and Pouring?

An important consideration in activities involving measuring or pouring, is whether the students **have familiarity with these procedures**. Younger students, less able students, and students with disabilities will function more efficiently if a period is provided for students to learn the specific techniques and use of the equipment. For example, students who lack familiarity with measuring tapes, measuring wheels, measuring cups, or syringes will benefit from a period in which their use is introduced prior to their use in the science activity. Have students who are familiar with these procedures assist those who are not. Start by assigning simple tasks, and develop skills until they are sufficient for the science activity you plan to undertake.

When undertaken as a specific unit, measurement is often introduced in the primary grades and includes activities intended to reinforce the concept of measurement, using such units as popsicle sticks, straws, and body parts. These activities help students learn what measurement is, and underlines the need for standardized instruments.

Such activities are likely to be very useful for students with disabilities; however, when making the transition, either in the unit or at later stages, be sure the students understand the relationships between the popsicle stick measurement activities and the use of more standardized and sophisticated measuring devices. The association may seem obvious to you, but it may not be for many students with disabilities.

For specific problem areas, assign **peer tutors** or **peer assistants**. However, students with disabilities should be encouraged to engage in all activities possible, even if it takes longer to do so.

If some students in a group have difficulty **counting**, have students **count as a group** while one student performs the physical operation.

How Can Pouring Activities Be Adapted?

The skill of pouring is important, but don't be surprised if many primary-aged students have little or no experience pouring liquids. Most students with disabilities will have some difficulty pouring, and some adaptations are available to make this task simpler. One obvious potential problem is spilling. To help avoid spills, supervise students carefully, especially those you believe are likely to spill. To reduce the danger of spills, conduct pouring activities over large **plastic tubs** or **trays with partitions**. In some cases, these trays can be attached to the student's wheelchair.

Whenever larger containers must be poured into smaller containers, or when vessels have small openings, **funnels** are likely to be useful.

Practice pouring and measuring using rice or unpopped popcorn before using liquids.

Students usually have an easier time **scooping** water from a large open container than they do getting it from the tap. For students with motor coordination difficulties, or impulsive or "accident-prone" students, **anchor receptacles** so that they can not be easily knocked over. This can be done by putting a **plastic bag full of wet sand** in the receptacle, or anchoring smaller glasses, etc. with **magnets**. **Velcro strips** may also be effective. Keep paper towels and sponges handy in anticipation of spills, and keep a container ready for discarding used liquids.

Syringes are included in some activities kits (e.g., SAVI/SELPH, FOSS) to facilitate pouring and liquid measurement. Syringes are usually very interesting to children, so you may wish to allow them a little time to experience them before assigning specific tasks. Syringes may be difficult for some individual students to operate, so consider allowing pairs of students to share holding and manipulating syringes.

As an alternative to pouring for measurement, consider using **solid volume indicators**, such as marbles or cubes.

If you have students with **emotional or affective problems** be aware of special fears concerning water or getting wet.

Specific recommendations for adapting pouring or liquid measurement activities for students with low vision include braille, raised print, or enlarged/highlighted print **labels** for cups, containers, and other measuring devices. Additionally, tactile adaptations of graduated cylinders and beakers are available from the FOSS project, Lawrence Hall of Science, Berkeley, CA.

How Can Activities With Scales and Balances Be Adapted?

Specific skills can be pretrained which may be helpful to students with disabilities. For instance, many students may benefit from training in estimating and sequencing placement of different weights on the balance (e.g., if one particular weight is too heavy, go to the next lighter weight).

Generally, **larger, simpler** balances will be easier for students with disabilities to use. Some simpler balances are more difficult to initially "balance" evenly. In such cases, try taping a paper clip to the bottom of one side.

The balance used in the FOSS materials has a **plastic guide** located at the scale of the balance, which may be helpful for students with visual impairments, as well as students with intellectual or cognitive difficulties. Such a guide could be constructed with other balances.

The American Printing House for the Blind (Louisville, KY) makes available braille **spring scales** that may be helpful for many visually impaired students.

Most equipment can be **labeled in braille** with a special stick-on label marker.

Scales can also be used to substitute for counting skills, when it is difficult to manipulate the things to be counted. Instead of counting washers, for example, students who have difficulty with grasping small things could weigh all the washers together and estimate the total number.

Adapt a regular balance scale by placing masking tape, sticky neoprene tape, pipe cleaners, or wire in the center of the bar about 1/2 inch above the balance bar. Students can feel when the tape (or other object) is covered by the balance indicator.

For students with visual impairments, water, sand, and mud can be used to explore weight, texture, and simple measurement.

How Can Linear Measurement Activities Be Adapted?

Many students can benefit from **pretraining** in use of rulers and measuring tapes. Lessons in rounding measurements, counting in between measured lines, and knowledge of the measurement system (e.g., metric), are all likely to be beneficial to students with disabilities.

For many students, **measuring wheels** may be easier to use for large measurements (e.g., size of classroom). Polygonal "wheels" which also click at each rotation of one meter, available from Delta Publishing, may be helpful for students with visual, intellectual or cognitive impairments.

For students with visual impairments, **braille** or **large print rulers** or measuring tape are available, for example, from the American Foundation for the Blind.

Students with physical disabilities may have difficulty manipulating both ends of a tape measure. In such cases, assign a peer assistant.

In some measurement activities, the same measurement standard is applied repeatedly, for example, planting a number of seeds at the same depth. For these activities, wind a **rubber band** around a dowel, ruler, or stick at the correct measurement, and demonstrate the use of the measuring device.

Charting, Graphing, and Recording Data

A large number of activities undertaken in science education classes involve charting, graphing, and recording data. Students chart, graph, and record data on a variety of scientific phenomena. These activities are usually a component of other scientific objectives. In this section are some recommendations for undertaking these activities with students with disabilities.

What Are Recommendations for Charting, Graphing, and Recording Data?

An important consideration in activities involving charting, graphing, and recording data, is whether the students **have prerequisite skills necessary to complete these procedures**. Younger students, less able students, and students with disabilities will function more efficiently if time is provided for students to learn the specific charting and recording techniques. It may be beneficial for teachers to provide students with practice using the specific materials to be used for charting and recording data. For example, students who lack familiarity with graph paper, bar charts, histograms, and frequency charts will benefit from a period in which their use is introduced prior to their use in the science activity. The National Science Resource Center materials have included some lessons for teachers to use with all students on charting, graphing, and recording data. These lessons are recommended for teachers to use prior to implementing the procedures within a science activity. Many teachers recommend distributing chart and graph paper that contain all the necessary information to students to eliminate the need for students to have to complete all the line drawing themselves. Teachers can have students who are familiar with these procedures assist those who are not. Start by assigning simple charts and graphs, such as simple bar charts, and develop skills until they are sufficient for the science activity you plan to undertake.

How Can Activities for Charting and Graphing Be Adapted?

There are a variety of ways to make charting, graphing, and recording data activities more successful for mainstreamed special education students. Some of these suggestions are now described.

Make the activity as concrete as possible. Some special education students may not understand the purpose of the charting and graphing of data. To increase meaningfulness of the activity use very concrete, simple examples initially. Use pieces of paper or other materials to represent the variable being measured to teach bar charting skills. Have students measure the growth of a plant using strips of construction paper. Then, use each strip of construction paper as a line on the bar graph. Students can then see the relationship between the measuring of the plant growth and the data on the chart. This technique can work well with visually impaired students, too. Or, use **three dimensional** materials and make three-dimensional bar charts for **visually impaired** students. Once students gain a conceptual understanding of the **purpose** of the charting and graphing activity, teachers can then teach a variety of types of charting and graphing.

Pictographs can be used to teach charting and graphing. For example, in an early activity, each student has a square of paper and decides if he or she would rather have a cat, dog, bird, or rabbit by drawing a picture of his or her choice on the small squares. Each small square is then pasted into a column to make a graph. The class graph can then be used to answer questions. Students are able to see that each square means one choice for the animal drawn. After several similar examples, teachers can switch to colors to represent different choices. Following that teachers can switch to similar bar graphs.

Teach all the necessary **prerequisite skills** for success. Then require students to complete small aspects of the task. Many mainstreamed students have difficulty with fine motor skills. Use blackboards initially and students can easily erase and correct errors. Collect and **record data on an organized data table** before graphing.

Use **language cards** when teaching about charting and graphing to assist in reinforcing the concepts underlying the activities for students with cognitive difficulties. Keep large charts and graphs displayed in the classroom as examples, using something familiar, like the weather as the variable of interest.

Provide mainstreamed students **paper that has the guidelines and labels for charting and graphing** displayed on the paper. This will allow those students to concentrate on placing the data in the correct spots, rather than having to also concentrate on drawing the chart or graph. The only skills required for this type of charting will be placing either check marks or tally marks in the correct spaces.

Schedule **extra help sessions** in charting and graphing data after school. Many mainstreamed students will want to perfect their skills, but sometimes are embarrassed to admit their weaknesses during class time. If sessions are held after school, they will have opportunities to obtain necessary prerequisite skills.

Make charts and graphs with **stickers, velcro** or **felt dots,** or **guide strips from computer paper**. The same charts can be reused to demonstrate different patterns of data for students. Additionally, **visually impaired students can feel the patterns of data** when textured materials are used for representing the data.

Rubber stamps with handles can be used by students with physical disabilities to record data on charts.

Use **raised line graph paper** for completeing charts and graphs to facilitate the learning for visually impaired students.

Braille graphs and charts and tactile dots can be made for and by students with visual impairments. A separate piece of braille paper can be used to represent each line of data on a bar graph.

Push pins, tiles, and golf tees can be used in making **histograms**. These three-dimensional graphs may help reinforce concepts for learning and cognitively disabled students.

Chicken wire and yarn can be used to make larger three-dimensional charts and graphs. The yarn can be woven through the wire at various intervals to represent the data.

Students with physical disabilities can use **velcro gloves** to pick up **velcro dots** and place them on **velcro strips** to represent data in a variety of formats.

Pieces of paper can be placed over a **plastic screen** (window screen) or **hardware cloth** and students can use crayons to draw the lines for histograms, charts, or graphs. This marking will produce a different texture that can be felt by students with visual difficulties.

Teachers can make **large print** charts, tables, and graphs and post them in prominent places. Periodic review on interpretation of the chart and graph will help reinforce concepts for mainstreamed students.

Cooperative learning groups can be used when completing charts and graphs. mainstreamed students will then have an opportunity to interact with their peers on developing and interpreting the charts and graphs. (See cooperative learning section in this manual).

Students can work with **peer assistants** during charting and graphing activities. Mainstreamed students with fine motor or visual disabilities can dictate information to peer assistants who can in turn record the data on charts and graphs. Later, roles can be reversed whenever possible.

Use **computer programs** that have simple charting and graphing components. Programs such as the SVE Autograph for Apple computers and MS Works, Lotus, or Excel for IBM computers can be useful. Variations of graphing and charting programs are available. Often students with disabilities can be very successful with using adaptive devices and computers.

For upper level science classes, computer programs are available that **collect and record data**. Information on these programs may prove invaluable to mainstreamed students with limited vision and physical abilities. For example, IBM has developed a Personal Science Laboratory which collects and records data.

Observing, Classifying, and Predicting

Observing, classifying, and predicting, as critical process skills, are applied and reinforced (or should be) throughout the curriculum. Some specific activities (e.g., attribute blocks, early observing, classifying, and predicting activities) are specifically intended to develop and emphasize these skills.

What Are Recommendations for Observation Activities?

Some of the observation activities used in the primary grades may involve distribution of examples of a common object (e.g., peanuts) and group discussion of its attributes. Careful, guided **prompting** can be very helpful in leading students with intellectual or cognitive impairments to make good observations. For example, the teacher could distribute peanuts to class members and ask, *"How can you describe your peanut?"* When students give responses (e.g., small, brown, rough), the teacher can prompt them to provide the **sense** they used to make that observation. Systematic **questioning, reviewing and summarizing** can be helpful in enforcing relevant concepts. When new objects (e.g., rocks) are used for observation activities, students should review their previous observation processes. The relationship to observation process in the present instance should be made clear to students. Finally, the observation process should be emphasized whenever careful observation is called for.

Since observation involves the uses of the **senses**, some adaptations must be made for students who may have limited use of one or more senses. Students who are unable to feel objects with their fingers may benefit from a **peer** or teacher placing the object against the cheek. Students with low vision can be provided with **bright lighting, magnifying lenses** or **closed circuit television**. Students with very limited or no vision can listen to the **descriptions** of other students, and compare these descriptions with information they gather from their other senses. **Color** discriminations may have to be provided by a peer. In some cases the use of a **light sensor** may be appropriate. Some students with restricted hearing may benefit from the use of the microphone for their FM receiver, a stethoscope, feeling vibrations with their hands, or placing the object (e.g., tuning fork) in water and observing sound waves. In these cases, students should also carefully consider what sense they are using for observation, and what information that sense is giving them.

What Are Recommendations for Classification Activities?

Classifying activities build upon observation skills and can start as early as the primary grades with students classifying common objects (e.g., buttons) and extend in later grades to sophisticated discriminations among similar scientific phenomena (e.g., rocks from minerals). Some materials (e.g., attribute blocks) are specifically designed for classification activities. Again, carefully structured **questioning** can be very helpful in promoting the appropriate skills, particularly in students with intellectual or cognitive difficulties. For example, for students who are unsure how to classify buttons, you could first ask them about the attributes of their buttons, using the observation skills they had previously been taught. If size is mentioned, for example, you could ask, *"Are they all the same size?"* If the student answers *"no,"* you could ask, *"How many different sizes are there?"* If the student is able to then say, *"small and large,"* you could prompt the student to place all the small buttons in one group and the large buttons in another group. Questioning could be **repeated** with other observations, e.g., color, pattern, number of holes. **Peers** can be used to provide additional practice.

Attribute cards and blocks can be used to teach classification and observation. Shapes of blocks can be felt by students with visual disabilities. Various textures can be placed on the surfaces of blocks to represent different colors. Students with limited vision or hearing could use modifications as described previously, or **peer assistants** when specific observations or manipulations are too difficult.

Make sure students are familiar with relevant **concepts** and associated **language** on which items will be compared. Distinctions such as rough/smooth, hard/soft, and light/heavy, should be communicated carefully, especially for students with language or hearing impairments. Use concrete examples and manipulatives as demonstrations for the students.

For students with low vision or physical impairments, use **sorting trays**, and provide guidance when needed on how to sort items. Color coded beakers or containers can be used to assist with compairson and classification activities.

Venn diagrams may seem very complicated to some students with disabilities. They may benefit from being provided very **specific examples** using familiar objects. Explanations and structured questioning can help ensure comprehension (e.g., *"How can a block be in with both the **green** area and the **triangle** area?"*), before students are given their own Venn diagrams to complete. Finally, practice with Venn diagrams will not be useful unless students learn to apply the same skills to other classifying activities. Make sure that the relationship between, for instance, classifying attribute blocks and classifying plants and animals, is made clear (e.g., *"Do you remember how we put the attribute blocks into groups? Now, we're going to do the same thing with these animals"*).

What Are Recommendations for Prediction Activities?

Prediction skills are typically based on observation skills, estimation skills, and charting/graphing skills, and require making an **inference** from what is known to what is not known. For students with intellectual or cognitive impairments, the **basis** for making this inference should be made explicit. For instance, students in an electricity activity may be asked to chart the relationship between number of turns of a wire around a core, and the number of washers picked up. The number of turns is recorded on the abscissa, and the number of washers on the ordinate. Even though charting may suggest a clear trend that seems easy to predict, students with intellectual or cognitive difficulties may not initially understand prediction on such a chart. Ask the student to use a ruler (if the line is straight) or a string (if the line is curved), and extend. Then look up how many turns is associated with how many washers. **Test** the prediction by adding turns and picking up the washers. Repeating the process several times would be helpful in reinforcing the concept. For students with physical or sensory disabilities on such a task, see the section on charting and graphing.

Predictions can also be made from direct observations. In these cases, be sure students are thinking of the **relevant variables**, and understand the general relationship (e.g., *"When the heat lamp is turned on, the lizards are more active"*), before they are asked more specific prediction questions. Students should be allowed to **test** their predictions, and discuss whether they were accurate. If so, review all concepts. If not, help the student think through the process, step by step, identify a problem, think of another possible relationship, and make another prediction. To assist students with predicting problems, ask them to tell you in what direction the change will happen. For example, say: *"Do you think it will pick up more washers or fewer washers?"* This will help you determine if the general concept has been understood. The next higher level of question would be: *"How many more washers will it pick up?"*

27

Mapping Activities

What Mapping Activities Are Done in Science Classes?

Many mapping activities are considered more a part of social studies than sicence. Nevertheless, map activities are highly relevant to the study of earth science, and are found as components of larger units in science. Students may examine a physical environment (e.g., the classroom or school yard), and create a three-dimensional map, describe locations to other students, create topographical maps, or examine and interpret aerial photos or weather maps. In some cases, mapping activities are used to help integrate learning in science and social studies.

What Adaptations Can Be Made in Mapping Activities?

Following are some suggestions for adapting mapping activities for students with special needs.

Before having students with visual impairments or some physical disabilities explore the classroom environment, **cover sharp edges** of furniture or large equipment with tape or foam rubber (This may be a good idea whenever such students are in the classroom).

Some students with visual impairments may have an **orienting and mobility instructor** that can assist and provide specific suggestions for outdoor map-creating activities.

Use **measuring wheels** to measure outdoor distances. Polygonal "wheels," and wheels that "click" for every rotation of the wheel are are also available and may be helpful to students with visual impairments.

Consider substituting a **written or verbal description**, or audiotaped tour of the area to be mapped for immobile students or students with visual impairments.

Topographic maps and **aerial photos** may not be appropriate for blind students. However, lights, magnifying lenses or closed circuit TV, and high-contrast, enlarged illustrations, may be helpful for low vision students. Try simplifying a topographic map and using **string** of different thicknesses or textures for contour lines. **Braille maps** are also available, as are **raised globes** and **illuminated globes**, to enforce concepts of maps.

Overhead transparencies can be made of most maps. These transparencies can be enlarged on screens and various colors can be added to highlight different features.

When transferring grid lines from areas to paper, consider using **tracing paper** instead of a direct grid-to-grid paper. Alternately, draw the grid on an **overhead transparency** and allow students to trace.

Some computer simulation programs (e.g., *Sticky Bear*, and *Voyage of the Mimi*) have map simulation activities that may provide extra practice.

Relief maps may be very helpful, not only for low vision students, but also for students who may have difficulty understanding the abstractions inherent in mapping.

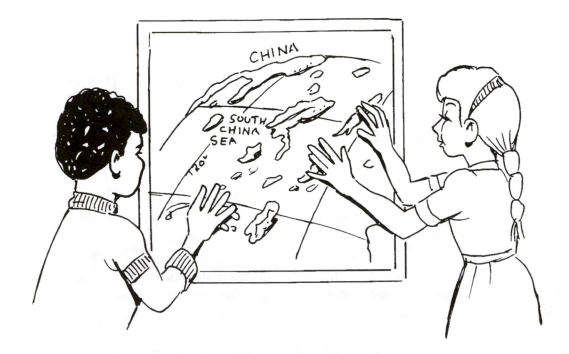

Be certain that all students **understand** the relationship between the mapping activity, and other earth science activities which are intended to build upon this activity. Demonstrate the relationships and ask students comprehension questions.

Use **map symbols** that are familiar to students, and question students on visual relationships between the map symbol and the phenomenon (e.g, river, railroad). Begin with symbols that are most like the concrete thing they are representing. Later, move on to more abstract symbols.

When place names on maps are **familiar** and are not extensive, most students with learning problems will exhibit adequate **spatial memory**. Illustrations of places are very helpful on two dimensional maps. **Mnemonic illustrations** of unfamiliar place names [e.g., Cumberland (keyword = cucumber) Plateau; see the section on mnemonic instruction] may be helpful when recall of these places is important.

Have all students **discuss and reflect on** the geologic form of the land. Students with visual impairments may be surprisingly knowledgeable about this topic.

28

Invention and Discovery Activities

What Are Invention and Discovery Activities?

In many instances in science education, students are encouraged to "discover" scientific concepts and regularities for themselves, rather than simply hearing them described by the teacher or reading them in a book. Discovery methods can be incorporated in every science activity, and for some activities, the content is of little importance compared with the process of "inventing." Such approaches are intended to promote active reasoning on the part of students, which, if developed, could potentially be applied to other areas of students' lives and lead to the promotion of more curious and thoughtful individuals. These are desirable educational objectives.

However, many special education teachers, especially teachers of students with intellectual or cognitive deficits, are concerned about the use of "discovery learning" in mainstream classrooms. Without denying the goals of this approach, special educators are concerned that their students will not have the reasoning ability, prior knowledge, or insight necessary to learn effectively under such circumstances. Nevertheless, these students potentially have much to gain from appropriate activities to enhance their thinking and reasoning skills.

How Can Invention and Discovery Activities Be Adapted?

Following are some guidelines for adapting invention or discovery activities.

1. Determine the **suitability of the information** for discovery activities. Many general principles in earth, life, and physical sciences, given the appropriate background, readily lend themselves to student inquiry. However, many other

aspects of science do not lend themselves to discovery, because the information reflects a human convention (e.g., names for scientific concepts or phenomena, classification systems, or steps in assembling a model), or because it reflects a truth that cannot be deduced (e.g., there are nine known planets in the solar system). Some discovery activities implicitly require students to "discover" the proper **procedures** for task completion. This may be difficult for some students, and not directly related to the inquiry task itself. When information is important for students to know, direct teaching is very effective and time-efficient. When information **can** be "discovered," and time allows for such activities, "indirect" teaching may be very appropriate.

2. Determine whether the **subject area is familiar** to students and determine whether they have existing misconceptions about the topic. Students are more able to think critically about subjects or materials with which they are familiar. If not, perhaps some general information or experience with the materials prior to discovery activities would be helpful.

3. Determine whether the task is **meaningful**. Activities which have little meaning to students outside the discovery process are less likely to be successful. For example, open-ended inquiry about imaginary life forms, hypothetical situations, or machines with no practical significance are less likely to be successful in promoting good reasoning skills for students with intellectual or cognitive impairments.

4. Ensure the level of **prior knowledge** is appropriate. Many reasoning activities require that students, first, retrieve relevant information and second, apply it appropriately to explain or solve the issue at hand. Many students with disabilities have less general knowledge and have had fewer experiences than their classmates have had. Question to ensure that all students possess necessary prerequisite information. If the information has previously been taught, it may have been forgotten by some students. Review relevant concepts to insure that all students have sufficient prior knowledge to make appropriate deductions. Build a discovery component into a unit you are teaching already. This will help ensure that students have the necessary prior knowledge for the discovery component.

5. Ensure that students **know what they are looking for**. For example, some students may waste time looking through a microscope at an eyelash or speck of dust if they do not have a general idea of what the specimen will look like. In this case, providing a general example may save valuable time.

6. **Open-ended questions** can be very appropriate when the methods are specified and the outcomes are obvious (e.g., "Drop the seltzer tablet in the BTB solution and tell me what you observe"). Directed questioning can help the student refine observations.

7. Some students may need more **specific prompting** when the methods are unknown (e.g., "Find a way to make the bridge hold this weight"). If students appear lost, structured questioning may help direct them into more productive responding (e.g., "What would happen if you connected the braces this way?").

8. Allow students to **practice** reasoning skills on simple problems. For example, if the student encounters the fact that the anteater has very strong claws on its front feet, you could ask the student (rather than provide the answer) why this is so. Further prompts could lead the student to the answer, as in the following table.

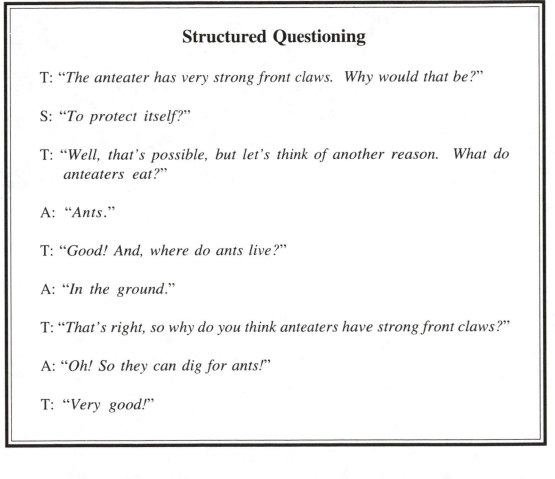

Structured Questioning

T: *"The anteater has very strong front claws. Why would that be?"*

S: *"To protect itself?"*

T: *"Well, that's possible, but let's think of another reason. What do anteaters eat?"*

A: *"Ants."*

T: *"Good! And, where do ants live?"*

A: *"In the ground."*

T: *"That's right, so why do you think anteaters have strong front claws?"*

A: *"Oh! So they can dig for ants!"*

T: *"Very good!"*

You may feel that this level of prompting is not very different from direct teaching; however, for students with intellectual or cognitive deficits, it can be very helpful in promoting their thinking skills.

9. **Review** discovery activities after they have been completed. Review the problem and the thinking that led to a solution. If reasoning errors were made, or incorrect hypotheses were considered, review the reasoning that evaluated or tested this thinking and how it led to better ideas. Discuss previous problem solving activities in the context of the present one.

10. **Monitor progress** on critical thinking. Keep records of thought processes and quality of thinking. Are students showing progress in critical thinking, inquiry, or problem solving? If not, modify procedures. Also, monitor student affect during these activities. If affect is negative, the students may perceive the problems as too difficult, and may need additional structuring or familiarity with the subject. Reinforce appropriate insights.

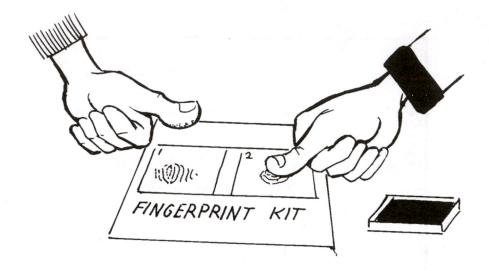

Assembling Kits and Models

Various kits and models are important, motivating components of the science curriculum. These types of activities appear at every grade level, beginning in kindergarten and appear in all aspects of the curriculum. Since the process of assembling is often as important as the completed model or kit, clearly stated directions and guidelines for that process often facilitate the successful completion of the project by mainstreamed students.

What Are Common Assembly Activities?

Some of the types of kits and models included in science range from assembling rockets, to making models of plants and animals, to building skeletons from owl pellets, to assembling bones of dinosaurs, to making models of vehicles or bridges, to assembling models of molecular structures. Typical materials used in kits include plastic, wood, clay, paper mache, string, glue, and paint. These activities can be completed individually or by small groups of students. Often, as students become older they actually design and assemble the model, rather than relying upon prepared kits with directions. Mainstreamed students can actively participate in these activities, which are usually very motivating activities. Careful, preplanning on the part of teachers can facilitate the successful completion of these activities.

What Are General Recommendations for Assembling Kits and Models?

Most mainstreamed students will benefit from the addition of structured directions to the task. A thorough task-analysis listing all the major steps involved in the process of assembling kits and models is a necessary first step. Teachers can list all the steps on individual self-monitoring sheets and explain to students the sequential order of steps for task completion. **Students can be required to show teachers the product at the end of each step prior to initiating the next steps.** Corrective feedback can be provided as necessary along each step. This process will help ensure more accurate assembling on the part of some students who may tend to rush and work carelessly.

Self-Monitoring and Task Analysis for Rocket Assembly

Step	Check-Out Date
1. Read directions and sort pieces	_____
2. Assemble engine	_____
3. Connect engine to rocket tube	_____
4. Connect tail fins to rocket tube	_____
5. Assemble nose cone, shock cord, & parachute apparatus	_____
6. Connect nose cone, shock cord, and parachute apparatus to rocket tube	_____
7. Paint one color at a time	_____
8. Place decals on rocket	_____

Some mainstreamed students would benefit from even further subdividing of the tasks involved in the rocket assembly activity. For example, each step beginning with the engine assembly step may need to be further subdivided for these students. This initial preplanning and monitoring of the task can help ensure that mainstreamed students complete projects successfully.

Cooperative learning groups can be helpful when tasks involve the assembly of kits and models. Mainstreamed students can actively participate, but need clearly defined roles during the assembly tasks. **Jigsaw components** may prove helpful in assembling kits and models. For example, during painting activities, each student can be given a different color to paint.

Peers can be used as tutors or as assistants with mainstreamed students during assembling activities. Peers can be especially helpful for students with physical disabilities, poor fine motor control, cognitive difficulties, and for students with visual impairments.

Prioritize objectives and determine whether the assembling of the model and kit is a necessary objective for the mainstreamed student. For example, is the objective the "process of assembling" (e.g. a model of a dinosaur skeleton), or is the objective something to do with the end product (e.g., observe and describe the completed model). This does not mean that the process objective is not valuable, but, given *all* of your science objectives, is this one a major objective to be mastered by the mainstreamed student? If the student has severe difficulties with motor skills, for example, determine whether the student can play an alternative role, such as be designated as the photo-journalist for describing the class progress on the assembling activity.

How Can Activities With Kits and Models Be Adapted?

There are also some very specific guidelines that may prove helpful when assembling kits and models during science. For example, **special clamps** can be used to help hold pieces of the model that need specialized work. Individual pieces can be held in clamps during painting activities. If clamps are unavailable, **clay** might be a useful alternative.

Students may benefit from careful directions on **how to handle** individual pieces from the kits. Often the individual pieces are very fragile and if broken or lost, the model cannot be completely assembled.

Mainstreamed students may benefit from additional assistance on **proper use of rubber band and tape**. Rubber bands and tape are frequently used to keep portions of the kits together initially.

Magnifying devices and big-eye lights can be placed over individual pieces to facilitate the vision of students.

Individual pieces can be **covered with different types of textured materials** to aid visually impaired students. For example, sand can be glued to one type of piece.

When individual pieces are initially connected to a central plastic form, it is often useful to keep some pieces connected until after they are painted. The ends of the plastic can be used as places where hands can go, or they can be placed into a clay mound until drying is complete.

Velcro gloves and velcro strips can be used to help some students with grasping the various pieces of the models.

Specific directions may need to be provided for **painting**. This may include proper handling of the brush and paint, as well as clean-up activities.

Specific guidelines can be provided for using **glue**. It is important that students be informed about the proper handling of glue. Some types of glue require specialized care during use. Teachers may need to model the correct amount of glue and handling procedures needed for the project. Sometimes glue sticks can be used.

Special areas can be designated for **drying** for both glue and paint.

Mainstreamed students may require **additional time to work** on the assembling of kits and materials. Some assembling, such as painting, can also be completed at home. This will allow students who need extra time to have the opportunity to complete the activity.

Estes has snap-together plastic rockets available which eliminates the need for gluing and painting. These types of models may be more suitable for some students with disabilities.

Human Anatomy

What Are Human Anatomy Activities?

Activities involving the study of the human body can begin as early as kindergarten, and extend throughout the grades. Early activities can include simple identification and measurement, such as tracing hands, feet, and outlining children's bodies on large sheets of wrapping paper. Other activities can include the stethoscope, crackers to describe the sense of taste and the digestive process, and examining the relationship between activity and heart beat. Older students assemble and examine anatomical models, study organ functions and write reports. The study of health and hygiene is often associated with human anatomy.

What Adaptations Can Be Made in Human Anatomy Activities?

Following are some recommendations for adaptations of human anatomy activities.

Some younger children or students with disabilities may not have a good image of their bodies. Use **photos** and **mirrors** to help enforce these concepts.

Some of the **vocabulary** used to describe body parts may not be familiar to some students. Question to determine familiarity. Language cards may be helpful for students with language or hearing impairments.

Make distinctions and relationships clear among photographs, drawings, and actual body parts. For example, demonstrate the relationships among a real hand, a drawn hand, and a photograph of a hand. This will help make the photographs and drawings more concrete for students.

Feeling and recording **pulse rates** at rest and after running in place are common activities. It may be helpful to practice counting and recording taps (of a pencil, etc.) prior to measuring heart beat. Some students with hearing impairments may not benefit from use of a traditional stethoscope. Students with visual impairments may be able to **feel** heartbeats, especially at the carotid, brachial, or femoral arteries. Students with physical disabilities may not be able to run in place; any physical exercise can be substituted (e.g., raising and lowering the body from the arms of a wheelchair). Some students with physical disabilities may need assistance keeping their fingers steady when feeling pulse.

Most science supply companies carry anatomical **illustrations, models or specimens**. All of these are likely to be helpful for students with disabilities, although three-dimensional models will be the most helpful for enforcing concepts, and providing tactual information for visually impaired students. When assembling models of the human body, consider changing the **texture** of different body parts (e.g. by adding sand to the paint or sanding surfaces), so that students with visual impairments can receive a different tactual stimulus. Also, use Braille or raised labels when needed.

Use **working models** of anatomy when available. The *Me Now* series (Hubbard) contains a large model of a boy ("Dudley") with simulated working heart, diaphragm, kidneys, etc., which has been found to be useful for younger students or students with intellectual or cognitive impairments.

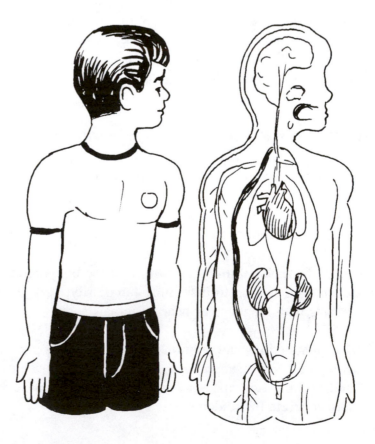

31

Activities With Plants and Animals

What Are Activities With Plants and Animals?

Activities with plants and animals are among the most motivating and rewarding of science activities. Typically, students collect, house, and care for animals. They also observe plant and animal growth and development, engage plants and animals in experiments and demonstration activities, and observe life cycles of particular plants or animals.

Some students with disabilities have negative affect or poor self-esteem. Caring successfully for plants or animals may help them feel more responsible and improve affect (such benefits are not certain, however).

Commonly used plants include corn, grass, peas or beans, tomatoes or petunias. Commonly used animals include ants, isopods (e.g., pill bugs), mealworms, earthworms, caterpillars/butterflies and moths, land snails, brine shrimp, goldfish, guppies, salamanders and newts, tadpoles/frogs, crayfish, lizards, snakes, turtles, eggs/chicks, hamsters, gerbils, mice, and albino rats. Other animals may be shown in travelling demonstrations or seen in zoos.

Students can conduct a number of experiments with plants, and learn not only about characteristics of plants, but also process skills such as controlling variables, hypothesizing, making predictions, and charting and recording data. Students observe and predict the effects of sunlight, water, and chemicals, including salt and detergent, on plant growth and development. With animals, students develop recording and observation skills, and test theories such as attraction to light or dark. Be cautious with animals requiring live food, as many students may react very negatively to that situation. Always determine the school and district policies on live animals prior to obtaining any. Include instructions on the use of live specimens and a basic respect for living things.

What Are Recommendations for Keeping Plants and Animals?

Some general considerations for choosing and keeping plants and animals are given in the table.

Recommendations for Selecting and Keeping Plants

- Even though plants may dry out faster in heated school buildings or very dry climates, plants die most frequently from **overwatering**. Keep to a strict watering schedule, especially if the plant does not have lots of sunlight.

- Keep plants out of extreme **heat or cold**. Keep plants in areas where they will not be **knocked over** by students. Except for certain plants, it is generally good to allow soil to **dry** periodically. You can often wait for visible signs that the plant needs water before watering. When watering is part of the experiment, however, water as directed and record results.

- If seedlings are growing under a **light source** during the day, switch the light off at the end of the school day, unless the temperature will drop below 45 degrees.

- If plants become **crowded** in their planting cups, remove all but two plants per cup.

Recommendations for Selecting and Keeping Animals

- Some animals (e.g., hamsters) are most active at night, when students are not in class to observe them. Some animals (e.g., goldfish, ants) frequently die from **overfeeding**. Maintain a strict feeding schedule.

- Reptiles will not eat if they are not **kept sufficiently warm**. Acquire a heat light or heat rock for their cage. Reptiles are also very susceptible to catching **colds**, so keep them out of drafts and cold temperatures.

- Snakes and lizards eat best if they are fed **live** animals (e.g., insects or mice). You may also need to keep a supply of these animals available.

- Newts also eat most readily if their food (e.g., small insects) is **live**. If preserved food is used, keep the water in the tank **clean and fresh** so the newts can locate the food easily. Sometimes newts also like to rest or come out of the water, so add some plastic or live aquatic plants.

- Crayfish are prone to **diseases** that spread rapidly. Isolate and quarantine crayfish as soon as they arrive for five days. Continue to examine them for any sign of red tinge to underside. If this is observed, isolate the crayfish and discard the housing it had used.

When you bring animals into the class also bring special books to help direct the care of the animals. This will not only help provide for the animals' needs, but will also help students see books used directly in deciding what should be done. For example, some animals may need special light sources or food sources in order to survive in the classroom environment.

What Adaptations Can Be Made With Plant Activities?

One problem with plant units is that time can be lost or students can lose interest, or train of thought because of the **length of time** it takes for plants to germinate and grow. Some students with disabilities may have difficulty sustaining attention or interest over such extended time periods. One possibility for dealing with this is to start separate plant projects **simultaneously**. Since **beans** grow faster and flower sooner than peas, you may wish to use beans in your experiments. Additionally, **Wisconsin Fast Plants**, which grow and develop much faster than ordinary plants, are available from Carolina Biological Supply Company. Finally, consider planting seeds, then turning to other science activities while plants grow.

Some students may have **allergies** associated with **molds and pollens** from some plants. If this is a problem, consider eliminating that plant or moving it as far as possible from the student.

Set up a very strict **watering schedule**, and be certain that students adhere to it. They should cooperate in keeping records that document when the plant was last watered, when it should be watered next, and which student will do the watering. Some students may benefit from using a **syringe** for watering plants. The syringe is easy to use, more difficult to spill, and can deliver controlled amounts of water.

Starting seeds in a "baggie" garden can help students more easily see daily growth changes at the roots and top.

Some students with visual impairments or physical impairments may be better able to observe plants with **magnifying lenses or closed circuit TV**.

Many students with disabilities may have difficulty **planting seeds** at a standard depth. Wrap a rubber band around a dowel at the appropriate distance and show students how to use it for planting.

Students with visual or physical impairments may benefit from using a **sorting tray** for separating seeds.

Students with visual impairments can record plant growth by drawing on a **screen board** (drawing with a crayon on paper over a screen) the size of the plant at different dates, or the relative sizes of plants under different experimental conditions. Alternately, they could construct **clay models** or complete graphs with **Braille numbers and raised lines**. Some three dimensional plant models are available.

For students with visual, physical, or motor coordination problems, **reinforce plants** with plant sticks and wire ties.

Students with visual impairments can be encouraged to **feel the sunlight** in front of the plant, and feel the effect of sunlight on the plant. They can also consider the direction of sunlight and note the plant bending toward the light. Videotape segments of the growth process for later review.

What Adaptations Can Be Made With Animal Activities?

Before creating a habitat for animals, consider **visiting a zoo** to observe large scale examples of animal habitats. When your class habitat is constructed, you can make direct comparisons with the zoo habitats.

Many students with disabilities can benefit from **prefamiliarization** activities. For example, tapioca soaked in water overnight feels like frog or salamander eggs, and may help prepare students with visual impairments for similar activities.

Show **pictures, charts, and models** of animals whenever possible. Media activities may also be very helpful.

Students with intellectual or cognitive impairments may understand development better if animals are selected that develop more rapidly. For example, the meal worm cycle is relatively short and could be repeated several times to ensure understanding.

Even after preparation and discussing rules, many students with disabilities should be **closely monitored** when first handling animals. Guide student hands with your own the first time, when appropriate. Students with visual impairments may need encouragement, and directions for handling specific animals. Students with emotional problems, impulsive students, or students with poor motor coordination should be observed to ensure they are handling animals appropriately. Students with some physical impairments may not be able to control their grasp and may risk either injuring the animal or allowing it to escape. Parent volunteers or aides can be used to help monitor the activities.

Braille dog tags are available from the Lawrence Hall of Science, University of California, Berkley, which may be useful in labeling different animal specimens (e.g., crayfish).

If animals are difficult to handle (e.g., they are difficult to catch without injury or if they bite or pinch), consider acquiring **models** of the animals and allowing students to hold the model and describe properties. Consider making **clay models** if more realistic ones are unavailable.

Enforce important **language concepts** for hearing impaired students and students with language learning difficulties. For example, cut out shapes of animals and place them on wallpaper of the same pattern to intensify the concept of "camouflage."

Some activities involve placing **isopods or mealworms** on runways and observing whether they prefer light or dark surfaces, observe paths of travel, and hypothesize about which senses they are using. **Practice** with runways prior to the activities with animals can help the students develop facility with that skill and allow them to concentrate on the animal behavior.

Counting and recording skills are prerequisite for these activities; be certain students have learned these or they can work with a skilled peer. Some students with less motor coordination may use "drop counting." Place the isopods in the students hands; they count them as they drop on the runway.

Students in wheelchairs may benefit from attaching a **deep tray** to their wheelchair, so that they can examine animals that live in the water, such as crayfish, more closely.

For students with physical or visual impairments, a **two-cup apparatus** for observing fish or water animals can be constructed. Get two paper cups and punch a hole in one. Place the cup with the hole inside the other cup and add water and the animal to be observed. As you lift the second cup out of the first, the animal stays in the cup, and can be replaced easily when it is time to return the animal to the water. This procedure can also be adapted to **aquariums**.

Three dimensional models of animals and cells are available and can help make learning more concrete for students with disabilities. *Carolina Biological Supply (CBS) Company* has a **pull-apart cell** that presents cross sectional layers of a cell which can be separated by students. An **insect identification kit** is also available from CBS. This kit illustrates insects and other small invertebrates on high contrasting backgrounds.

Some activities may involve examining **owl pellets**. Since owl pellets and the bones contained in them are very small, **magnifying lenses** such as the **Big Eye Light** can help visibility. Students with fine motor difficulties may need extra time and assistance while removing the bones from the pellet and while attempting to assemble the bones. To assist students with identifying the bones, large, clear illustrations of the bones in the pellets would be helpful.

Some students may be **allergic** to certain animals. Determine whether such allergies exist prior to bringing animals into the classroom.

32

Activities With Microscopes

Many activities in the science curriculum employ the use of microscopes. Microscopes are valuable pieces of scientific equipment that enable students to see parts of their world that are unavailable to them without the use of microscopes. Since many types of microscopes exist, ranging from small, inexpensive magnifying lenses to very large, expensive projecting microscopes, it is possible to use a number of these variations with students across all ages. For example, kindergarten teachers may use projecting microscopes to show students enlarged versions of specimens, while students at older age ranges may use microscopes independently during units observing small things. During microscope units students often examine specimen such as insect parts, plant cells, cheek cells, single celled organisms, and multi-celled organisms.

What Are Recommendations for Activities With Microscopes?

The use of microscopes and stereoscopes can be very **motivating** for mainstreamed students. Teachers can use participation in these activities as rewards for performance in class. Since they are valuable pieces of equipment, **special directions** may need to be provided to reinforce the careful use of the equipment. This may be especially important during distribution of microscopes to students. **Allow plenty of space** in the classroom when completing microscope activities. In more advanced classes, students may be required to make their own slides and therefore have to use fine motor skills in obtaining and distributing appropriate amounts of dye prior to placing slide covers on their slides. Students may need to be reminded about **safety rules** while handling breakable materials.

Provide initial practice and additional practice with the materials students will be using during microscope activities. Mainstreamed students may require additional time exploring materials and practicing the proper ways to handle the materials. Materials that students may need to become familiarized with include: magnifiers, eye droppers, cover slips, slides, lens paper, dye, petri dishes, pocket scopes, and various microscopes.

Cooperative learning groups may be helpful during activities using microscopes. Depending upon the group size, all students can have opportunities to view the specimen, while a few students could have the responsibilities for getting the materials together. For example, if following the FOSS cooperative learning guidelines, only a single student from each group would be responsible for getting all materials, another for recording all information, another for reading all materials, and another for starting the activity. This process would allow most mainstreamed students opportunities for successfully completing the activities.

Peer tutors and peer assistants may also be helpful for working with mainstreamed students during microscope activities. Peers can help mainstreamed students use the microscope, identify specimen, and record observations of the specimen. Even though some mainstreamed students may be unable to complete each step necessary in using the microscope, due to physical disabilities, these students can still participate fully in the looking, observing, describing, and recording information stages of the activity.

Prioritize learning objectives during activities involving microscopes. It is important to determine what the learning objectives are during activities involving microscopes. Teachers need to clarify whether the **use of microscopes** and/or **viewing specimen** are major objectives. For example, is learning how to use a microscope the major objective? Or, is learning about the specimen you observe the major objective? Or, is being able to prepare slides and appropriate use of dye and slide covers the objectives? Once teachers determine the major objectives of the activities involving microscopes, they can determine whether that objective is an appropriate objective for mainstreamed special education students. For example, if the study of the specimen is the major objective, and not use of a microscope, then teachers can use adaptive equipment and alternative procedures and microscopes for assisting mainstreamed students in mastering those objectives.

How Can Activities With Microscopes Be Adapted?

Microscopes can be **stabilized securely** for all mainstreamed students, but especially for those students with physical disabilities. Special **clamps** can be used to secure the microscopes to tables, or to tables attached to wheelchairs.

Sturdier microscopes are available and can be substituted for less sturdy ones. For example, the **Brock microscope (Magiscope)** is made of heavy cast iron and is almost indestructible. This microscope operates without the use of a light or mirror, but has a special **lumarod** that collects light. This type of microscope would be especially helpful to use with students who have motor difficulties or are less careful than most. Additionally, this microscope is **easy to focus**, as there are no knobs to turn.

Special **adaptive devices** can be used with microscopes so that students could use a head device to focus a microscope like the **Brock microscope**. Other adaptive devices can be employed to assist with **grasping objects**.

Slatted trays can be used to hold various pieces of equipment while using microscopes. Each compartment of the tray can hold a separate item needed during the activity.

Staining slides and putting on slide covers appropriately can be very difficult tasks for students with fine motor difficulties. If slides contain too much or too little dye, students will be unable to see the specimen appropriately. If staining abilities are not the major objectives of the lesson, then teachers may want to stain students' slides. Or, teachers can assign a **peer assistant** to aid with the staining process.

Projecting microscopes or microprojectors can be used instead of traditional microscopes. These microscopes project the image from the slide onto larger areas, including overhead screens. This type of microscope would ensure that all students were viewing the correct specimen. Additionally, these microscopes lessen the need for physical abilities for successful task completion.

Closed circuit television systems can be hooked up to microscopes to enlarge the view. These systems can help visually impaired students participate more fully in microscope activities.

Stereoscopes can be used to ensure students are seeing the correct specimen.

Once enlarged images are projected from the projecting microscopes, the **images can be traced onto raised-line paper.** The raised-line representation can be used by visually impaired students as a tactile substitute.

Three-dimensional models can be made of whatever the specimen are for visually impaired students. Different **textured materials** can be used to represent different parts of the objects. For example, sand, string, paper clips, etc. can be glued onto a representational drawing of the specimen. Different types of seeds can be glued to a line drawing of the specimen, and each type of seed can represent a different part of the specimen. This can then be used manually by visually impaired students.

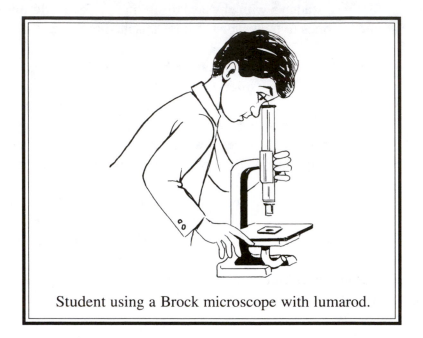

Student using a Brock microscope with lumarod.

Braille descriptions of the microscope activities can be completed and provided for visually impaired students. These students can complete **braille laboratory booklets** that contain descriptions of all of the microscope activities.

Descriptive video components of class activities during microscope activities can be completed. These can be completed using either a video camera or a tape recorder, and can provide detailed descriptions of all events, especially of the specimen.

Photographs of specimens can be shown to students so they can accurately find specimen when looking through microscopes, or can be used when students are unable to see through microscopes. Multiple copies of high-quality microphotographs are available from science supply companies.

Additional time may be required to complete activities using microscopes for mainstreamed students.

Often many small items, including tweezers, eye droppers, slides, and slide covers, need to be manipulated during some microscope activities. Substitute larger items if possible for students with fine motor difficulties.

33

Water Activities

How Are Water Activities Used in Science Classes?

Activities involving water are common in science classes. Water is very familiar to students, easily available, and safe to use. At the same time, important scientific concepts can be illustrated with water activities. Using water, students study the relative size and shapes of drops of different solutions, examine surface tension, investigate evaporation, examine water pressure, create bubbles, observe solutions rising through blotter paper, and make clay boats.

What Are Adaptations for Water Activities?

Some science curricula contain science activities that are less directly relevant to studying the properties of water, and teachers may wish to **prioritize objectives** in these areas. For instance, activities involving making water colors, or investigating sounds made by water may be more difficult for students with extreme visual or hearing impairments. Perhaps there are other relevant activities with water that the whole class can benefit from.

When investigating water sounds with students with hearing impairments, **amplify** sounds, or use materials that enhance sounds (e.g., pouring water into an aluminum pan rather than a plastic container).

Water is likely to **spill** in any classroom, and is very likely to spill if students with disabilities are investigating water. Turn to the section on "Measuring and Pouring" for specific recommendations for measuring and containing spills.

Studying the relative size and shapes of drops of various solutions may be a very difficult task for students with visual impairments. Try creating **clay models** of larger-than-life drops, or try obtaining high quality videos and show them on enlarged screens.

Students with visual impairments can **feel** Petri dishes or other containers to check for evaporation. They will learn the concept better if only a small amount of water is used, and is allowed to evaporate completely.

Provide **specific procedures** for comparing weights of various liquids, when comparing weights of liquids is the primary objective. Students with intellectual or cognitive impairments may have difficulty "discovering" how to do this. Alternately, when reasoning through possible measurement systems is the primary objective, provide **guided questioning** to help the student arrive at an appropriate conclusion.

Surface tension experiments may require good fine motor control. Students with physical disabilities or visual impairments may require **peer assistance** in, e.g., floating a paper clip or turning a beaker of water upside down. Guide the hand of students with physical disabilities or visual impairments so they can experience the process of the experiment.

Tactile markers can be used to indicate various water levels for students with visual impairments.

For water pressure experiments, students with visual impairments can **feel**, e.g., rather than see, the relative pressure of water coming from holes punched in a container at different elevations.

When engaging in "clay boat" activities (constructing boats out of clay, testing their buoyancy, and drawing conclusions about buoyancy), many students with disabilities may benefit from **additional time** in order to manipulate boat construction, floating/sinking activities, and recording activities.

Visually impaired students can test buoyancy by placing a **hand under the boat**, before launching, and feeling whether it sinks.

For lifting washers and sinkers in and out of boats, physically impaired students may benefit from a **magnet attached to a dowel rod**.

Students with physical disabilities may have difficulty manipulating clay. Before assigning a peer assistant, try **softening the clay** by manipulating it in your hand or laying it in the sun. **Aluminum foil** may be a helpful alternative to clay.

For water activities involving measuring the temperature of the water, use adapted or large thermometers. Adapted thermometers can be purchased from *Lawrence Hall of Science*, or braille labels can be added to traditional thermometers (those which indicate the temperature with a free-moving pointer). When temperatures are not excessive, it may be possible for students to feel the temperature of the water.

34

Powders, Mixtures, and Solutions

A large number of science activities involve the use of powders, mixtures, and solutions for completing scientific experiments. Powders, mixtures and solutions are studied to learn about chemical properties, solutions, chemical changes, saturation, concentrations, and separating liquids. These types of activities can be enjoyable for all students. In this section are some recommendations for completing these activities with mainstreamed special education students.

What Are Recommendations for Powders, Mixtures, and Solutions?

An important consideration in completing activities using powders, mixtures, and solutions is **safety**. It may be important to review and reinforce the safety procedures while using these substances. For example, mainstreamed students may need to be reminded: to never taste anything; to immediately clean up any spilled materials; to avoid physical contact with any of the powders, mixtures, and solutions being used; to rinse off any areas that have contacted the substances immediately; to wash hands after using the substances; to avoid blowing into the substance because it might fly into their eyes; and to follow special rules if heat sources are being used. Teachers may want to provide extra security for some mainstreamed students while using any chemicals in the class. This may be particularly important for students with visual impairments, physical disabilities, or students with behavior problems. Special peer assistants can be asked to provide extra support and guidance for some mainstreamed students.

The room can be arranged to allow **space** for movement to and from the sink and the materials distribution point. Additionally, the lab tables should be at an appropriate height for students to be able to interact effectively with the materials while seated.

There are also a variety of materials and tools that are usually necessary for completing activities with powders, mixtures, and solutions. A sample listing of materials includes: hand lenses, syringes for measuring, funnels, spoons, balances, screens, filters, burners, gravel, diatomaceous earth, salt, citric acid, baking soda, iodine, sterno, vinegar, calcium carbonate, sugar, laundry starch, and plaster of paris. Adaptive devices for using many of these tools and materials may be available. Teachers may therefore, want to **priortize the learning objectives** for mainstreamed students. Are students required to demonstrate mastery with **mixing and pouring skills**? Or, are the students required to demonstrate **mastery of the concepts** covered? Or, are there other main objectives? Once teachers have clarified the **main objectives** for mainstreamed students, they will be better able to decide on appropriate allocations of time and corresponding modifications in instruction.

How Can Activities With Powders, Mixtures, and Solutions Be Adapted?

Many of these activities rely upon visual observations for seeing similarities and differences among the various powders, mixtures, and solutions. It is important to tell students to rely upon **all senses (except taste), including the sense of smell** while completing these activities. This guideline will be especially important for visually impaired students, but will also benefit other mainstreamed students. Some of the combinations of powders, mixtures, and solutions produce very definite smells.

Students should also be encouraged to use the sense of **hearing** when making observations during units involving powders, mixtures, and solutions. Often mixing various substances together results in **fizzing noises**. Sound observations can also be recorded, and described for hearing impaired students. For example, when a fizzing noise occurs, teachers can **place a microphone nearby to amplify the sound**. Other students can attempt to describe the fizzing sound in concrete verbal forms for students with hearing impairments.

When powders, mixtures, and solutions are **not harmful**, students can be encouraged to **feel** the substances and to observe similarities and differences. This adaptation could be helpful for students with visual impairments. Students can be asked to describe any observations noted through the tactile sense. Some powders may be fine and soft, while others are hard and grainy. Additionally, some chemical changes produce **heat** and that heat can be felt by placing a hand on the beaker or container. These observations can be combined with observations made visually.

Light sensors may be used to assist visually impaired students ability to detect **color changes** in various solutions and mixtures.

All observations can be recorded **descriptively** either on audiotapes or videotapes for later review. Observations can also be recorded in **braille formats** for some students.

During activities that require filtering solutions, students can be encouraged to **touch the filter** before and after the filtering process. Students will then be able to describe whether they can feel any residue materials. This will again encourage students to use the **tactile** sense for observations.

During activities that require the mixing of substances to form solutions, students can be asked to **use straws to feel for any undissolved materials** in the bottom of the solutions.

As with many activities, it is important to **stabilize all materials to avoid spillage**. The bottoms of containers can be weighted to help control spillage.

Teachers can color code different containers to assist ensuring students appropriately label the right containers.

When making **colored solutions** have containers next to a contrasting background to enhance visibility.

Use **eyedroppers** for adding colors to solutions. This will allow the change process to occur more slowly and enhance students' observations of the process.

Strainers with handles can be used in place of flat screens for filtering or separating mixtures.

Funnels can be used to assist with **pouring** activities. The addition of funnels may make it possible for mainstreamed students to participate in the mixing and pouring components of the activities.

Some concepts in these units may be difficult for mainstreamed students. The use of **language cards** and clear concrete **descriptions and examples** will help facilitate understanding.

Substitute **coffee stirrers** for **tooth picks** for mixing powders in small cups. Coffee stirrers are somewhat larger and easier to hold.

Teachers can **add sand to mixtures and solutions** and have visually impaired students **feel the sand** to help teach the concepts of mixtures and solutions and concentrations.

Adaptive devices, including special balances, magnifying lenses, Big Eye Lights, syringes, and handles for spoons can be employed during these activities to facilitate the complete mainstreaming of students with disabilities.

Cooperative learning groups can be employed to facilitate the mainstreaming and participation of students in powders, mixtures, and solution activities. Students can be assigned various roles in the group to maximize their participation and learning. See the cooperative learning section for additional information.

Peer assistants and tutors can be employed to assist mainstreamed students in completing these activities. Many special education students may need to be able to **complete these activities several times** in order to fully comprehend the purpose of the activity. Recall that redundancy is an important instructional variable for most mainstreamed special education students.

When completing activities involving Bunsen burners, hot plates, or other items using heat, place wire guards around those objects. Use insulated tongs to hold containers over heat. Carefully monitor any activities using heat.

Cylindrical foam padding and triangular finger grips can be used to build up handles for students wtih fine motor difficulties.

35

Weather
Activities

What Are Weather Activities?

Weather is a subject that is familiar to virtually all learners, lends itself to direct observations, and therefore may be very beneficial for students with special needs. In common weather activities, younger students may go outdoors and observe and describe elements of the weather. Older students can measure temperature in various locations, experiment with barometers, calculate relative humidity, construct weather vanes, and calculate wind speed and direction. Students also read weather maps, forecast weather or operate electronic media to communicate about weather with students in other parts of the country.

What Adaptations Can Be Made With Weather Activities?

Some **caution** should be applied to activities involving certain types of weather apparatus. For example, in some investigations, students compute relative humidity by swinging wet and dry thermometers which are attached to strings. Students with behavior problems and students who are prone to impulsivity or motor coordination problems should be carefully **supervised**.

Adapted thermometers for visually impaired students are available from the Lawrence Hall of Science. Thermometers with plastic or metal backs are more cost effective and resist breakage more than glass-type thermometers.

Adapted graduated cylinders and beakers, and tactile floating scales are available from Lawrence Hall of Science for measuring rainfall.

Some concepts in the study of weather (e.g., temperature) are already familiar to most students. However, others, such as humidity or barometric pressure, may be more difficult for students with intellectual or cognitive disabilities. **Evoking prior experience** with hot showers or boiling water vs. oven heat can help enforce the concept of humidity; the concept of air pressure can be discussed with respect to any experiences with fast moving elevators or airplane trips. Placing a barometer in a container with a rubber top that can be used to increase and decrease barometric pressure may also be helpful. Finally, sections of the *Voyage of the Mimi* videotapes effectively demonstrate temperature, humidity, and air/water pressure.

Students with intellectual or cognitive impairments may have difficulty using charts for computing relative humidity or wind speed. Spend some time **practicing** using the charts before using them to calculate weather phenomena. For other suggestions on graphing and charting, see the relevant section of this manual. For suggestions on construction of simple weather measuring apparatus (e.g., weathervane), refer to the section on building and assembling models.

Students with visual impairments can be taught about the composition of clouds by describing air from vaporizers or fog. Cotton or polyester stuffing of the type found in stuffed animals can be used to share with students the way clouds **appear** to sighted persons. Ensure that students understand the difference between the properties of clouds and the appearance of clouds from a distance.

Videotape actual weather forecasts from the weather channel or local television channel. Use those examples to demonstrate collecting and recording weather data and making predictions. The shows can also be reviewed to determine the accuracy of the predictions.

Maintain individual journals and allow students to record the weather data in those journals. The journals could be written, pictorial, or audio-taped accounts of weather activities.

36

Rocks, Minerals, and Fossils

What Are Activities With Rocks, Minerals, and Fossils?

Students have all seen rocks and minerals in their environment, but have rarely investigated them in depth. In rocks and minerals activities, students observe the properties of rocks and minerals, perform scratch tests, observe the interaction of calcite and vinegar, examine mineral components in rocks, and look for rock and mineral specimens on field trips. They can also observe and classify fossil specimens.

To facilitate understanding of the properties of **rocks**, FOSS has developed a lesson entitled "*Mock Rocks*." In this lesson, teachers create their own rocks as a combination of such ingredients as aquarium gravel, sand, oyster shell, food coloring, flour, and water. Students make and record surface observations. They break the rocks apart, separate like components into piles, and place the smallest particles into vials containing water. When the vials settle, different components emerge.

What Are Adaptations for Activities With Rocks, Minerals, and Fossils?

Activities such as "*Mock Rocks*" can be very helpful for many students in learning the properties of rocks, particularly for students with visual, cognitive, or intellectual deficits. For students with visual or physical impairments, **substitute larger particles**. Students with visual impairments can take a "core" sample of the dissolved rock solution with a **straw**, and feel the ingredients. After other students have made observations, they can **feel the residue** left in evaporating dishes. With impulsive or aggressive students, **monitor carefully** (or assign to other students) the use of nails or other sharp objects.

Models of "sedimentary rock" can be constructed with layers of different colored gravel and white glue or plaster of paris in plastic cups.

Many **different examples** of rocks, minerals, and fossils are available from scientific supply companies. Larger, more obvious specimens that can be handled (vs. glued on a page) are generally easier to learn from.

Students with visual impairments should observe rock specimens in **segmented trays** with Braille or raised line labels. For scratch tests, they could **feel the spot to be scratched** before scratching. This may make it easier to feel the scratch.

Many other properties of minerals may be directly observable **tactually** to students with visual impairments, and this type of observation should be encouraged. Cleavage, for example, and cleavage direction can be easily determined with samples of **mica**. **Fracture** is another property that can be felt easily, as can **heft** and **crystal faces**. Luster, color, and streak will be difficult for students with visual impairments to experience, although illumination, magnifying lenses and closed circuit television may be helpful for students who have some vision. However, only two of these three properties are particularly meaningful -- color is not a consistent property in many specific minerals.

Rocks, Minerals, and Fossils

Fossils may also provide excellent specimens for students with visual impairments to feel. With little prompting, they should be able to make out the plant or animal impression.

If rocks, fossils, and mineral samples are small, either try to obtain larger samples, or use a "Big Eye Light" or magnifying lens to assist visually impaired students.

Students with visual impairments may be able to **hear** the calcite fizzing in vinegar. If the calcite and vinegar is placed in a clear plastic cup, it may be visible to students on the **overhead projector**, so they can compare the teacher's observations with their own.

Large charts or tables can be made to include observations on the rocks, minerals, and fossils.

37

Earth Science/ Landform Activities

What Are Earth Science/Landform Activities?

Students explore, record, and replicate sections of land near the school. They construct landforms with different types of materials in stream tables and simulate water erosion. They also may simulate beach erosion and wind erosion in stream tables with "waves" and sand, and "wind" from breath and sand. They may construct models of plate movement on the earth's crust, construct model "volcanoes," or examine seismographs.

What Are Adaptations for Earth Science/Landform Activities?

Landform activities may be more understandable for students who have previously completed **mapping** activities. Refer to the mapping section for recommendations concerning building three dimensional models of landscapes.

For hearing impaired students, accompany any reference to earth or earth matter with a **globe**.

Students with visual impairments can carefully **feel changes from erosion** in landform activities, but supervision may be necessary so that the model is not altered. Most activities undertaken in earth science/landform areas can be directly experienced by students with visual impairments.

Be certain students with intellectual or cognitive impairments understand the relation between the landform **model** and the actual phenomena being studied. Ask for specific examples, and point out relationships with observable land (e.g., outside the classroom window).

Students with physical disabilities may need **physical assistance,** from teacher or peers, in all aspects of construction of landform models, earth plate models, and model volcanoes.

Supervise carefully (or assign peer assistant) students prone to impulsivity or aggressive behavior when developing landform earth/science models. Volcano activities may be particularly stimulating to some students.

Water in a shallow basin can be used to demonstrate effects of wind. Students can blow into the basin and make waves.

Sand dunes can be made by having sand in a basin and using a hair dryer to blow the sand.

Ant farms and terrariums can be used to demonstrate some land form concepts.

Use blue food coloring to highlight changes in a stream table activity for students with visual disabilities. This will enhance the contrast between eroded and noneroded areas.

38

Astronomy
Activities

What Are Astronomy Activities?

Astronomy is a little more difficult than some activities, because stars and planets are best observed at night, when students are not in school. Nevertheless, many activities are possible, as the moon can often be seen during the day. Students can construct or observe models of the sun and planets, determine relative size of stars and planets, and relative distance of stars from each other or the planets from the sun. They can construct models of eclipses, or the effects of planetary motion on the seasons. Students can also observe media presentations, visit a planetarium, and study space travel.

What Are Adaptations for Astronomy Activities?

Many different three dimensional, moving **models** of the sun and planets are available from scientific supply companies. Alternately, you could construct (or have students construct) models with different sized spheres (volleyball, ping pong ball, pea) and wire. Students can more easily absorb concepts involving relative movement or relative distance with such models. Teachers are reminded to check the accuracy of the models being used.

Moon and planet globes, star charts, galaxy models, and posters are generally available and will help greatly in enhancing interest and promoting understanding for normally sighted students.

Other **three-dimensional** models available from science supply companies that may be helpful for visually impaired students include lunar surface models and solar system models.

If **telescopes** are used, either as an after-school activity, or as a daytime demonstration of their use, set the telescope up and focus it on a particular object ahead of time. Without specific training, many students with disabilities may have difficulty focusing, finding an object, or sighting. Show students what they will be looking at, inform them that the image will be upside down (when appropriate), have them look in the lens without touching the telescope. Help the student steady his or her head if necessary. Students with visual impairments may benefit from verbal descriptions and raised line drawings of the object being viewed. Remember, never use telescopes or binoculars to look at the sun.

Although students with visual impairments may benefit from **planaterium** visits, it may not be the best use of their time. Check ahead with the planetarium concerning accomodations for students with visual impairments.

Computer progams, such as that found in *The Voyage of the Mimi II*, can provide additional practice learning concepts of relative motion. Many planetarium software applications are available. Refer to the section on computer-assisted instruction for additional recommendations.

Games, such as "Space Hop," that require attention directed to a visual representation of the solar system and careful consideration of its charactics, can be beneficial activities in providing experience and redundancy. Remember, when using pictures or models of the universe, point out that they might not be drawn or made to true scale.

On sunny days, students with visual impairments can be reminded of the **warmth of the sun** as indicator of its energy intensity, and informed that the universe contains unnumerable instances of these, too far away to be felt.

Braille labels or raised letters can be attached to models of the solar system. Be sure to place the labels in the same place for each planet. String can be glued or taped on paper to indicate planetary orbits.

Shadows can be marked on the pavement with colored chalk and measured over time to show the movement of the earth relative to the sun.

Use a heat lamp to help explain day and night and the earth's rotation. Have the student move around the lamp and note observations from the amount and light.

39

Magnetism and Electricity Activities

What Are Magnetism and Electricity Activities?

In magnetism and electricity activities, students learn about electromagnetic principles by observing magnets and constructing open and closed circuits, series and parallel circuits, using batteries, switches, lights, and motors. They create electromagnets and predict and test the relation between turns of a coil around a core and magnetic strength, and create simple telegraphs.

What Are Adaptations for Magnetism and Electricity Activities?

For activities involving scales and magnets, in which washers are placed in cups to break the magnetic force, provide **necessary assistance or supervision** so that students will add washers carefully.

Students who have physical disabilities or who lack good fine motor coordination may find that **alligator clips** are much easier to use than Fahnstock clips, when attaching wires.

Wires can be permanently attached to the main pieces of the circuit for students with severe physical disabilities.

Strip wires before class starts or use bare wire, especially for students who may have difficulty doing this.

For students with visual impairments, **substitute small electric motors** for electric lights when constructing electrical circuits.

When comparing the magnetic attraction of the different numbers of turns of wire around a core, have the students all **count together** as one student performs the operation. This will help focus the attention of the group, and enforce the concept being investigated.

If you have students with physical disabilities who use **special equipment** using electricity, this may be a good unit to have them demonstrate this.

For students with hearing impairments, have them **feel** the vibration of the motor. Alternately, place a **paper flag** on the electric motor, so students with hearing impairments can observe when the motor is operating.

Students with more limited intellectual and cognitive abilities will benefit from **pretraining on the "code"** that they will use to communicate on the telegraph. Practice creating the code and communicating with it using pencil taps before using it on the telegraph.

For students with hearing impairments, attach a **bulb** to flash when the telegraph circuit is connected.

Construct holders for small items, including bulbs, batteries, and wires.

Use **compass** with **raised letters** indicating North, South, East, West.

Use **stethoscopes** to hear iron filings move across a surface during activities with magnets. Or place objects on a thin surface and have students with visual disabilities place their hands underneath the table to feel the iron filings move during the activity. Do not use iron filings unless they are in sealed containers.

40

Force and Motion Activities

Force and motion activities can include completing experiments with inclined planes, small paper airplanes, levers and pulleys, and other small machines. These types of activities can be fun and motivating, but simultaneously contain concepts and vocabulary that are abstract and difficult.

What Are Recommendations for Force and Motion Activities?

Provide initial practice and additional supplemental practice with the materials students will be using during force and motion activities. Mainstreamed students may require additional time exploring materials and practicing the proper ways to handle the materials. Some students may experience difficulties with the manipulation of some of the pieces of equipment. FOSS recommends allocating additional time for students to set up the lever and pulley materials. Mainstreamed students may require repeated opportunities to set up and explore these materials, before they are able to acquire the necessary facility.

Cooperative learning groups may be helpful during force and motion activities. All students can have opportunities to observe the pulleys, levers, and small machines, while a few students could have the responsibilities for getting the materials together. For example, if following the FOSS cooperative learning guidelines, only a single student from each group would be responsible for getting all materials, another for recording all information, another for reading all materials, and another for starting the activity. This process would allow most mainstreamed students opportunities for successfully completing the activities.

Peer tutors and peer assistants may also be helpful for working with mainstreamed students during force and motion activities. Peers can help mainstreamed students set up materials, identify critical observations, and record observations. Even though some mainstreamed students may be unable to complete each step necessary in setting up the activities, due to physical disabilities, these students can still participate fully in the looking, observing, describing, and recording information stages of the activity.

Prioritize learning objectives during force and motion activities. It is important to determine what learning objectives are most important. Teachers need to clarify whether the **use of simple machines** and/or **observing simple machines** are major objectives. For example, is learning how to set up a simple lever the major objective? Or, is learning about levers the major objective? Once teachers determine the major objectives of the activities involving force and motion, they can determine whether that objective is an appropriate objective for mainstreamed special education students. Teachers can use adaptive equipment and alternative procedures for assisting mainstreamed students in mastering those objectives.

How Can Force and Motion Activities Be Adapted?

The materials, including levers, fulcrums, pulleys, and whirly birds can be **stabilized securely** for all mainstreamed students, but especially for those students with physical disabilities. Special **clamps** can be used to secure the materials to tables, or to tables attached to wheelchairs. General educators should request that adaptive materials such as these be acquired for use during mainstreamed science instruction.

Larger, sturdier examples of some items are available and can be substituted for less sturdy ones. For example, a **large clothesline pulley system from a hardware store** can be used as a substitute for the smaller pulley systems to aid in handling materials and to aid in observing the activities for mainstreamed students.

Toys such as toy carts, cars, wagons, balls, and planes can be used to demonstrate concepts of force, inertia, motion, and gravity.

Special **adaptive devices** can be purchased. For example, the American Printing House for the Blind has a **braille spring scales system** that can be used with visually impaired students.

Additional **adaptive devices** may be available to aid in **grasping** some of the materials employed during force and motion activities.

Light sensors can be used to assist students with visual impairments detect movement of pendulums during force and motion activities. Student can count the beaps and thus observe the number of swings for various objects.

Students can be allowed to **place their hands over the person executing the experiment** during many force and motion activities. This will help reinforce what actions have been completed.

Strings can be attached to objects when activities require bouncing, rolling, launching, and tossing to help students detect the motion of the objects.

Real world examples of levers can be used with students to reinforce the concrete aspects of newly presented concepts. For example, use objects around the room as examples (e.g., brooms, pliers, bottle openers) and discuss and discover the types of levers that are represented by such objects.

Slatted trays can be used to hold various pieces of equipment while using force and motion activities. Each compartment of the tray can hold a separate item needed during the activity.

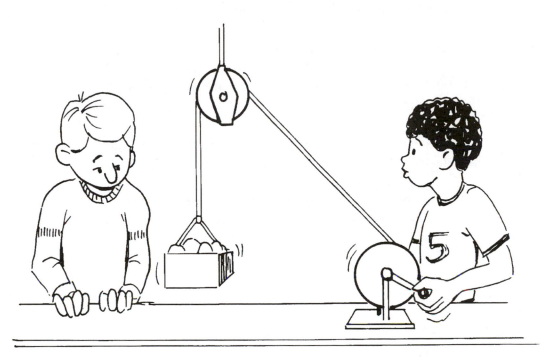

Computer programs, such as the Miner's Cave can be used to supplement the instruction of difficult to learn concepts. In this program students are provided opportunities to manipulate fulcrums, loads, and levers, as well as adjust the size and length of pulley systems.

Lego type materials are available to help teach more concrete examples of small machines. These types of activities can help make the concepts more concrete and meaningful for students. Several companies are making oversized building materials that may be easier to manipulate for some students.

Closed circuit television systems can be hooked up to observe the experiments using force and motion to enlarge the view. These systems can help visually impaired students participate more fully in force and motion activities.

Once enlarged images can be projected from experiments and the **images can be traced onto raised-line paper.** The raised-line representation can be used by visually impaired students as a tactile substitute.

Three-dimensional models can be made of the specimen for visually impaired students. Different **textured materials** can be used to represent different parts of the objects. For example, sand, string, paper clips, etc. can be glued onto a representational drawing of the types of levers.

Braille descriptions of the force and motion activities can be completed and provided for visually impaired students. These students can complete **braille laboratory booklets** that contain descriptions of all of the activities.

Descriptive video components of class activities during force and motion activities can be completed. These can be completed using either a video camera or a tape recorder, and can provide detailed descriptions of all events, especially of the specimen.

Place magnets in objects being used on inclined planes so students can more easily feel the friction during movement.

Use **glue** and make dots for each quarter turn of rotating parts of pulleys. Then students can feel and count the dots during activities using motion. Hot glue is quick and easy.

Physics
of Sound

What Are Physics of Sound Activities?

In physics of sound activities, students can observe and compare the sounds of different objects, observe the volume of different sounds, observe the pitch of sounds using tuning forks, investigate sounds traveling through strings, manipulate changes in pitch with rubber bands and strings of differing tension and thickness, and make whistles of different pitch. Students may also experiment with vacuum chambers.

What Are Adaptations of Sound Activities?

For most students with disabilities, sound activities present few difficulties and can be a particularly important unit. For students with hearing impairments, sound activities present particular problems. In some cases, sufficient sound can be generated to the student if **amplifying devices** are employed and activities are **sufficiently loud**. For students with very low hearing, further adaptations are required.

Use **musical instruments** to demonstrate pitch and volume. Involve students in the band. Allow students to feel the vibrations from the musical instruments.

Adjustments may need to be made to hearing aids and phonic ear devices during sound activities.

Students may be able to observe and feel vibrations in, e.g., **rubberbands** and **gongs**.

Consider attaching a tiny **watchspring** or other small spring to the tuning fork to show different vibrations.

Place the tuning fork in **water** to show the effect of the vibrations on the water. However, when you do this, watch closely, for the sound will dissipate rapidly due to the higher density of water. Also, place the tuning fork in the water carefully, because some water motion may result from the immersion of the tuning fork, and not the vibration.

Hearing impaired children may be able to **feel** the vibrations of a bell system in a vacuum chamber. Alternately, show vibration along physical objects (e.g., metal rods) when connected and disconnected, and explain analogy to air.

Students with visual impairments should have relatively fewer difficulties in sound activities. However, when varying tension or size of sound stimulus, make sure the student is actively participating, or is otherwise **informed** of the manipulations being performed. For example, in some activities, "waterphone bottles" containing different amounts of water are made to produce sound. Use **tactile markers** to indicate the level of water for each bottle. Place the markers on the same side of each bottle.

Use an **oscilloscope**, if available, to make variations in sound waves visible.

Some activities require that students **infer** the nature of objects placed in boxes, based on the sound each makes. This may not be an appropriate activity for students with severe hearing impairments.

Use a **piano** to demonstrate vibrations. Allow students to view the inside of the piano and to observe the vibrations of the various lengths of the wires. Students could feel the vibrations by touching the sides of the piano.

Solids/
Liquids/Gases

What Are Activities With Solids, Liquids, or Gases?

Students engaging in these activities may observe water in solid, liquid, and gaseous states, and/or examine the freezing/melting points of known and unknown liquids. Students may collect gases using solutions of baking soda, bromothymol blue, and vinegar in a bottle with a balloon over the opening.

What Are Adaptations of Activities With Solids, Liquids, or Gases?

Most students with disabilities can participate in these activities.

Water in different states can be observed by visually impaired students by **feeling**. After water has evaporated inside containers, students with visual impairments should be able to feel the condensation as one indication of evaporation. Similarly, **ice cubes** can be touched and melted to demonstrate various stages of matter.

Provide **supervision** when students use hot water to facilitate melting.

Braille or raised line thermometers are available to facilitate temperature measurement by visually impaired students.

Students with visual impairments can observe color changes in gas-producing solutions with the **light sensor**. Students with visual impairments can observe the expansion of carbon dioxide by **feeling** the balloon growing larger. Additionally, they can observe the chemical reactions by placing a **stethoscope** on the bottle.

Provide **physical assistance or guidance** to students with physical disabilities when needed.

Light and Color

What Are Activities With Light and Color?

To learn about light and color, students experiment with prisms, mix food colorings, separate pigments with paper chromatomography, investigate color and black and white printed pictures with magnifying lenses, use color filters, mix different colored light beams, investigate afterimages, illusions, and construct and use color wheels.

What Adaptations Can Be Made With Light and Color Activities?

These activities should be very helpful for most students with disabilities. They should provide excellent learning opportunities for students with hearing impairments, if **concepts** learned and relevant **language** is closely tied to the activities.

Students with visual impairments, especially those with some residual vision, can benefit from adaptations of some of these activities. However, for very low vision or blind students, it may be important to **prioritize** the activities the students are expected to undertake. Since light and color are necessarily less meaningful to such students, would they learn more from a different set of activities? Although learning can certainly occur, you may wish to consider whether **more** learning will occur with different science topics.

For students with some limited vision, **intensify** the light stimulus, using large, intense colors, magnifying lenses, closed circuit television, and high illumination.

Certain color changes are detectable using the **light sensor**. Determine before the activity what changes can and cannot be detected with the light sensor, and use this information in planning the activity. Students with visual impairments can also detect whether light bulbs are transmitting light by placing a hand near the bulb and feeling warmth. (Remember, some bulbs are hot).

If you are turning classroom lights off to demonstrate lighting, be aware of specific **fears** your students may have. Let them know ahead of time what will happen, and turn the light off only briefly, if some students are fearful of the dark.

In some activities, the **light sensor** is used as an activity for the whole class. Students with hearing impairments may be able to use the light sensor to detect differences in light intensity, if they place their fingers near the speaker of the light sensor.

Heat lamps can be used to demonstrate some activities involving light and intensity of light for visually impaired students.

A **spray bottle filled with water** can be used to demonstrate light rays.

Mirrors can be used to demonstrate reflection of light.

Ribbons of different thicknesses and textures can be used to represent different colors for students with visual disabilities.

Relevant References

Abruscato, J., Fossaceca, J.W., Hassard, J., & Peck, D. (1986). Holt science, Teacher's edition 2. New York: Holt, Rinehart & Winston.

Abruscato, J., Fossaceca, J.W., Hassard, J., & Peck, D. (1986). Holt science, Teacher's edition 4. New York: Holt, Rinehart & Winston.

Alexander, P., Fiegel, M., Foehr, S.K., Harris, A.F., Krajkovich, J.G., May, K.W., Tzimopoulos, N., & Voltmer, R.K. (1987). Silver Burdett & Ginn Earth science, Teacher's edition. Morristown, N.J.: Silver Burdett & Ginn.

Alexander, P., Fiegel, M., Foehr, S.K., Harris, A.F., Krajkovich, J.G., May, K.W., Tzimopoulos, N., & Voltmer, R.K. (1987). Silver Burdett & Ginn life science, Teacher's edition. Morristown, N.J.: Silver Burdett & Ginn.

Allen, E.E. (1931). Opening windows on nature for blind boys and girls. School Life, 17(2), 21-23.

Allen, V.L. (1976). Children as teachers: Theory and research on tutoring. New York: Academic Press.

American Association for the Advancement of Science. (1991). Barrier free in brief: Access in word and deed. Washington, D.C.: Author.

American Association for the Advancement of Science. (1991). Barrier free in brief: Access to science literacy. Washington, D.C.: Author.

American Association for the Advancement of Science. (1991). Barrier free in brief: Laboratories and classrooms in science and engineering. Washington, D.C.: Author.

American Association for the Advancement of Science. (1991). Barrier free in brief: Workshops and conferences for scientists and engineers. Washington, D.C.: Author.

American Foundation for the Blind. (1968). An introduction to development of curriculum for educable mentally retarded visually handicapped adolescents. Washington, DC: U.S. Department of Health, Education & Welfare.

Anderson, M.A. (1985). Cooperative group tasks and their relationship to peer acceptance and cooperation. Journal of Special Education, 18(2), 83-86.

Andrews, F.M. (1934). The biology laboratory period. The Teachers Forum, 6(5), 82-83.

Armstrong, B., Johnson, D.W., & Balow, B. (1981). Effects of cooperative vs. individualistic learning experiences on interpersonal attraction between learning disabled and normal-progress elementary school students. Contemporary Educational Psychology, 6, 102-109.

Barber, M., & Kissamis, K.S. (1990). Scott, Foresman Earth science, Teacher's annotated edition. Glenview, IL: Scott, Foresman.

Barman, C., Dispezio, M., Guthrie, V., Leyden, M.B., Mercier, S., Ostlund, K., & Armbruster, B. (1992). Addison-Wesley science, Teacher's edition 1 (2nd ed.). Menlo Park, CA: Addison-Wesley.

Barman, C., Dispezio, M., Guthrie, V., Leyden, M.B., Mercier, S., Ostlund, K., & Armbruster, B. (1992). Addison-Wesley science, Teacher's edition 2 (2nd ed.). Menlo Park, CA: Addison-Wesley.

Barman, C., Dispezio, M., Guthrie, V., Leyden, M.B., Mercier, S., Ostlund, K., & Armbruster, B. (1992). Addison-Wesley science, Teacher's edition 3 (2nd ed.). Menlo Park, CA: Addison-Wesley.

Barman, C., Dispezio, M., Guthrie, V., Leyden, M.B., Mercier, S., Ostlund, K., & Armbruster, B. (1992). Addison-Wesley science, Teacher's edition 4 (2nd ed.). Menlo Park, CA: Addison-Wesley.

Barman, C., Dispezio, M., Guthrie, V., Leyden, M.B., Mercier, S., Ostlund, K., & Armbruster, B. (1992). Addison-Wesley science, Teacher's edition 5 (2nd ed.). Menlo Park, CA: Addison-Wesley.

Barman, C., Dispezio, M., Guthrie, V., Leyden, M.B., Mercier, S., Ostlund, K., & Armbruster, B. (1992). Addison-Wesley science, Teacher's edition 6 (2nd ed.). Menlo Park, CA: Addison-Wesley.

Barr, B.B., & Leyden, M.B. (1989). Addison-Wesley life science, Teacher's edition. Menlo Park, CA: Addison-Wesley.

Baughman, J., & Zollman, D. (1977). Physics labs for the blind. The Physics Teacher, 15(6), 339-342.

Benedetti, D.M. (1984). The effectiveness of an instructional adaptation on the acquisition of science information by middle school learning disabled students. Unpublished doctoral dissertation, University of Washington, Seattle.

Bennett, L.M., & Downing, K. (1971). Science education for the mentally retarded. Science Education, 55(2), 155-162.

Berger, N., & Clark, J.R. (1978-79, Fall/Winter). Science education and the physically handicapped. Science Education News, p. 1-12.

Berhow, B.F. (1978). A Kindergarten science program for handicapped children: Adapting existing curricula. Paper presented at National Science Teachers Association, Arlington, VA.

Berres, M.S. & Knoblock, P., (1987). Program models for mainstreaming: Integrating students with moderate to severe disabilities. Rockville, MD: Aspen.

Bina, M.J. (1986). Social skills development through cooperative group learning strategies. Education of the Visually Handicapped, 18(1), 27-40.

Biological Sciences Curriculum Study (BSCS) (1989). Science for life and living: Integrating science, technology, and health, Grade 1 teacher's guide, Parts A-B. (Experimental Ed.). Dubuque, IA: Kendall/Hunt.

Biological Sciences Curriculum Study (BSCS) (1989). Science for life and living: Integrating science, technology, and health, Grade 2 teacher's guide, Parts C-D. (Experimental Ed.). Dubuque, IA: Kendall/Hunt.

Biological Sciences Curriculum Study (BSCS) (1989). Science for life and living: Integrating science, technology, and health, Grade 3 teacher's guide, Parts C-D. (Experimental Ed.). Dubuque, IA: Kendall/Hunt.

Biological Sciences Curriculum Study (BSCS) (1989). Science for life and living: Integrating science, technology, and health, Grade 4 teacher's guide, Parts C-D. (Experimental Ed.). Dubuque, IA: Kendall/Hunt.

Biological Sciences Curriculum Study (BSCS) (1989). Science for life and living: Integrating science, technology, and health, Grade 5 teacher's guide, Parts C-D. (Experimental Ed.). Dubuque, IA: Kendall/Hunt.

Biological Sciences Curriculum Study (BSCS) (1989). Science for life and living: Integrating science, technology, and health, Grade 6 teacher's guide, Parts C-D. (Experimental Ed.). Dubuque, IA: Kendall/Hunt.

Bleck, E. E., & Nagel, D. A. (Eds.). (1982). Physically handicapped children: A medical atlas for teachers (2nd ed.). New York: Grene & Stratton.

Bluhm, D.L. (1968). Teaching the retarded visually handicapped. Philadelphia: W.B. Saunders.

Boekel, N., & Steele, J.M. (1972). Science education for the exceptional child. Focus on Exceptional Children, 4(4), 1-15.

Boggess, J. (Speaker). (1985). The hearing impaired student in the normal hearing classroom. [Videotape]. West Lafayette, IN: Purdue University Continuing Education.

Booth, J.H., Krockover, G. H., & Woods, P. R., (1982). Creative museum methods and educational techniques. Springfield, IL: Charles C. Thomas.

Borron, R. (1978). Modifying science instruction to meet the needs of the hearing impaired. Journal of Research in Science Teaching, 15(4), 257-262.

Brigham, F.J., Bakken, J., Scruggs, T.E., & Mastropieri, M.A. (1992). Cooperative behavior management: Strategies for promoting a positive classroom environment. Education and Training of the Mentally Retarded, 27(1), 3-12.

Brigham, F.J., Scruggs, T.E., & Mastropieri, M.A. (1992). Teacher enthusiasm in learning disabilities classrooms: Effects on learning and behavior. Learning Disabilities Research and Practice 7(2), 68-73.

Brown, D.R. (1978). Science instruction of visually impaired youth: A research and review of relevant literature. American Foundation for the Blind Practice Report. New York: American Foundation for the Blind.

Bryan, A.H. (1951). Physics for the blind. Science Education, 35(5), 271-274.

Bryan, A.H. (1951). Sciences for the blind. Baltimore Bulletin of Education, 29(1), 14-15.

Bryan, C.A. (1956). Secondary school sciences for the blind. The Education of the Blind, 6(1), 11-18.

Bunner, W.R., & Bunner, R.T. (1968). What about your visually defective students? The American Biology Teacher, 30(2), 108-109.

Bybee, R.W. (1972). A review of literature on science for the deaf. Science Education, 56(2), 237-242.

Bybee, R.W. (1979). Helping the special student fit in. The Science Teacher, 45(7), 25-26.

Bybee, R.W., & Hendricks, P.A. (1972). Teaching science concepts to preschool deaf children to aid language development. Science Education, 56(3), 303-310.

California School for the Blind Staff. (1929). The teaching of nature study. The Teachers Forum, 2(1), 6-7.

Callahan, W.P. (1979). Science for the mentally retarded - Goals and assumptions. Biological Sciences Curriculum Study, 2(3), 3-5.

Cantrell, R.P., & Cantrell, M.L. (1976). Preventive mainstreaming: Impact of a supportive services program on pupils. Exceptional Children, 42(7), 381-386.

Carter, J.F. (1989). Prereferral intervention systems: An empirical link between regular and special education. Unpublished doctoral dissertation, University of Oregon, Eugene.

Carver, T.R. (1968). The design and use of a light probe for teaching science to blind students. Research Bulletin/ American Foundation for Blind, 16, 79-91.

Cawley, J.F., Miller, J.H., Sentman, J.R., & Bennett, S. (in preparation). Science for all children: An activity-based program. State University of New York at Buffalo: Amherst, NY.

Cohen, B., & Jones, H.L. (1969). Establishing a science curriculum for aggressive children. The Science Teacher, 36(8), 61-63.

Collea, F.P. (1976). Science in sounds. Science and Children, 13(6), 34.

Conway, R.N.F., & Gow, L. (1988). Mainstreaming special class students with mild handicaps through group instruction. Remedial and Special Education, 9(5), 34-41.

Cook, S., Scruggs, T.E., Mastropieri, M.A., & Casto, G.C. (1985-1986). Handicapped students as tutors. Journal of Special Education, 19, 483-492.

Cooke, N.L., Heron, T.E., & Heward, W.L. (1983). Peer tutoring. Implementing classwide programs in the primary grades. Columbus, OH: Special Press.

Coon, N. (1953). The place of the museum in the education of the blind. New York: American Foundation for the Blind.

Cooper, E.K., Blackwood, P.E., Boeschen, J.A., Giddings, M.G., & Carin, A.A. (1989). HBJ science, Teacher's edition, Level 3 (Green). (Nova Ed.). Orlando: Harcourt Brace Jovanovich.

Cooper, E.K., Blackwood, P.E., Boeschen, J.A., Giddings, M.G., & Carin, A.A. (1989). HBJ science, Teacher's edition, Level 6 (Brown). (Nova Ed.). Orlando: Harcourt Brace Jovanovich.

Cooper, J.O. (1974). Measurement and analysis of behavioral techniques. Columbus, OH: Charles E. Merrill.

Cooper, K.E., & Thier, H.D. (1974, April). Do you have to see it to believe it?: Laboratory science for visually impaired children. Learning, pp. 54-55.

Cooperative Learning Series (1990a). Learning to work together [Videotape]. Alexandria, VA: Association for Supervision and Curriculum Development.

Cooperative Learning Series (1990b). Planning and implementing cooperative lessons [Videotape]. Alexandria, VA: Association for Supervision and Curriculum Development.

Cooperative Learning Series (1990c). Teaching social skills [Videotape]. Alexandria, VA: Association for Supervision and Curriculum Development.

Cooperman, S. (1980). Biology for the visually impaired student. The American Biology Teacher, 42(5), 293-294, 304.

Corn, A.L., & Torres, I. (1990). When you have a handicapped child in your classroom: Suggestions for teachers (2nd ed.). New York: American Foundation for the Blind.

Corrick, M.E. (Ed.). (1981). Teaching handicapped students science. Washington, D.C.: National Education Association.

Cosden, M.A. (1989). Cooperative groups and microcomputer instruction: Combining technologies. The Pointer, 33(2), 21-26.

Cosden, M., Pearl, R., & Bryan, T.H. (1985). The effects of cooperative and individual goal structures on learning disabled and nondisabled students. Exceptional Children, 52(2), 103-114.

Cramer, T.V. (1967). Liquid level indicator for the blind. Popular Electronics, 26(5), 59-60.

Crockett, M.C. (1958). The field trip. The Education of the Blind, 7(4), 136-137.

Danglade, R., & Ball, D.W. (1978). Science for someone special. Science and Children, 16(3), 23-24.

Davis, S.J. (1990). Applying content study skills in co-listed reading classrooms. Journal of Reading, 33(4), 277-281.

Dawson, J.R. (1958). Biology for the blind. The American Biology Teacher, 20(2), 42-44.

deHaaff, S.J. (1977). A creative science project for blind children. Visual Impairment and Blindness, 71(10), 458-459.

DeLucchi, L., Malone, L., & Thier, H.D. (1980). Science activities for the visually impaired: Developing a model. Exceptional Children, 46(4), 287-288.

DeWalt, P. (1968). Adaptations of the scientific method for the deaf child. The Volta Review, 70(6), 394-398.

Diebold, T.J., & Waldron, M.B. (1988). The effects of verbal and pictorial instructional formats on the comprehension of science concepts by hearing impaired subjects. American Annals of the Deaf, 133(1) 30-35.

Donahue, M. (Speaker). (1986). Communicative styles of learning disabled children: Some implications for classroom discourse. [Videotape]. West Lafayette, IN: Purdue University Continuing Education.

Educational aids for visually handicapped. (1969). Louisville: American Printing House for the Blind.

Egelston, J.C. (1975). Editorial comment on adapting science materials for the blind (ASMB): Student outcomes. Science Teacher Education, 59(2), 235-236.

Egelston, J.C., & Mercaldo, D. (1975). Science education for the Handicapped: Implementation for the hearing-impaired. Science Education, 59(2), 257-261.

Ehly, S.W., & Larsen, S.C. (1980). Peer tutoring for individualized instruction. Boston: Allyn & Bacon.

Eichenberger, R.J. (1974). Special students: Teaching science to the blind student. Science Teacher, 41(9), 53-54.

Ellis, S.S. (1989/1990). Introducing cooperative learning. Educational Leadership, 47(4), 34-37.

Fariel, R.E., Hinds, R.W., & Berey, D.B. (1989). Addison-Wesley Earth science, Teacher's edition. Menlo Park, CA: Addison-Wesley.

Fenner, S.W. (1979). A comparison of programs and techniques for teaching science to handicapped elementary students. Unpublished doctoral dissertation, University of Missouri, Kansas City.

Ferraro, E., Lee, M.T., & Anderson, O.R. (1977). The effects of structure in science communications on knowledge acquisition and conceptual organization by students of varying mental maturity. Journal of Research in Science Teaching, 14(5), 441-447.

Flexer, C. (Speaker). (1989). The relationship of hearing and hearing loss to academic performance. [Videotape]. West Lafayette, IN: Purdue University Continuing Education.

Francoeur, P., & Eilam, B. (1975). Teaching the mammalian heart to the visually handicapped. The Science Teacher, 42(10), 8-11.

Franks, F.L. (1970). Measurement in science for blind students. Teaching Exceptional Children, 3(1), 2-11.

Franks, F.L., & Baird, R.M. (1971). Geographical concepts and the visually handicapped. Exceptional Children, 38(4), 321-324.

Franks, F.L, & Butterfield, L.H. (1977). Educational materials development in primary science: Simple machines. Education of the Visually Handicapped, 9(2), 51-55.

Franks, F.L. & Huff, R. (1976a). Educational materials development in primary science: The pull-apart cell. Education of the Visually Handicapped, 8, 16-20.

Franks, F.L., & Huff, R. (1976b). Educational materials development in primary science: Insect identification kit. Education of the Visually Handicapped, 8, 57-62.

Franks, F.L., & Huff, R. (1976-77). Educational materials development in primary science: Dial thermometer instructional unit. Education of the Visually Handicapped, 8(2), 120-128.

Franks, F.L., & Huff, R. (1977). Educational materials development in primary science: Linear measurement unit for young blind students. Education of the Visually Handicapped, 9(2), 23-28.

Franks, F.L., & Murr, M.J. (1978). Biological models for blind students. Visual Impairment and Blindness, 72(4), 121-124.

Franks, F.L., Sanford, L.R. (1976). Using the light sensor to introduce laboratory science. Science and Children, 13(6) 48-49.

Fuchs, D. (1987). Prereferral intervention for difficult-to-teach students: Mainstream assistance teams--Years 1 and 2. (Contract No. G008530158). Washington D.C.: Office of Special Education (ED).

Fuchs, D., Fuchs, L., & Bahr, M.W. (1990). Mainstream assistance teams: A scientific basis for the art of consultation. Exceptional Children, 57(2), 128-139.

Fuchs, D., Fuchs, L., Bahr, M.W., & Fernstrom, P. (1988, February). Accommodating difficult-to-teach pupils in regular education through prereferral intervention. Pennsylvania Resources and Information Center for Special Education Reporter, pp. 7-12.

Fuchs, D., Fuchs, L., Bahr, M.W., Fernstrom, P., & Stecker, P.M. (1990). Prereferral intervention: A prescriptive approach. Exceptional Children, 56(6), 493-513.

Fuchs, D., Fuchs, L., Bahr, M., Reeder, P., Gilman, S., Fernstrom, P., & Roberts, H. (1990). Prereferral intervention to increase attention and work productivity among difficult-to-teach pupils. Focus on Exceptional Children, 22(6), 1-8.

Fuchs, D., Fuchs, L., Gilman, S., Reeder, P., Bahr, M., Fernstrom, P., & Roberts, H. (1990). Prereferral intervention through teacher consultation: Mainstream assistance teams. Academic Therapy, 25(3), 263-276.

Fulk, B.J.M., Mastropieri, M.A., & Scruggs, T.E. (1992). Mnemonic generalization training with learning disabled adolescents. Learning Disabilities Research and Practice, 7, 2-10.

Fulker, W.H., & Fulker, M. (1968). Techniques with tangibles - A manual for teaching the blind. Springfield, IL: Charles C. Thomas.

Garcia, S.B., & Ortiz, A.A. (1988, June). Preventing inappropriate referrals of language minority students to special education. National Clearinghouse for Bilingual Education: New Focus, pp. 1-12.

Garner, J.B., & Campbell, P.H. (1987). Technology for persons with severe disabilities: Practical and ethical considerations. The Journal of Special Education, 21(3), 122-132.

Gearheart, B.R., Weishahn, M.W., & Gearheart, C.J. (1992). The exceptional student in the regular classroom. (5th ed.). New York: Merrill.

Gilmore, G., Orndorff, J., & Wilder, M.S. (1990). Scott, Foresman life science, Teacher's annotated edition. Glenview, IL: Scott, Foresman & Company.

Girl Scouts of America, (1990). Focus on ability: Serving girls with special needs. New York: Girl Scouts of the United States of America.

Graden, J.L. (1989). Redefining "prereferral" intervention as intervention assistance: Collaboration between general and special education. Exceptional Children, 56(3), 227-231.

Grant, W.D. (1975). Me Now and Me and My Environment: Science for the Exceptional Student. Science Education, 59(2), 249-254.

Grinder, A.L., & McCoy, E.S. (1985). The good guide: A sourcebook for interpreters, docents and tour guides. Scottsdale, AZ: Ironwood.

Groff, G. with Gardner, L. (1989). What museum guides need to know: Access for blind and visually impaired visitor. New York: American Foundation for the Blind.

Guy, R.G., Miller, R.J., Roscoe, M.J., Snell, A., & Thomas, S.L. (1991). Scott, Foresman discover science, Teacher's annotated editions 1-6. Glenview, IL: Scott, Foresman.

Hadary, D.E. (1975). Picking up good vibrations from science for the handicapped. The Science Teacher, 42(10), 12-13.

Hadary, D.E. (1977). Science and art for visually handicapped children. Visual Impairment and Blindness, 71(5), 203-209.

Hadary, D.E. (1978). Laboratory science and art for blind and deaf children: A mainstream approach. Working Conference on Science Education for Handicapped Students, National Science Teachers Association, Arlington, VA.

Hadary, D.E., & Cohen, S.H. (1978). Laboratory science and art for blind, deaf, and emotionally disturbed children: A mainstreaming approach. Baltimore: University Park Press.

Hadary, D.E., Cohen, S.H., Haushalter, R., Hadary, T.D., & Levine, R. (1976). Interaction and creation through laboratory science and art for special children. Science and Children, 13(6), 31-33.

Hadary, D., Haushatter, R., & Rosenberg, R. (1976). Breaking sound barriers for the deaf child. Science and Children, 14(3), 33.

Hallahan, D.P. & Kauffman, J. M. (1991). Exceptional children: Introduction to special education. Englewood Cliffs, NJ: Prentice-Hall.

Hamilton, D.W. (1932). The laboratory in schools for the blind. American Association of Instructors of the Blind, 31, 775-777.

Hance, R.T. (1935). Laboratory work for the blind. The Science Counselor, 1(4), 4-5, 34.

Hebbeln, H.J. (1932). Some uses of hearing in the study of physics. The Teachers Forum, 4(5), 91.

Hebbeln, H.J. (1941). Adaptation in teaching physics to the blind. The Teachers Forum, 13(2), 54-58

Heimler, C.H., & Neal, C.D. (1986). Principles of science, Book one, Teacher's annotated edition. Columbus, OH: Charles E. Merrill.

Heimler, C.H., & Neal, C.D. (1986). Principles of science, Book two, Teacher's annotated edition. Columbus, OH: Charles E. Merrill.

Heisler, W.T. (1944). Tree study. Outlook for the Blind, 38(6), 160-162.

Henderson, D.R. (1964). Laboratory methods in physics for the blind. Unpublished master's thesis. University of Pittsburgh, Pittsburgh, PA.

Hill, O.J. (1940). How scaled models are used to teach the blind. American Association of Instructors of the Blind, 35, 145-147.

Hofman, H.H. (1978). A working conference on science education for handicapped students: Proceedings (April 3-5). National Science Teachers Association. Washington, D.C.

Hofman, H.H., & Ricker, K.S. (1979). Sourcebook: Science Education and the Physically Handicapped. Washington, DC: National Science Teachers Association.

Holloway, B.L. (1989). Improving elementary LD students' recall of social studies and science vocabulary using mnemonic instruction. Ed.D. Practicum Report, Nova University. (ERIC Document Reproduction Service No. ED 315 962)

Hoover, W.C. (1937). The teaching of physics instruction for the blind. The Teachers Forum, 9(4), 73-78.

Humphrey, J.H. (1972). The use of motor activity learning in the development of science concepts with slow learning fifth grade children. Journal of Research in Science Teaching, 9(3), 261-266.

Hurst, A.D. (1933). Ways and means of teaching general science to blind students. The Teachers Forum, 6(2), 34-37.

Jernigan, K. (Ed.). (1992). What you should know about blindness, services for the blind, and the organized blind movement. Baltimore: National Federation of the Blind.

Johnson, D.W. & Johnson, R.T. (1982). The effects of cooperative and individualistic instruction on handicapped and nonhandicapped students. Journal of Social Psychology, 118, 257-268.

Johnson, D.W. & Johnson, R.T. (1983). The socialization and achievement crises: Are cooperative learning experiences the solution? Applied Social Psychology Annual, 4, 119-164.

Johnson, D.W., & Johnson, R.T. (1984). Building acceptance of differences between handicapped and nonhandicapped students: The effects of cooperative and individualistic instruction. Journal of Social Psychology, 122(2), 257-267.

Johnson, D.W. & Johnson, R. T. (1985). Mainstreaming hearing-impaired students: The effect of effort in communicating on cooperation and interpersonal attraction. Journal of Psychology, 119(1), 31-44.

Johnson, D.W., & Johnson, R.T. (1989). Cooperative learning: What special education teachers need to know. The Pointer, 33(2), 5-10.

Johnson, D.W., & Johnson, R.T. (1989/1990). Social skills for successful group work. Educational Leadership, 47(4), 29-33

Johnson, D.W., & Johnson, R.T. (1991). Learning together and alone: Cooperative, competitive, and individualistic learning, Third edition. Englewood Cliffs, NJ: Prentice Hall.

Johnson, R.T., Johnson, D.W., DeWeerdt, N., Lyons, V., & Zaidman, B. (1983). Integrating severely adaptively handicapped seventh-grade students into constructive relationships with nonhandicapped peers in science class. American Journal of Mental Deficiency, 87(6), 611-618.

Johnson, D.W., Johnson, R.T., & Holubec, E.J. (1990). Circles of learning: Cooperation in the classroom, Third edition. Edina, MN: Interaction Book Company.

Johnson, D.W., Johnson, R.T., & Holubec, E.J. (1991). Cooperation in the classroom, Revised. Edina, MN: Interaction Book Company.

Johnson, D.W., Johnson, R.T., & Maruyama, G. (1983). Interdependence and interpersonal attraction among heterogeneous and homogeneous individuals: A theoretical formulation and a meta-analysis of the research. Review of Educational Research, 53(1), 5-54.

Johnson, R. T., Johnson, D.W., Scott, L. E., & Ramolae, R. A. (1985). Effects of single-sex and mixed-sex cooperative interaction on science achievement and attitudes and cross-handicap and cross-sex relationships. Journal of Research in Science Teaching, 22(3), 207-22.

Johnson, R.T., Johnson, D.W., & Stanne, M.B. (1986). Comparison of computer-assisted cooperative, competitive, and individualistic learning. American Educational Research Journal, 23(3), 382-392.

Johnson, D.W., Johnson, R.T., Tiffany, M., & Zaidman, B. (1983). Are low achievers disliked in a cooperative situation? A test of rival theories in a mixed ethnic situation. Contemporary Educational Psychology, 8(2), 189-200.

Jones, A., & Barnett, A. (1980). Science for the physically handicapped. Special Education: Forward Trends, 7(3), 25-28.

Karp, R.S. (1991). Library services for disabled individuals. Boston: G.K. Hall & Co.

Kaschner, S.K. (1978). Viewing the earth with closed eyes. Science Activities, 15(3), 12-13.

Kaufman, A.S. (1971). Tutoring a visually handicapped student in high school chemistry. The New Outlook for the Blind, 65(10), 313-317.

Kenny, A.P. (1980). Access to the past. Nashville, TN: American Association for State and Local History.

Kerr, M.M. & Nelson, C.M. (1989). Strategies for managing behavior problems in the classroom. (2nd ed.). Columbus, OH: Merrill.

King-Sears, M.E. (1989). Mnemonic and nonmnemonic science vocabulary instruction with mildly handicapped students. Unpublished doctoral dissertation, University of Florida, Gainesville, FL.

Lamendola, A. (1976). Science and the emotionally disadvantaged child: A case study. Science and Children, 13(6), 17-20.

Lang, B., Smith, B., & Wolf, J. (undated). Cooperative learning level I: Handbook. Mesa, AZ: Mesa Public Schools.

Lang, H.G. (1973). Teaching physics to the deaf. The Physics Teacher, 11(9), 527-531.

Lang, H.G. (1978). Mainstreaming: A new challenge in science education for the deaf. Midwest Education Review, 10(3), 13-27.

Lang, H.G. (1978). Some educationally significant traits of hearing-impaired physics students and implications for teachers in the mainstream. Paper presented at Working Conference on Science Education for Handicapped Students, Arlington, VA.

Laufenberg, R., & Scruggs, T.E. (1986). Effects of a transformational mnemonic strategy to facilitate digit span recall by mildly handicapped students. Psychological Reports, 58, 811-820.

Lazarowitz, R. (1991). Learning biology cooperatively: An Israeli junior high school study. Cooperative Learning, 11(3), 19-21.

Leitman, A. (1968). Science for deaf children. Washington, D.C.: Alexander Graham Bell Association for the Deaf.

Levin, J.R., Dretzke, B.J., McCormick, C.B., Scruggs, T.E., McGivern, J.E., & Mastropieri, M.A. (1983). Learning via mnemonic pictures: Analysis of the presidential process. Educational Communication and Technology Journal, 31, 161-173.

Levin, J.R., Morrison, C.R., McGivern, J.E., Mastropieri, M.A., & Scruggs, T.E. (1986). Mnemonic facilitation of text-embedded science facts. American Educational Research Journal, 23, 489-506.

Lew, M., Mesch, D., Johnson, D.W., & Johnson, R. (1986). Positive interdependence, academic and collaborative-skills group contingencies, and isolated students. American Educational Research Journal, 23(3), 476-488.

Lewis, R. B. & Doorlag, D. H. (1991). Teaching special students in the mainstream. (3rd ed.) New York: MacMillan.

Leyden, M.B., Johnson, G.P., & Barr, B.B. (1988). Addison-Wesley introduction to physical science, Teacher's edition. Menlo Park, CA: Addison-Wesley.

Liem, T.L. (1990). Invitations to science inquiry. Chino Hills, CA: Science Inquiry Enterprises.

Lifson, S., Scruggs, T.E., & Bennion, K. (1984). Passage independence in reading achievement tests: A follow-up. Perceptual and Motor Skills, 58, 945-946.

Linn, M.C. & Thier, H.D. (1975). Adapting science material for the blind (ASMB): Expectation for student outcomes. Science Education, 59(2), 237-246.

Lippitt, P. (1975). Students teach students. Bloomington, IN: The Phi Delta Kappa Educational Foundation.

Lloyd, J.W., Crowley, E.P., Kohler, F.W., & Strain, P.S. (1988). Redefining the applied research agenda: Cooperative learning, prereferral, teacher consultation, and peer-mediated interventions. Journal of Learning Disabilities, 21(1), 43-52.

Lombardi, T.P., & Balch, P.E. (1976). Science experiences and the mentally retarded. Science and Children, 13(6), 20.

Lovitt, T., Rudsit, J., Jenkins, J., Pious, C., & Benedetti, D. (1985). Two methods of adapting science materials for learning disabled and regular seventh graders. Learning Disability Quarterly, 8, 275-285.

Lovitt, T., Rudsit, J., Jenkins, J., Pious, C., & Benedetti, D. (1986). Adapting science materials for regular and learning disabled seventh graders. Remedial and Special Education, 7(1), 31-39.

Lucker, G.W., Rosenfield, D., Sikes, J., & Aronson, E. (1976). Performance in the interdependent classroom: A field study. American Educational Research Journal, 13(2), 115-123.

Madden, N.A., & Slavin, R.E. (1983). Effects of cooperative learning on the social acceptance of mainstreamed academically handicapped students. Journal of Special Education, 17(2), 171-182.

Maheady, L., Mallette, B., Harper, G.F., & Sacca, K. (1991). Heads together: A peer-mediated option for improving the academic achievement of heterogeneous learning groups. Remedial and Special Education, 12(2), 5-33.

Maheady, L., Sacca, M.K., & Harper, G.F. (1987). Classwide student tutoring teams: The effects of peer-mediated instruction on the academic performance of secondary mainstreamed students. The Journal of Special Education, 21(3), 107-121.

Majewski, J. (1987). Part of your general public is disabled: A handbook for guides in museums, zoos, and historic houses. Washington, D.C.: Smithsonian Institution.

Majewski, J. (1987). Disabled museum visitors: Part of your general public [videotape]. Washington D.C.: Smithsonian Institution, Office of Museum Programs.

Maley, P.V. (1950). Suggestions for using the senses in teaching science. American Association of Instructors of the Blind, 40, 125-127.

Mallinson, G.G. (1967). Programmed learning materials for the blind. Final Report. Kalamazoo: Western Michigan University.

Mallinson, G.G., Mallinson, J.B., Smallwood, W.L., & Valentino, C. (1987). Silver Burdett science, Teacher's edition 1. Morristown, N.J.: Silver Burdett & Ginn.

Mallinson, G.G., Mallinson, J.B., Smallwood, W.L., & Valentino, C. (1987). Silver Burdett science, Teacher's edition 3. Morristown, N.J.: Silver Burdett & Ginn.

Maloff, C., & Wood, S.M. (1988). Business and social etiquette with disabled people. Springfield, IL: Charles C. Thomas.

Malone, L., & DeLucchi, L. (1979). Life science for visually impaired students. Science and Children, 16(5), 29-31.

Marcuccio, P.R. (Ed.). (1976). Science for the handicapped, [Special issue]. Science and Children 13(6).

Martin, G., & Pear, J. (1988). Behavior modification: What it is and how to do it. (3rd ed.). Englewood Cliffs, NJ: Prentice Hall.

Mastropieri, M.A., Emerick, K., & Scruggs, T.E. (1988). Mnemonic instruction of science concepts. Behavioral Disorders, 14(1), 48-56.

Mastropieri, M.A., Jenkins, V., & Scruggs, T.E. (1985). Academic and intellectual characteristics of behaviorally disordered children and youth. Severe Behavior Disorders Monograph, 8, 86-104.

Mastropieri, M.A., Jenne, T., & Scruggs, T.E. (1988). A level system for managing problem behaviors in a high school resource program. Behavioral Disorders, 13, 202-208.

Mastropieri, M.A., & Scruggs, T.E. (1983). Maps as schema for gifted learners. Roeper Review, 6, 107-111.

Mastropieri, M.A., & Scruggs, T.E. (1984). Generalization: Five effective strategies. Academic Therapy, 19, 427-432.

Mastropieri, M.A., & Scruggs, T.E. (1987). Effective instruction for special education. Austin: Pro-Ed.

Mastropieri, M.A., & Scruggs, T.E. (1988). Increasing the content area learning of learning disabled students: Research implementation. Learning Disabilities Research, 4, 17-25.

Mastropieri, M.A., & Scruggs, T.E. (1989). Constructing more meaningful relationships: Mnemonic instruction for special populations. Educational Psychology Review, 1, 83-111.

Mastropieri, M.A., & Scruggs, T.E. (1989). Mnemonic social studies instruction: Classroom applications. Remedial and Special Education, 10, 40-46.

Mastropieri, M.A., & Scruggs, T.E. (1989). Reconstructive elaborations: Strategies for adapting content area information. Academic Therapy, 24, 391-406.

Mastropieri, M.A., & Scruggs, T.E. (1989). Reconstructive elaborations: Strategies that facilitate content learning. Learning Disabilities Focus, 4, 73-77.

Mastropieri, M.A., & Scruggs, T.E. (1990). Memory and learning disabilities. Learning Disability Quarterly, 13, 234-235.

Mastropieri, M.A., & Scruggs, T.E. (1991). Teaching students ways to remember: Strategies for learning mnemonically. Cambridge, MA: Brookline Books.

Mastropieri, M.A., & Scruggs, T.E. (in press). Science for students with disabilities. Review of Educational Research.

Mastropieri, M.A., Scruggs, T.E., Bakken, J., & Brigham, F. J. (1992). A complex mnemonic strategy for teaching states and capitals: Comparing forward and backward associations. Learning Disabilities Research and Practice, 7, 96-103.

Mastropieri, M.A., Scruggs, T.E., & Fulk, B.J.M. (1990). Teaching abstract vocabulary with the keyword method: Effects on recall and comprehension. Journal of Learning Disabilities, 23, 92-107.

Mastropieri, M.A., Scruggs, T.E., & Levin, J.R. (1983). Pictorial mnemonic strategies for special education. Journal of Special Education Technology, 6(3), 24-33.

Mastropieri, M.A., Scruggs, T.E. & Levin, J.R. (1985). Maximizing what exceptional students can learn: A review of research on the keyword method and related mnemonic techniques. Remedial and Special Education, 6(2), 39-45.

Mastropieri, M.A., Scruggs, T.E., & Levin, J.R. (1985). Mnemonic strategy instruction with learning disabled adolescents. Journal of Learning Disabilities, 18(2), 94-100.

Mastropieri, M.A., Scruggs, T.E., & Levin, J.R. (1986). Direct vs. mnemonic instruction: Relative benefits for exceptional learners. Journal of Special Education, 20, 299-308.

Mastropieri, M.A., Scruggs, T.E., & Levin, J.R. (1987). Learning-disabled students' memory for expository prose: Mnemonic versus nonmnemonic pictures. American Educational Research Journal, 24(4), 505-519.

Mastropieri, M.A., Scruggs, T.E., & Levin, J.R. (1987). Mnemonic strategies in special education. In M. McDaniel & M. Pressley (Eds.), Imagery and related mnemonic processes (pp. 358-376). New York: Springer-Verlag.

Mastropieri, M.A., Scruggs, T.E., Levin, J.R., Gaffney, J., & McLoone, B. (1985) Mnemonic vocabulary instruction for learning disabled students. Learning Disability Quarterly, 8, 57-63.

Mastropieri, M.A., Scruggs, T.E., McLoone, B., & Levin, J.R. (1985). Facilitating learning disabled students' acquisition of science classifications. Learning Disability Quarterly, 8, 299-309.

Mastropieri, M.A., Scruggs, T.E., Whittaker, M., & Bakken, J.P., (in press). Mnemonic science applications with mentally handicapped students. Remedial and Special Education.

McCarney, S.B., & Cummins, K.K. (1988). The pre-referral intervention manual: The most common learning and behavior problems encountered in the educational environment. Columbia, MO: Hawthorne Educational Services.

McElroy, K.B. (1989). A taste of cooperativeness within an elementary school. The Pointer, 33(2), 34-38.

McIntyre, M. (1976). Science is for all children. Science and Children, 13(6), 50-51.

McLoone, B.B., Scruggs, T.E., Mastropieri, M.A., & Zucker, S. F. (1986). Memory strategy instruction and training with LD adolescents. Learning Disabilities Research, 2, 45-53.

Menhusen, B.R., & Gromme, R.O. (1976). Science for handicapped children - why? Science and children, 13(6), 35-37.

Merry, F.K. (1930). A study of the merits of animal models used in teaching blind children. [Monograph]. The Teachers Forum, 2, 12-14.

Metropolitan Museum of Art (1979). Museums and the disabled. New York: Metropolitan Museum of Art.

Moores, D. F. (1987). Educating the deaf: Psychology, principles, and practices (3rd ed.) Boston: Houghton Miffli

Napier, G.D. (1973). Special subject adjustments and skills. In B. Lowenfield (Ed.), The visually handicapped child in school. (pp. 221-253). New York: John Day.

National Science Resources Center (1988). Science for children: Resources for teachers. Washington, D.C.: National Academy Press.

Neal, A. (1987). Help for the small museum: Handbook of exhibit ideas and methods. (2nd ed.). Boulder, CO: Pruett.

Olsen, J. (1970). Viewing solar crescents, Science and children, 7(5), 21.

Osguthorpe, R.T., & Scruggs, T.E. (1986). Special Education students as tutors: A review and analysis. Remedial and Special Education, 7(4), 15-25.

Ossler, A., Bader, J.A., Heck, M.C., & Walsh, S. (1990). School prereferral intervention strategies for students experiencing learning problems. Preventing School Failure, 34(2), 23-31.

Owsley, P.J. (1961, September). Teaching science to deaf children. Paper presented at meeting of The Council for Exceptional Children, Detroit, MI.

Owsley, P.J. (1968). Development of the cognitive abilities and language of deaf children through science. The Volta Review, 389-393.

Parker, R.E. (1985). Small-group cooperative learning: Improving academic, social gains in the classroom. NASSP Bulletin, 69(479), 48-57.

Pease, L.C. (1946). The science laboratory in the elementary school for the blind. The New Outlook, 40(6), 159-164.

Pierce, M.M., Stahlbrand, K., & Armstrong, S.B. (1984). Increasing student productivity through peer tutoring programs. Austin, TX: PRO-ED.

Post, T.R., Humphreys, A.H., & Pearson, M. (1976). Laboratory-based mathematics and science for the handicapped child. Science and Children, 13(6), 41-43.

Pressley, M., Scruggs, T.E., & Mastropieri, M.A. (1989). Memory strategy instruction for learning disabilities: Present and future directions. Learning Disabilities Research, 4, 68-77.

Pugach, M.C., & Johnson, L.J. (1989). Prereferral interventions: Progress, problems, and challenges. Exceptional Children, 56(3), 217-226.

Putnam, J.W., Rynders, J.E., Johnson, R.T., & Johnson, D.W. (1989). Collaborative skill instruction for promoting positive interactions between mentally handicapped and nonhandicapped children. Exceptional Children, 55(6), 550-557.

Ramsey, W.L., Gabriel, L.A., McGuirk, J.F., Phillips, C.R., & Watenpaugh, F.M. (1986). Holt science, Teacher's edition 7. New York: Holt, Rinehart & Winston.

Ramsey, W.L., Gabriel, L.A., McGuirk, J.F., Phillips, C.R., & Watenpaugh, F.M. (1986). Holt science, Teacher's edition 8. New York: Holt, Rinehart & Winston.

Redden, M.R. (1979). Science education for handicapped children. Education Unlimited, 1(4), 44-46.

Sachse, T.P. (1989). Making science happen. Educational Leadership, 47(3), 18-21.

Salend, S.J. (1990). Effective mainstreaming. New York: MacMillan.

Salend, S.J., & Washin, B. (1988). Team-assisted individualization with handicapped adjudicated youth. Exceptional Children, 55(2), 174-180.

Schatz, D., Franks, F., Thier, H.D., & Linn, M.C. (1976). Hands-on science for the blind. Science and Children, 13(6), 21-22.

Schatz, D., Thier, H.D. (1976). Increasing the accessibility of hands-on science for blind students. The New Outlook, 70(2), 61-63.

Schniedewind, N., & Salend, S.J. (1987). Cooperative learning works. Teaching Exceptional Children, 19(2), 22-25.

Schulz, J.B., Carpenter, C.D., & Turnball, A.P. (1991). Mainstreaming exceptional students: A guide for classroom teachers. Needham Heights, MA: Allyn & Bacon.

Scruggs, T.E. (1988). Psychology of computer use: VI. Effectiveness of computer-assisted instruction in expository writing. Perceptual and Motor Skills, 67, 871-877.

Scruggs, T.E., Bennion, K., & Lifson, S. (1985). An analysis of children's strategy use on reading achievement tests. Elementary School Journal, 85, 479-484.

Scruggs, T.E., Bennion, K., & Lifson, S. (1985). Learning disabled students' spontaneous use of test-taking skills on reading achievement tests. Learning Disabilities Quarterly, 8, 205-210.

Scruggs, T.E., & Brigham, F.J. (1991). Utility of musical mnemonics. Perceptual and Motor Skills, 72, 881-882.

Scruggs, T.E., & Brigham, R. (1990). The challenges of metacognitive instruction. Remedial and Special Education, 11, 16-18.

Scruggs, T.E., & Laufenberg, R. (1986). Transformational mnemonic strategies for retarded learners. Education and Training of the Mentally Retarded, 27, 165-173.

Scruggs, T.E., & Lifson, S.A. (1985). Current conceptions of test-wiseness: Myths and realities. School Psychology Review, 14, 339-350.

Scruggs, T.E., & Lifson, S.A. (1986). Are learning disabled students 'test-wise'?: An inquiry into reading comprehension test items. Educational and Psychological Measurement, 46, 1075-1082.

Scruggs, T.E., & Marshing, L. (1988). Teaching test-taking skills to behaviorally disordered students. Behavioral Disorders, 13, 240-244.

Scruggs, T.E., & Mastropieri, M.A. (1984). Improving memory for facts: The "keyword" method. Academic Therapy, 10, 159-166.

Scruggs, T.E., & Mastropieri, M.A. (1984). Issues in generalization: Implications for special education. Psychology in the Schools, 21, 397-403.

Scruggs, T.E. & Mastropieri, M.A. (1984). Use content maps to increase children's comprehension and recall. The Reading Teacher, 37, 807.

Scruggs, T.E., & Mastropieri, M.A. (1985). Cooperative vs. competitive performances of behaviorally disordered American Indian adolescents. Journal of Instructional Psychology, 12(1), 31-33.

Scruggs, T.E., & Mastropieri, M.A. (1985). Illustrative aids improve reading. Reading Horizons, 25(2), 107-110.

Scruggs, T.E., & Mastropieri, M.A. (1986). Improving the test-taking skills of behaviorally disordered and learning disabled students. Exceptional Children, 53, 63-68.

Scruggs, T.E., & Mastropieri, M.A. (1988). Acquisition and transfer of mnemonic strategies by gifted and non-gifted students. Journal of Special Education, 22, 153-166.

Scruggs, T.E., & Mastropieri, M.A. (1988). Are learning disabled students "test-wise"?: A review of recent research. Learning Disabilities Focus, 3(2), 87-97.

Scruggs, T.E., & Mastropieri, M.A. (1989). Mnemonic instruction of learning disabled students: A field-based evaluation. Learning Disability Quarterly, 12, 119-125.

Scruggs, T.E., & Mastropieri, M.A. (1989). Reconstructive elaborations: A model for content area learning. American Educational Research Journal, 26, 311-327.

Scruggs, T.E., & Mastropieri, M.A. (1990). Mnemonic instruction for students with learning disabilities: What it is and what it does. Learning Disability Quarterly, 13, 271-281.

Scruggs, T.E., & Mastropieri, M.A. (1990). The case for mnemonic instruction: From laboratory investigations to classroom applications. Journal of Special Education, 24, 7-32.

Scruggs, T.E., & Mastropieri, M.A. (1992). Classroom applications of mnemonic instruction: Acquisition, maintenance, and generalization. Exceptional Children, 58, 219-229.

Scruggs, T.E., & Mastropieri, M.A. (1992). Effective mainstreaming strategies for mildly handicapped students. Elementary School Journal, 92, 389-409.

Scruggs, T.E., & Mastropieri, M.A. (1992). Teaching test-taking skills: Helping students show what they know. Cambridge, MA: Brookline Books.

Scruggs, T.E., & Mastropieri, M.A. (in press). Academic interventions for mildly handicapped students. In R. A. Gable, (Ed.), Advances in mental retardation and developmental disabilities (Vol. 5). London: Kingsley.

Scruggs, T.E., & Mastropieri, M.A. (in press). Current approaches to science education: Implications for mainstream instruction of students with disabilities. Remedial and Special Education.

Scruggs, T.E., & Mastropieri, M.A. (in press). Issues in intervention research: Secondary students. In S. Vaughn & C. Bos (Eds.), Learning disabilities research: Theory, methodology, assessment, and ethics. New York: Springer-Verlag.

Scruggs, T.E., & Mastropieri, M.A. (in press). Special education for the 21st century: Integrating learning strategies and thinking skills. Journal of Learning Disabilities.

Scruggs, T.E., & Mastropieri, M.A. (Eds.) (in press). Advances in learning and behavioral disabilities (Vol. 7). Greenwich, CT: JAI.

Scruggs, T.E., Mastropieri, M.A., Bakken, J.P., & Brigham, F.J. (in press). Reading vs. doing: The relative effectiveness of textbook-based and inquiry-oriented approaches to science education. Journal of Special Education.

Scruggs, T.E., Mastropieri, M.A., Brigham, F.J., & Sullivan, G. S. (1992). Effects of mnemonic reconstructions on the spatial learning of adolescents with learning disabilities. Learning Disability Quarterly, 15, 154-162.

Scruggs, T.E., Mastropieri, M.A., & Levin, J.R. (1985). Vocabulary acquisition by mentally retarded students under direct and mnemonic instruction. American Journal of Mental Deficiency, 89, 546-551.

Scruggs, T.E., Mastropieri, M.A., & Levin, J.R. (1986). Can children effectively re-use the same mnemonic pegwords? Educational Communication and Technology Journal, 34, 83-88.

Scruggs, T.E., Mastropieri, M.A., & Levin, J.R.(1987). Implications of mnemonic strategy instruction for theories of learning disabilities. In H. L. Swanson (Ed.), Memory and learning disabilities: Advances in learning and behavioral disabilities: (pp. 225-244). Greenwich, CT: JAI Press.

Scruggs, T.E., Mastropieri, M.A., Levin, J.R., & Gaffney, J.S. (1985). Facilitating the acquisition of science facts in learning disabled students. American Educational Research Journal, 22(4), 575-586.

Scruggs, T.E., Mastropieri, M.A., Levin, J.R., McLoone, B., Gaffney, J.S., & Prater, M.A. (1985). Increasing content-area learning: A comparison of mnemonic and visual-spatial direct instruction. Learning Disabilities Research, 1, 18-31.

Scruggs, T.E., Mastropieri, M.A., McLoone, B.B., Levin, J.R., & Morrison, C.R. (1987). Mnemonic facilitation of learning disabled students' memory for expository prose. Journal of Educational Psychology, 79, 27-34.

Scruggs, T.E., Mastropieri, M.A., & Richter, L.L. (1985). Peer tutoring with behaviorally disordered students: Social and academic benefits. Behavioral Disorders, 10, 283-294.

Scruggs, T.E., Mastropieri, M.A., & Veit, D. (1986). The effects of coaching on the standardized test performance of learning disabled and behaviorally disordered students. Remedial and Special Education, 7(5), 37-41.

Scruggs, T.E., Mastropieri, M.A., Veit, D.T., & Osguthorpe, R. T. (1986). Behaviorally disordered students as tutors: Effects on social behaviors. Behavioral Disorders, 12, 36-44.

Scruggs, T.E., & Osguthorpe, R.T. (1986). Tutoring interventions within special education settings: A comparison of cross-age and peer tutoring. Psychology in the Schools, 23, 187-193.

Scruggs, T.E., & Richter, L. (1988). Tutoring learning disabled students: A critical review. Learning Disability Quarterly, 11, 274-286.

Scruggs, T.E., White, K., & Bennion, K., (1986). Teaching test-taking skills to elementary grade students: A meta-analysis. Elementary School Journal, 87, 69-82.

Scruggs, T.E., & Wong, B.J.L. (Eds.)(1990). Intervention research in learning disabilities. New York: Springer-Verlag.

Sharan, Y., & Sharan, S. (1989/1990). Group investigation expands cooperative learning. Educational Leadership, 47(4), 17-21.

Sherman, L. W. (1988). A comparative study of cooperative and competitive achievement in two secondary biology classrooms: The group investigation model versus an individually competitive goal structure. Journal of Research in Science Teaching, 26(1), 55-64.

Shugrue, S.K., Morris, W.M, & Kuhne, C.H. (1968). Braille trail model. Science and Children, 6(2), 23-25.

Shultz, O.A. (1973). Planetarium astronomy for the hearing-impaired. The Science Teacher, 40(4), 45-46.

Slavin, R.E. (1983). Cooperative learning. New York: Longman.

Slavin, R.E. (1984). Team assisted individualization: Cooperative learning and individualized instruction in the mainstreamed classroom. Remedial and Special Education, 5(6), 33-42.

Slavin, R.E. (1988). Student team learning: An overview and practical guide, Second edition. Washington, DC: National Education Association of the United States.

Slavin, R.E. (1989). Comprehensive cooperative learning models for heterogenous classrooms. The Pointer, 33(2), 12-19.

Slavin, R.E. (1991). Synthesis of research on cooperative learning. Educational Leadership, 48(5), 71-82.

Slavin, R. E., Leavey, M. B. & Madden, N. A. (1984). Combining cooperative learning and individualized instruction: Effects on student mathematics and achievement, attitudes, and behaviors. The Elementary School Journal, 84(4), 409-422.

Slavin, R. E., Madden, N. A., & Leavey, M. (1984a). Effects of cooperative learning and individualized instruction on mainstreamed students. Exceptional Children, 50, 434-443.

Slavin, R. E., Madden, N. A., & Leavey, M. (1984b). Effects of team assisted individualization on the mathematics achievement of academically handicapped and nonhandicapped students. Journal of Educational Psychology, 76, 813-819.

Slavin, R.E., Madden, N.A., & Stevens, R.J. (1989/1990). Cooperative learning models for the 3 R's. Educational Leadership, 47(4), 22-28.

Slavin, R.E., Stevens, R.J., & Madden, N.A. (1988). Accommodating student diversity in reading and writing instruction: A cooperative learning approach. Remedial and Special Education, 9(1), 60-66.

Smith, J.P. (1990). How to solve student adjustment problems. West Nyack, N.Y.: The Center for Applied Research in Education.

Smithsonian Institution (1977). Museums and handicapped students guidelines for educators. Washington, D.C.: Author.

Sprick, R. (1981). The Solution book. Chicago: Science Research Associates.

Sprick, R. (1985). Discipline in the secondary classroom: A problem by problem survival guide. West Nyack, NY: Center for Applied Research in Education.

Stelle, M. (1946). The introduction of science in the intermediate grades. American Association of Instructors of the Blind, 38, 67-72.

Stern, V.W., Lifton, D.E., & Malcom, S.M. (1987). Resource directory of scientists and engineers with disabilities. Washington, D.C.: American Association for the Advancement of Science.

Stevens, R. J. & Slavin, R. E. (1991). When cooperative learning improves the achievement of students with mild disabilities: A response to Tateyama-Sniezek. Exceptional Children, 57(2), 276-280.

Sugai, G. (1988). Educational assessment of the culturally diverse and behavior disordered student: An examination of critical effect. Paper presented at the Ethnic and Multicultural Symposia, Dallas, TX.

Sunal, C.S., & Sunal, D.W. (1981). Adapting science for hearing impaired early adolescents. Final Report. Morgantown: West Virginia University, College of Human Resources and Education.

Sund, R.B., & Bybee, R.W. (1973). Becoming a Better Elementary Science Teacher. Columbus, OH: Charles E. Merrill.

Sund, R.B., Adams, D.K., Hackett, J.K., & Moyer, R.H. (1985). Accent on science, Level six (Teacher's Annotated Ed.). Columbus, OH: Merrill.

Sund, R.B., Adams, D.K., Hackett, J.K., & Moyer, R.H. (1985). Accent on science, Level two (Teacher's Annotated Ed.). Columbus, OH: Merrill.

Tateyama-Sniezek, K. (1990). Cooperative learning: Does it improve the academic achievement of students with handicaps? Exceptional Children, 56(5), 426-432.

Taymans, J.M. (1989). Cooperative learning for learning-disabled adolescents. The Pointer, 33(2), 28-32.

Thier, H.D. (1971). Laboratory science for visually handicapped elementary school children. The New Outlook for the Blind, 65(6), 190-194.

Thier, H.D., & Hadary, D.E. (1973). We can do it, too. Science and Children, December, 7-9.

Thomas, B. (1977). Environmental ed for the blind. Instructor, 86(5), 106-107.

Tolfa, D., Scruggs, T.E., & Bennion, K. (1985). Format changes in reading achievement tests: Implications for learning disabled students. Psychology in the Schools, 22, 387-391.

Tolfa, D., Scruggs, T.E., & Mastropieri, M.A. (1985). Attitudes of behaviorally disordered students toward tests: A replication. Perceptual and Motor Skills, 61, 963-966.

Tombaugh, D. (1972). Laboratory techniques for the blind. The American Biology Teacher, 34(5), 258-260.

Tombaugh, D. (1973). Biology for the Blind. Euclid, OH: Euclid Public Schools.

Vance, J., Lind, K., & Wilder, M. (1987). Science and technology: Changes around us, Teacher's edition. San Diego: Coronado.

Vance, J., Lind, K., & Wilder, M. (1987). Science and technology: Changes we make: Teacher's edition. San Diego: Coronado.

Vance, J., Lind, K., & Wilder, M. (1987). Science and technology: On planet Earth: Teacher's edition. San Diego: Coronado.

Vance, J., Lind, K., & Wilder, M. (1987). Science and technology: Things around us, Teacher's edition. San Diego: Coronado.

Veit, D.T., & Scruggs, T.E. (1986). Can learning disabled students effectively use separate answer sheets? Perceptual and Motor Skills, 63, 155-160.

Veit, D.T., Scruggs, T.E., & Mastropieri, M.A. (1986). Extended mnemonic instruction with learning disabled students. Journal of Educational Psychology, 78(4), 300-308.

Walrich, R.G. (1980). The development of a science handbook for teachers of educable mentally handicapped children. Unpublished doctoral dissertation, University of Michigan, Ann Arbor.

Walsh, E. (1977). The handicapped and science: Moving into the mainstream. Science, 196, 1424-1426.

Welch, M., Judge, T., Anderson, J., Bray, J., Child, B., & Franke, L. (1990). A tool for implementing prereferral consultation. Teaching Exceptional Children, 22, 30-31.

Wellington, J.A., & Morgan, D.H. (1940). Visual aids in the teaching of astronomy to the blind. The Teachers Forum, 12(4), 66-67.

West, J.F., & Cannon, G.S. (1988). Essential collaborative consultation competencies for regular and special educators. Journal of Learning Disabilities, 21(1), 56-63.

Whitfield, E. (1976). Experiments on tape. Science and Children, March, 13(6), 47. Wielert, J.S., & Retish, P. (1983). Mainstreaming and the science teacher. School Science and Mathematics, 83(7), 552-559.

Wilcox, J., Sbardellati, E., & Nevin, A. (1987). Cooperative learning groups aid integration. Teaching Exceptional Children, 20(1), 61-63.

Wilson, J.T., & Koran, J.J. (1973). Science curriculum materials for special education students. Education and Training of the Mentally Retarded, 8(2), 30-32.

Winkler, A., Bernstein, L., Schachter, M., Wolfe, S., & Natchez, G. (1984). Concepts and challenges in science, Book 1, Teacher's edition (2nd Ed.). Newton, MA: CEBCO.

Witteborg, L.P. (1981). Good Show! A practical guide for temporary exhibitions. Washington, D.C.: Smithsonian Institution Traveling Exhibition Service.

Wood, J.W. (1989). Mainstreaming: A practical approach for teachers. Columbus: Merrill.

Worcester College for the Blind. (1973). The science laboratory in a school for the blind: general science -- a suggested two year syllabus. In The teaching of science and mathematics to the blind. Second edition. (pp. 35-48). Oldbury, England: R. Jones.

Wright, J., Coble, C.R., Hopkins, J., Johnson, S., & Lattart, D. (1991). Prentice Hall life science, Annotated teacher's edition. Englewood Cliffs, NJ: Prentice Hall.

Wright, R.B. (1978). Laboratory exercises for visually handicapped botany students. Visual Impairment and Blindness, 72(10), 67-68.

Yau, M. (1988). Alternative service delivery models for learning disabled students. (Report No. 188). Toronto, Ontario, Canada: Toronto Board of Education (Ontario), Research Department. (ERIC Document Reproduction Service No. ED 309 601)

Zins, J.E., Graden, J.L., & Ponti, C.R. (1988). Prereferral intervention to improve special services delivery. Special Services in the Schools, 4(3/4), 109-130.

Index

INDEX: ALL T = info in table; P = info in picture;
(T) = info in table and script; (P) = info in picture and script

A

Academic Deficiency
  Emotional disturbance 29
  Learning disabilities 8
  Mental retardation 20
  Physical disabilities 45

Accessibility
  Behavior disorder 201T
  Communication disorder 201T, 202T, 203T
  Hearing impairments 200, 201T, 202T, 203T, 222T
  Learning 203T, 223T
  Mental retardation 203T, 223T
  Mobility 219(T)-220
  Physical disabilities 60(P)-61(P), 64(T), 97, 200, 201T,
    202T, 203T, 219(T), 243, 265
  Visual impairments 200, 201T, 202T, 203T, 220(T)-221,
    243, 286

Accountability
  Student 82-85, 86, 88T, 89, 91T

Acting-Out
  see Behavior

Activities
  Structuring tasks 251-253
  Teaching of 227-229, 228T, 238
  see also specific activity type

Activities-Oriented Approaches 77, 78(T), 85, 86-87T,
    89, 101, 108(T), 109, 111, 113, 114T, 146, 228
  Concrete manipulatives illustrate concepts 162T, 168
  Hands-on programs 180

Learning disabilities
  mainstreaming techniques 10

Adaptations
  Alternative devices 64(T), 200
  Audio components 220
  Audio tape (tape record) 60, 63, 199T
    assessment 50, 51T, 115T, 116T, 117, 118T
    attention increase 140
    descriptive 164, 166, 167, 168, 176, 201T, 244,
      268, 275
    field trips and demonstrations 49, 212, 244
    listening center 165
    note taking 183, 275, 278
    peer assistance 96, 98, 165
    reading 9, 162T, 164-165, 171, 173, 175, 176
    variable speed cassettes 164
  Big Eye Lamps 254, 276
  Blackboards 181, 236
  Bookholders 63
  Bookmarks 164
  Braille 52, 53T, 96, 162, 166, 167, 168, 171, 174,
      175, 176, 183, 221, 234, 237, 244, 256, 261,
      262, 268, 275, 280, 287, 292, 294, 297
    booklets 163, 165
    braille descriptions 166, 167, 168, 176, 268, 294
    braille label marker 166
    braille like symbols 162
    labelers 52, 233
    labels 52, 233
    laboratory manuals 52, 53T, 268, 294
  Bulletin boards 167
  Calculators 63
  Carbon paper 96, 98
  Charts and diagrams 167-168
  Clear photographic cubes 63
  Clear plastic folder 64
  Clipboards 62
  Closed caption 97

Adaptations (cont.)
  Closed circuit T.V.
    scanners 163
  Communication 51T
    boards 16, 18, 63
  Compressed speech machine 63, 165
  Computers 16, 18, 117, 174, 196, 213-216
    extra large monitors 53(T)
  Controlled vocabulary and syntax materials 163
  Corrugated cardboard 62
  Descriptive video 50, 51T, 96, 169, 205T, 220T, 221, 225, 268, 275, 294
  Development of materials 69, 70, 71
  Enlarge examples 166, 237
  Enlarged type 52, 163, 221, 234
  Films 199T
    use in attention increase 140, 141
  Filmstrip 199T
    use in note-taking 181
  Handling classroom materials 59T
  High interest, low vocabulary materials 163
  Highlight 174-175
  Illustrations 162T, 165-166
    glue 166
    3-D 166
  Kurtzweil reading machine 163
  Language cards 11, 18, 39, 236, 255, 276
  Large print books 163, 220T
  Light sensors 53(T), 240, 275, 292, 298, 300
  Lower readability level material 163
  Magnets 62, 232
  Magnifying glasses 163
  Magnifying lamp 163
  Major modifications 119T
    allocated time 12T, 23T, 49T, 119T, 215
      see also Allocated Time
    presentation format 12T, 23T, 43T, 49T, 119T, 152-161
    response format 12T, 43T, 49T, 57T, 119T
    scoring procedures 12T, 23T, 119T
    test format 12T, 23T, 43T, 119T
    test-taking skills 12T, 119T, 186-189(T)
    written format 119T
  Microprojectors 53(T)
  Modified input technology 199
    see also Computers
  Modeling 165
  Movies 96, 97
  Multi-level text 163
  NCR copy paper 96, 98
  Opticon 163
  Oral reports 117
  Organizational pictures, maps, diagrams 166-167, 176
    audio-taped description 167
    braille description 167
    colors 167
    enlarge 167
    3-D 167
  Outline 175, 178T
  Overhead transparencies 163, 165, 166, 174, 180T, 181
    color 140, 141, 244
  Pads of paper 62
  Page turners 63, 164

Paper produces raised line 166, 167
Photocopies inserted into books 165
Polaroid camera 179
Practice golf ball 62
Reading and studying 59T, 63
"Rebus" writing 165
Role play/pantomime 165
Rubber stamps 62
Rubberbands 62, 254
Screen/text reader 169, 212
Secretaries 117
Slides 199T
  use in attention increase 140, 141
  reading aid 170
Speech synthesizer 16, 18
Stabilizers 64(T), 275
  feltpads 64
  slatted trays 64
  velcro 64, 232
Study guides 176
Summary charts and tables 167-168
  audio-taped description 168
  braille descriptions 168
  contain pictures of information 168
  enlarge 168
  large print 167, 168
  photocopied 167, 168
Talking books 63
Tape 62, 254
Tubing 62
Typewriters 199T, 200, 204
  electric 63
  eraser buttons 63
  pointer sticks 63
Underline 173
Velcro
  dots 237
  gloves 254
  strips 254
Videodiscs 169, 181, 199T
  curriculum 169
Videos/Videotape 199T, 268
  interactive 199T
  use in
    assessment 115T
    field trips/demonstrations 224(T), 278
    reading 169
    peer assistance 96, 97
    note-taking 181
Write into separate booklet 173

Adaptive Equipment/Devices 209-213, 210(T), 211(T)
  see also Adaptations
  see also each individual disability

Advance Organizers 162T, 170, 179, 205T

Affect 2, 191-198
  Attributions 2
  Improvement of 191-198, 257
  Self-esteem 2
  see also Behavior

Aggression
see Behavior

Allergies 260, 263

Allocated Time 122T, 123, 228(T), 254, 266, 268, 271, 291

Animal Activities 261-263
Adaptations for
examining animals 263
handling animals 262, 257-259
insect identification 263
isopod or mealworm behavior 261, 263
labeling specimens 262
language concepts 262
pictures, charts, models, use of 262
prefamiliarization activities 261
studying habitats 261
Adaptive equipment
braille dog tags 262
charts, models, pictures 261, 263
two-cup apparatus 263
wall paper 262
wheelchair tray 263
Commonly used species 257-258
Handling animals 262
Models, use of 262
Practice, need for 260-261
Process skills needed 257
Selecting and keeping animals 259T, 260T
Student self-esteem 257

Anxiety 89, 125

Arthrogryposts 56T
see also Physical Disabilities

Astronomy Activities 285-287
Adaptations for
computer programs 286
games 286
planetarium visits 286
planetary models 285
telescopes 286
visual aids 285, 287
visually impaired 286
Adaptive equipment
braille labels 287
colored chalk, 287
computer program, Voyage of Mimi II 286
galaxy models 285
games, "Space Hop" 286
heat lamp 287
moon and planet globes 285
plastic form for painting 254
posters 285
rubber bands 254
star charts 285
tape 254
textured materials 254
Types of 285

Attention 2, 139-143, 145, 167, 169, 170, 193
Attending strategies 167, 169, 170, 198
Head injury 56T
Hearing impairments
mainstreaming technologies 42
Learning disabilities
characteristics 8
mainstreaming technologies 12T
Maintaining attention 126, 131T
enthusiasm 75
Mental retardation
characteristics 20-21
Sources of attention problems 139
Strategies for increasing attention 139-143
Suggestions for
emotionally disturbed 2
hearing impairment 139
learning disabilities 2, 8, 9, 13
mental retardation 2, 21
physical disabilities 56T, 139
visual impairments 139

B

Balance Activities
see Scales and Balance Activities

Behavior
Affect 2
Attributions 2
Behavior management 30-31(T), 91T, 121-137
Cooperative learning 79-82
Decreasing problem behaviors 79-82
acting out 79
aggression 82
conflicts 79
non-compliance 79
passive 79, 81, 89
positive and negative statements 191-193
In relation to
emotional disturbance 28, 29, 123
hearing impairments 122, 123
learning disabilities 9, 123
mental retardation 122, 123
physical disabilities 122
visual impairments 122
On-task 133, 204
contracts for improvement 128
self-monitor 132T, 133T
Peer tutors 108
Self-esteem 2, 89
Social
acceptance 2, 9, 21, 89
interaction 2, 9, 21, 29, 30, 82, 95T

Behavior Disabilities
Cooperative learning 90T
Laboratory techniques 273, 277, 279
Safety 273, 277, 279
Visual accessibility 201T

Behavior Disabilities (cont.)
see Emotional Disturbance
see Learning Disability

Behavior Management 79-82, 81T, 91T, 121-137, 143, 192, 193
  Behavior expectations 79
  Behavioral goal 128(T), 129(T)
  Classroom environmental factors 111, 113
  Complex strategies 127(T)
    combinations of group and individual reward systems 127T, 137
    good behavior game 127T, 136(T)
    individual contracting 127T, 128(T)-130, 129(T)
    level systems 127T, 134-135(T)
    response cost systems 127T, 134
    school-wide systems 127T, 137
      assertive discipline 137
    self-monitoring 127T, 130-133T, 131T, 132T
    time out 127T, 135-136(T)
    token systems 127T, 133-134T
  Cooperative group 136
  Emotional disturbance
    laboratory techniques 31, 32T
    mainstreaming techniques 29, 30T
  Learning disabilities
    mainstreaming technologies 10, 12T
    positive and negative ways of correcting behavior 192
    reinforcement 196
  Model appropriate behavior 123
  Peer response 122T, 123
  Proximity 124, 125T, 140
  Reinforce inappropriate behavior 123
  Simple strategies 11, 123-126(T), 125T
  Teacher response 122T, 123

Big Eye Lamps 254, 276

Blackboards/Markerboards 12(T), 199T, 200, 204

Blind
see Visual Impairment

Braille 52, 53T, 96, 162, 166, 167, 168, 171, 174, 175, 176, 183, 221, 234, 237, 244, 256, 261, 262, 268, 275, 280, 287, 292, 294, 297
  Braille descriptions 166, 167, 168, 176, 268, 294
  Braille like symbols 162
  Brailler 175
  Labeled diskettes 210T
  Labelers 52, 233
  Labels 52, 233
  Laboratory manuals 52, 53T, 268, 294
  Perkin's brailler 162
  Pocket computer 210T
  Printers 210T

Bulletin Board 165

C

Calculators 199T, 200, 204
  Talking 210T

Cerebral Palsy 15, 54T
see also Physical Disabilities

Charting and Graphing 236-238
  Adaptations for
    computer programs 238
    concept review 236
    concrete activities 236
    cooperative learning groups 238
    extra help sessions 237
    peer assistants 238
    prerequisite skills 235
  Adaptive equipment
    blackboard 236
    braille 237
    chicken wire and yarn 237
    computer paper guide strips 237
    computer programs 238
    computers and adaptive devices 238
    construction paper 236
    felt dots 237
    golf tees 237
    hardware cloth 238
    language cards 236
    large print 238
    paper, window screen, crayons 238
    plastic screen 238
    predrawn and labeled forms 236
    push-pin histograms 237
    raised-line paper 237
    rubber stamps 237
    textured surfaces 237
    tiles 237
    velcro 237

Classification 240-241
  Adaptations for
    concepts and associated language 241
    peer assistants 240
    structured questioning 240
    systematic questioning, review, summaries 240
    Venn diagrams, presentation of 241
  Adaptive equipment
    attribute blocks 241
    buttons 240
    sorting trays 241

Classroom Environment 95, 121, 273
  Common disability characteristics 1
  Emotional disturbance
    mainstreaming techniques 29, 30T
  Hearing impairments
    mainstreaming techniques 43T
  Physical disabilities 58, 59T, 60(P)-61(P)
  Visual impairments 47, 52, 57T

Classroom Organization 9-10, 38-39
  Audio-Visual 10, 38
    closed caption 38
  Class rules 29
  Demonstrations 10, 44
    visibility 38T
  Emergency procedures 42, 47, 58(T)
  Groups
    activities 10
    cooperative learning 77-91
    discussions 10, 39
    projects 10
    see also Cooperative Learning
  Physical environment 47
    access 47, 60(P)-61(P)
  Suggestions for
    emotional disturbance 29
    hearing impairment 38(T)-39
    learning disabilities 9-10
    physical disabilities 56, 60(P)-61(P)
    visual impairment 47, 51T

Closed Captioned Television and Video 38

Closed Circuit Television 239, 244, 261, 267, 280, 293, 299

Closed Circuit Television Scanners 52, 53T, 163, 210T, 293

Collaboration with
  Media specialist 69
  Occupational therapist 58
  Physical therapist 58
  Same grade level teacher 69(T)
  School Nurse 57
  Science specialist 69
  Special education teacher 3, 4, 9, 11, 17, 18, 39, 58, 68(T), 83, 171, 214
  Speech-language teacher 17, 18

Communication
  Communication boards 16, 18, 63
  Computer 16
  Speech synthesizers 16, 18, 63

Communication Disorders 15-18
  Attributes/characteristics 15-16
  Auditory accessibility adaptations 202T
  Brain injury 15
    apraxia 15
    dysarthria 15
  Cleft palate 15
  Cooperative learning 89, 90T
  Definition 15
  Evaluation adaptations 118
    written communication disabilities 117
  Field trips 98
  Incidence 15, 16T
  Instructional media adaptations 206
  Laboratory activity recommendations 18(T), 227-229, 236-238, 239-242, 243-244, 253, 256, 265-267, 270, 274, 278, 279-280, 284

Language disorder 15, 16
  echolalia 16
  elective mutism 16
  morphology 16
  nonverbal 16, 17
  phonology 16
  pragmatics 16
  semantics 16
  syntax 16
Mainstreaming techniques 17(T)-18
  adaptive communication devices 16, 17(T), 18
  patience 17(T)
  questioning 17(T)
  reports, oral 17(T)
  support services 17
  vocabulary 255
Manipulability and task performance 203T
Neurological damage 15
  cerebral palsy 15
Nonverbal students 16, 17
Peer mediation 17, 98-99
Reading adaptations 165
Science project preparation adaptations 185-186
Speech disorder 15, 16T
  articulation 15, 16T
  fluency 15, 16T
  voice 15, 16T
Visual accessibility 201T

Companies
  see Appendix B: Related Organizations and Resources

Comprehension 172-178(T), 183-184(T), 228

Compressed Speech Devices 63, 165

Computer-Assisted Instruction 209-216
  see also Computers

Computers 117, 169, 175, 199, 200, 204, 209-216
  Adaptations for 209-213, 210T, 211T
    communication disorders 212
    hearing impaired 212
    learning disabilities 212
    mental retardation 212
    physical disabilities 211(T)-212
    visual disabilities 210T
  Adaptive keyboards
    braille overlays 169
    expanded keyboard 211
    keyguards 211(T)
    membrane keyboard 211(T)
    miniature keyboard 211(T)
  Foot pedals 211(T)
  Modified input devices 211T
    adapted switches 211T
    adaptive firmware card 212
    footpedal 211(T)
    headsticks 211T
    joysticks 211(T)
    keyboard membranes 211(T)
    keyguards 211(T)

Computers (cont.)
 light pens 211T
 miniature keyboards 211(T)
 mouth sticks 211T
 scanning devices 211T
 software 200, 211, 212
 touch screens 210, 211T, 212
 voice recognition 211T, 212
 Monitors
 enlarged 210T
 larger and darker fonts 210T
 large screen as monitors 51T, 169
 with different colors and resolution 210T
 Opaque projectors 199T
 Programs/Software 205, 211, 212, 213, 214, 238, 286
 astronomy activities 286
 charting and graphing 238
 Excel 238
 force and motion 293
 Lotus 238
 mapping activities 244
 Miner's Cave 293
 MSWorks 238
 Personal Science Laboratory 238
 Sticky Bear 244
 SVE Autograph 238
 Twinkle 199, 211
 Voyage of the Mimi 206, 244, 278, 286
 Voyage of the Mimi II 205, 213
 see Instructional Media
 Software systems
 electronic mail systems 214(T), 215(T)
 optical reader and character recognition 210T
 Text readers 169, 210T

Concepts
 Abstract concepts, keywords 152
 Teaching scientific concepts 6, 228, 229, 255
 Teaching suggestions for 40, 48(T), 50, 165, 168
 hearing impaired 39
 learning disabilities 10
 mental retardation 22
 visually impaired 51T, 50

Cooperative Learning 77-91, 78T, 80T, 81T, 83T, 84T, 85T, 87T, 88T, 90T, 91T, 238, 252, 266, 276, 291
 Behavior management 79, 121, 124, 129T, 131T, 136
 Computer
 delivered instruction 214(T)
 supplements to instruction 215(T)
 Effective instruction
 guided practice 76
 independent 76
 present new information 74
 review 73
 Enhancing comprehension
 summarize information 174
 Hearing impairments
 laboratory techniques 44(T)
 Improving attention 141
 Instructional media
 teacher modification 207

Learning disabilities
 mainstreaming techniques 10
Peer assistance benefits 97
Presentation format adaptations
 organizational structure of reading material 171
 vocabulary and concept acquisition 171
Suggestions for activities
 assembling kits and models 238
 charting and graphing 238
 force and motion 291
 microscopes 266
 powders, mixtures, and solutions 276

Corrective Feedback 75T, 76, 95, 100T, 103T, 104T, 105(T), 107T, 108T, 252(T)

D

Deaf
 see Hearing Impaired

Demonstrations
 see Exhibits/Demonstrations

Descriptive Video 50, 69, 169, 268, 275, 294

Direct Appeal 124, 125T

Discovery Activities
 see Invention Activities

E

Earth Science (Landform Activities) 283-284
 Activities for
 astronomy 285
 landforms 283, 284
 mapping 243
 rocks, minerals, and fossils 279
 weather 277
 Adaptations for
 cognitive impairment 283, 284
 hearing impaired 283
 mapping 283
 physically disabled 284
 supervision of 284
 visually impaired 283
 Adaptive equipment
 globe 283
 model 283

Educational Activity Objectives
 Assembling 253
 Charting, graphing, recording data 235
 Determination of 227
 Force and motion 292
 Invention and discovery 247
 Measurement 231
 Microscopes 266-267

Educational Activity Objectives (cont.)
Observation 239
Powders, mixtures, solutions 274
Water activities 269

Effective Instruction 73-76, 75T
Implications for mainstream instruction 5(T)

Electricity Activities
see Magnetism and Electricity Activities

Emergency Procedures
see Safety

Emotional Disturbance (SEH) 27-33
Adaptations for activities
animals 262
powders, mixtures, and solutions 273
rocks, minerals, and fossils 279
weather 277
Affect and social behavior 2
Attributes/characteristics 28-29
academic deficiency 29
affect 2, 28, 29
aggression 28, 29
attention 2
knowledge base 29
motor (gross and fine) 2
psychosomatic illness 28
social behavior 2, 28, 29
withdrawal 28
Definition 27T
exclusions 27(T)
Field trips 99
Incidence 28
Laboratory activity recommendations 31-33, 32T,
227-229, 232, 238, 239-242, 243-244, 250, 253, 256,
265-267, 274, 277-278, 279-280, 284, 300
alternative activities 32T
awareness of fears 32(T)
behavior contingencies 31, 32T, 72
peer assistant 31, 32(T)
Mainstreaming techniques 29-31, 30T
behavior management 29-30T
classroom rules 29
peer cooperation 30(T)
positive environment 29, 30T
resource personnel 30T
Peer assistance 98-99
Safety 31, 32T, 99, 233
see also Learning Disabilities

Enthusiasm 75T, 140, 141, 193-194(T)
Learning disabilities
teacher presentation 10

Environmental Activities
Animals 259T, 261-263
Landforms 283-284
Mapping 243-245
Plants 258T, 260-261

Water 269-271
Weather 277-278

Epilepsy 56T
see Health Impairments

Evaluation (assessment)
see Testing

Exhibits/Demonstrations 168, 194-195(T), 217-225, 257
Accessibility 61
Demonstration videotaped 220T
Enrichment activity 217
Hearing impaired 221-222
Large group demonstration 217
Learning Disabilities 222-223(T)
mainstreaming techniques 10
Outdoor considerations 225
Physical disabilities 219(T)-220
Possibilities 218T
Preparation/planning
facility 217-223
students 223-225
Speakers 218, 222
Teacher guidelines 223-225, 224T
Visual impairments 49, 52, 220(T)-221

F

Field Trips 96, 98, 99, 217-225(T)
Behavioral expectations 219T
Hearing needs 219T, 221-222(T)
Learning needs 219T, 222-223(T)
Medical needs 219T, 223
Mobility requirements 219(T), 220T, 223
Museums 96, 98, 99, 182, 205, 206T, 209, 210,
212(T), 213
curators 218
docents 218, 219, 220
outdoor activities 225
science 194, 218T
special tours 217
Planetarium 286
Previsit 217
Student preparation 223-225, 224T
Tour guides 218, 219(T), 220, 221, 222, 223
Transportation 223
Visual needs 219T, 220(T)-221
Zoos 217, 218T, 257, 261

Force and Motion Activities 291-294
Adaptations for 292-294
computer programs 293
forces 292
material handling 292
material substitution 292
simple machines 292
visually impaired 292-293

Force and Motion Activities (cont.)
Adaptive equipment
  braille descriptions 294
  braille laboratory booklets 294
  braille spring scale system 292
  clamps 292
  closed circuit television 293
  clothesline pulley system 292
  computer program, Miner's Cave 293
  descriptive video 294
  glue dots 294
  grasping, adaptive devices for 292
  lego materials 293
  light sensor 292
  magnets 294
  raised line paper 294
  slatted trays 293
  string 293
  toys 292
  textured materials 294
  three dimensional models 294
Additional time 291
Recommendations 291-292
Types of activities 291

FOSS (Full Option Science System) 78(T), 80T, 82, 87T, 89, 113
Cooperative learning model 78(T)
Mock Rocks 279
Pouring activity 233
Sample lesson 80T
Student accountability 82

G

Gas Activities
see Solids/Liquids/Gases Activities

Graphic Organizers 176-178T

Graphing Data 25, 81
see also Charting and Graphing

Groups
Effective instruction 76
Group oriented 10
Group size 86
Jigsaw components 85T, 86, 87, 89
Laboratory 238
Roles 18(T), 31, 78T-85, 80T, 81T, 83T, 84T
Suggestions for
  communication disorders 18(T)
  emotional disturbances 31, 32T
  hearing impairment 44
  learning disabilities 10
see also Cooperative Learning

Guided Practice 76
General disability characteristics
  effective instructional technique 5(T)

H

Hard of Hearing 35
see also Hearing Impaired

Head Injury 56T
see also Physical Disabilities

Headpointers 211

Health and Hygiene
see Human Anatomy/Health

Health Impairments 55-64
Definitions 55, 56T
Epilepsy 56T, 62(T)
Incidence 55
Medical considerations 57(T), 62(T)
  diabetic coma 57T
  insulin shock 57T
  medication 57T
  seizures 57T, 62(T)
Resources 55
see also Physical Disabilities

Hearing Impairment 35-44
Attributes/characteristics
  academic achievement 36-37
  intellectual/cognitive 1-2, 36
  language 1, 36
  social 37
Auditory accessibility 202T
Causes of 36
Classroom environment 122-123
Closed caption 38, 97
Communication
  feigning comprehension 41
  hearing aid 38, 39
  intercom 41, 96
  interpreter 42
  lip-reading 36, 39
  oral communication 36
  sign language 41
  speech reader 36, 39(T)
  total communication 36, 42
  wireless FM 38
Computer adaptive devices 212-213
Cooperative learning 44, 78, 89, 90T
Definition
  adventitious (acquired) 36
  congenital 36
  deaf 35-36
  hard of hearing 35-36
  prelingual 36
  postlingual 36
Diagnosis 35(T)-36
  decibels (dB) 35
  frequency 35
  Hertz (Hz) 35
  pure-tone audiometer 35
Evaluation adaptations 118

Hearing Impairment (cont.)
  Fatigue 41, 96
  Field trip/demonstration needs 97, 221-222(T)
  Groups 44, 78, 89, 90T
  Incidence 36
  Instructional media modifications/accessibility
      200-203T, 206
  Interpreter 42, 221-222(T)
    use in testing 42
  Laboratory activity recommendations 44(T), 96,
      227-229, 236-238, 240, 241-242, 253, 256, 265-267,
      274, 275, 283, 290, 299-300
    animals 262
    classifying 240
    earth science (landforms) 283
    human anatomy 256
    light and color 299
    magnetism and electricity 290
    observing 239
    physics of sound 295-296
    powders, mixtures, and solutions 275
    water 269
  Levels of 35T, 36
  Listening partners 41
  Mainstreaming techniques 38-43T, 39T, 40T
    classroom organization 38-39, 43T
    reading strategies 161, 163, 165, 168, 169
    vocabulary 40(T), 247
    teacher presentation 39-42, 40T, 43T
    testing 42, 43T
  Manipulability and task performance 203T
  Myths 42
  Note-taking, study skills strategies 183
  Peer assistant 39, 42, 44, 96-97, 163
  Safety 42, 95, 96, 97
  Source of attention problem 139
  Speech and language services 15
  Students with low hearing 202T
  Use of mnemonics with 137
  Visual accessibility 201T

Highlighting Skills 166T, 170T, 171, 172

Human Anatomy/Health Activities 255-256
  Adaptations for 255-256
    anatomical illustrations, models, specimens 256
    assembling human body models 256
    body image 255
    pulse rate 256
    vocabulary 255
  Adaptive equipment 255-256
    anatomical illustrations, models, specimens 256
    braille labels 256
    "Dudley" Me Now Series 256
    language cards 255
    mirrors 255
    photographs 255
    raised labels 256
    sand in paint or glue 256
    working model of anatomy 256
  Body image 255

  Models, use of 256
  Pulse rate 256
  Vocabulary 255

Hydrocephalus 56T
  see also Physical Disabilities

Hyperactivity 8
  see also Emotional Disturbance
  see also Learning Disabilities

I

IEP (Individualized Education Plan) 99
  Implications for mainstream instruction 3
  Special education teacher as resource 68(T)

Illustrations 176, 178T, 184(T)
  Hearing impairments
    laboratory techniques 44(T)
    mainstreaming techniques 39, 43T
  Journals 176
  Learning disabilities
    teacher presentation 10, 12T
  Log booklets 176
  Mental retardation
    laboratory techniques 24
    mainstreaming techniques 21, 23T
  Multi-textured materials 176
  Skills for studying illustrations 184(T)
  3-D 176

Instructional Delivery
  see Presentation/Delivery
  see Presentation Format

Instructional Media 199(T)-207
  Accessibility 200-203T
  Audiotapes 199T, 204, 205
  Compact discs 199T
  Computers
    see Computers
  Descriptive video 50
  Films 199T, 200, 205
  Filmstrips 199T, 204
  Language cards 1, 11, 18, 21, 39, 40, 43T, 135, 228,
      236, 255, 276
  Learning centers 200
  Legos 293
  Media centers 206
  Me Now 256
  Mock rocks 279
  Modifications 204-207, 205T
    advance organizers 205(T)
    outlines 205T, 206
    peers 205T, 207
    preview 205(T)
    review 205T, 207
    summaries 205T, 206

Instructional Media (cont.)
Mr. Wizard videotapes 194
Overhead transparency 204, 205, 206
Photocopied 204, 206
Slides 199T, 204
Software 202, 204
Miner's Cave 282
Sticky Bear 244
Voyage of the Mimi 206, 244, 278, 286
Voyage of the Mimi II 205, 213
see Computer (software)
Videodiscs 199T, 204
Videos 199T, 204, 205
Wisconsin Fast Plants 260

Instructional Objective 213, 214T, 227, 228T, 266, 269, 274, 292

Invention and Discovery Activities 247-250
Adaptations for
thinking and reasoning skills 247-250

J

Jigsaw Procedure 85T, 86, 87, 89, 252

Joystick 211(T)

K

Keywords 148(P)-153(P)
Abstract concept learning 152(P)
Attribute illustration 152(P)
Building on one another 151(P)
Interaction with each other 148-149(P)
Word part learning 150(P)

Kit Activities
see Model and Kit Activities

Kurtzweil Reading Machine 163

L

Laboratory Techniques 13(T), 18(T), 24-26(T), 227-229
Demonstration 44, 51
Directions/steps 13(T), 24, 26T, 44(T)
outline 44
Groups 18, 44
roles 18
see also Cooperative Learning
Materials (apparatus) 13(T), 31, 52, 53(T)
Peer assistance 23T, 24, 44, 51
Self-monitoring 13, 24
Structured questioning and directions 25(T)
see also each specific disability listings

Landform Activities
see Earth Science Activities

Language
Communication devices 60
Language cards 11, 18, 39, 236, 255, 276
Strategies
mnemonics 18, 146-159, 245
vocabulary 11-12, 18
Suggestions for
communication disorders 17-18
hearing impaired 1, 36, 137
learning disabilities 1
visually impaired 1, 45
Verbalisms 50
see also Vocabulary

Language Cards 11, 18, 39, 236, 255, 276

Language Disorders
see Communication Disorders

Learning Disabilities 7-13
Adaptations for activities
animals 262
graphing 236-237
mapping 244-245
rocks, minerals, and fossils 279
Attention and memory 2
Attributes/characteristics 8-9
academic problems 8
attention 2, 8
behavior 9, 10
generalization/application 9
hyperactivity 8
impulsivity 13
memory 2, 8, 11
motor (gross and fine) 2
reading disability 9
Classroom environment 123
Computer adaptive devices 200
Cooperative learning 78, 80, 90T
Definition 7
Discovery learning 247-250
Discrepancy 8
Evaluation adaptations 117, 118
Field trip/demonstration 99, 222-223(T)
Identification 8
Incidence 7, 8
Instructional media adaptations 206, 237-238, 278
Laboratory activity recommendations 13(T), 227-229, 236-238, 239-242, 243-244, 253, 256, 265-267, 270, 274, 278, 279-280, 284
Mainstreaming techniques 9-12
classroom organization 9-10, 12T
teacher presentation 10-11, 12T
tests 11, 12T
text adaptations 9
Note-taking and study strategies 183, 278

Learning Disabilities (cont.)
Peer assistants 98-99
note-taking 98
oral reporting 98
reading 98
writing 98
Reading adaptations 152T-166T
Related terms/labels 7T
Science project preparations 174
Speech-language services 15
Student affect 257

Letter Strategies
Acronyms 157-158P
Acrostics 158(T)-159(T)

Library Specialist
see Media Specialist

Life Science Activities
Activities for
animals 259T, 260T, 261-263
human anatomy 255-256
microscopes 267-268
plants 258T, 260-261

Light and Color Activities 299-300
Adaptations for
concepts and language 299
fear of dark 300
visually impaired 299-300
Adaptive equipment
closed circuit television 300
heat lamp 300
high intensity lights 300
light sensor 300
magnifying lenses 300
mirrors 300
ribbons 300
Types of activities 299

Light Sensor 53, 240, 275, 292, 298, 300

Linear Measurement 234
Adaptations for
peer assistants 234
repeated measurements 234
rulers, use of 234
Adaptive equipment
braille rulers 234
large print rulers 234
measuring wheels 234
rubber band around dowel 234

Listening Center 165

Listening Guide 180, 181

Liquid Activities
see Solids/Liquids/Gases Activities

Low Vision
see Visually Impaired

M

Magnetism and Electricity Activities 289-290
Adaptations for
adapting circuits for visually impaired 289
attaching wires 289
construction of magnetic wire core 290
demonstration of physically disabled student's
electrical equipment 289
electric circuits 290
electric motor for hearing impaired 289
magnetic force activities 289, 290
telegraph activities 290
Adaptive equipment
alligator clips 289
iron filings 290
paper flag for electric motor 290
stethoscope 290
Types of activities 289

Magnifying Lamps 163

Magnifying Lenses 163, 220T, 244, 254, 276, 280, 299
For standard monitor screens 198T

Mainstreaming 3-6, 9-12, 17-18, 21-24, 29-31,
57(T)-59(T), 58T
Implications 3-4
expectations 3
IEP 3
individual 3
rewards 4, 74
Modifications and adaptations for 69, 70, 71
Techniques 5(T)
communication disorders 17-18
computer use 201-204
emotional disturbance 29-30(T)
hearing impairments 38-43(T)
learning disabilities 9-12
mental retardation 21-24, 23T
objectives 6, 64
physical disabilities 57(T)-59(T), 58T
redundancy 6, 10, 26, 75T
visually impaired 47-51(T)
Time and Resource Management 65-71
community resources 71(T)
school resources 69, 70T
special education teacher 68(T)
university resources 70(T)
see also Time and Resource Management

Manual Grasp 62, 64, 254
Gripping pencil 62
Handling cards 63
Securing paper 62
Velcro use 64, 254

Mapping Activities 243-245
  Adaptations for
    audiotaped description 244
    computer simulations 244
    landforms 244
    map symbols 245
    orienting and mobility instructor 243
    relationship of map symbol to landform 245
    safety 243
    type of map 244
  Adaptive equipment
    audiotaped description 244
    braille map 244
    closed circuit television 244
    computer simulation programs 244
    foam rubber 243
    high-contrast, enlarged illustrations 244
    illuminated globes 244
    lights 244
    magnifying lenses 244
    measuring wheel 243
    mnemonic illustrations 245
    overhead transparency 244
    raised-surface globe 244
    relief maps 244
    simplified topographic map 244
    tape 243
    tracing paper 244
    two-dimensional maps 245

Measuring Wheel 234, 243

Media Specialist
  As mainstreaming resource 69

Memory 2, 20, 145-160
  Causes of problems 145
  Learning disabilities
    characteristics 8
    mainstreaming techniques 10-11, 12T
  Mental retardation
    mainstreaming techniques 20
  Strategies for improvement 145-147
    mnemonic strategies 147-160

Mental Retardation 19-26
  Adaptations for activities
    animals 262
    charting and graphing 237-238
    earth science (landforms) 283
    human anatomy 256
    invention and discovery 247
    magnetism and electricity 290
    mapping 244
    predicting 241-242
    rocks, minerals, and fossils 279-280
    scales and balances 233-234
    water 270
    weather 278
  Attention and memory 2
  Attributes/characteristics 20-21
    academic skills 20

affect 2, 240
appearance 20
attention 2, 21
generalization 21
intellectual/cognitive 1-2, 19-20
language 1, 20
memory 2, 20
motor (gross and fine) 2, 21
social behaviors 2, 21, 250
frustration 21
Auditory accessibility 202T
Classroom environment 122, 123
Computer adaptive devices 212-213
Cooperative learning 89, 90
Definition 19(T)
  adaptive behavior 19(T)
Discovery learning 247-250
Field trip/demonstration 89, 222-223(T)
Identification 19-20
Incidence 19
Instructional media adaptations 206, 227
Laboratory recommendations 24-26(T), 227-229, 233, 234, 239-242, 243-244, 253, 256, 265-267, 274-278, 279-280, 284
  direct instruction 25
  "discovery" method demands 25, 26T
  open ended question 25, 26
  structured questioning 25(T)
Levels 20T
  mild 20(T), 21
  moderate 20(T), 26
  profound 20(T), 26
  severe 20(T), 26
Mainstreaming techniques 21-24
  teaching 21-24, 23T
  testing 23T, 24
Manipulability and task performance
  accessibility 203T
Mild mental disabilities
  peer assistance 100
Note-taking adaptations 183
Peer assistants 21, 24, 25, 26T, 98-99, 100
Reading adaptations 165, 169
Related terms/labels 19
Science project preparation strategies 185-186
Severe disabilities 101
Speech-language services 15
Visual accessibility 201T

Microscope Activities 265-268
  Adaptations for 267-268
    additional time 268
    manipulation equipment 267
    photographs, use of 268
    staining slides 267
    use of 265
    visually impaired 268
  Adaptive equipment
    alternative to standard microscopes 267
    braille descriptions 268
    braille laboratory booklets 268
    Brock microscope 267

Microscope Activities (cont.)
    closed circuit television 267
    descriptive video 268
    microprojector 267
    microscope clamps 267
    projecting microscope 53, 166, 265, 267, 268
    raised line paper 268
    slatted trays 267
    specimen photographs 268
    textured materials 268
    three-dimensional models 268
  Recommendations 265-267
  Uses of 265

Microscopes 265-268
  Adaptations 267-268
  Brock microscope 267, 268P
  Projection microscope 53, 166, 267, 268
  Recommendations 265-267
  Stereoscopes 265, 267
    uses of 265

Miner's Cave
  see Instructional Media

Mixture Activities
  see Powders, Mixtures, and Solutions Activities

Mnemonics 18, 235
  Comprehension 147
  Mental retardation 22
  Techniques 146-147
  Strategies 147-160, 171
    alternatives to teacher drawn pictures 160T
    keyword method 148(P)-153
    letter strategies 157-159(T)
    pegword method 153(T)-157(T)
    time saving suggestions 160T
    use with graphic organizer 176

Mobility Aids
  see Physical Disabilities

Mobility 85, 87, 207

Model and Kit Activities 251-254
  Adaptations for
    additional time to work 254
    designated drying areas 254
    glue, use of 254
    how-to-handle directions 253
    magnifying devices 253
    painting 254
    planning 251-252
    textured materials 254
  Adaptive equipment
    Big Eye Lamps 254
    clamps 253
    clay 253
    glue sticks 254
    magnifying devices 254

    sand and glue 254
    snap together models 254
    textured material 254
    velcro gloves 254
    velcro strips 254

Models 256, 294

Motion Activities
  see Force and Motion Activities

Motivation 10, 13, 165, 169, 191-198, 213, 216, 265
  Emotionally disturbed 29
  Kits and models 251
  Mental retardation 24
  Microscopes 265
  Plants and animals 257
  Successful experiences 24, 29

Muscular Dystrophy 56T
  see also Physical Disabilities

N

Note-taking Skills 179-189, 206

O

Observations 239-240
  Adaptations for
    color 240
    guided prompting 239
    low vision 240
    sense of touch, cheek 240
    sense used and information obtained 240
    systematic questioning, review, summaries 239
    verbal description 240
    vibrations 240
  Adaptive equipment 240
    bright lights 240
    closed circuit television 240, 261
    FM system with stethoscope/tuning fork 240
    light sensor 240
    magnifying lenses 240, 261

Opticon 163

Opticon II 210T

Oral Reading 163, 165

Organizations and Companies
  American Association of Mental Retardation (AAMR) 19
  American Foundation for the Blind 234
  American Printing House for the Blind 52, 162, 163, 233, 292
  American Speech-Language-Hearing Association (ASHA) 15

Organizations and Companies (cont.)
  Bank Street College of Education 205
  Brock 267
  Carolina Biological Supply Company 260
  Children's Press 163
  Delta 234
  Hubbard 256
  IBM - National Support Center for Persons with
    Disabilities 209
  Icom Designs 199
  FOSS 232, 233, 279, 291
  Lawrence Hall of Science 232, 262, 277
  Library of Congress 162
  Mesa Public Schools, Arizona 195
  National Science Resource Center 176, 235
  Phoenix Learning Resources 163
  Prentke Romich Company 64
  Public Television 169
  SAVI/SELPH 232
  Steck Vaughn Publications 163
  Wendall Foster 64
  see also Appendix B: Related Organizations and
    Resources

Orthopedic Handicap
  see Physical Disabilities

Oscilloscope 296

Osteoarthritis 56T
  see also Physical Disabilities

Osteogenesis Imperfecta 56T, 58
  see also Physical Disabilities

Osteomyelitis 56T
  see also Physical Disabilities

Outlining 178T, 179-181, 183-184T, 205T, 206
  Learning disabilities
    teacher presentations 10

Overhead Projector 10, 17, 41, 43T, 140, 141, 146, 148, 165, 180T, 181, 199T, 200, 204, 206

P

Page Turners 164, 212

Partitioned Trays 232, 263, 267, 280, 293

Parents
  As mainstreaming resource 71(T)
  Conferences 3
  Behavior contracts 130

Passive Behavior
  Cooperative learning 79, 81, 89
  see also Behavior

Peer Assistance 80T, 83-91, 109, 171, 174, 185, 213, 214T, 215(T), 228, 232, 240, 253, 266, 270, 271, 273, 276, 291
  Audio-visuals 96-97, 205T, 207
  Benefits for students with disabilities 95-99
  Definition 93
  Emergency procedures 95
  Field trips 96, 97, 98, 99
  Fine motor difficulties 238, 267, 268, 276, 293
  Implementation 94-95(T)
  In activities 228
    assembling 253
    charting and graphing 235, 238
    chemicals, use of 273
    classification 240
    force and motion 291-292
    landforms 284
    magnetism and electricity 289
    measuring and pouring 232, 234
    microscopes 266, 267
    observing 239
    powders, mixtures, solutions 276
    water activities 270
  Manipulation 87, 239, 253, 266, 276, 291-292
  Mobility 95, 97
  Observations 239, 266
  Oral presentation 96, 98
  Peer notes 183
  Peer secretaries 89, 98
  Practice opportunities 98, 207, 215(T)
  Reading 96, 98, 163, 165, 174, 177
    taped textbooks 163, 164, 165
  Recording data 64, 238
  Secretarial tasks 64, 96, 97, 98
  Special consideration 99-100T
  Suggestions for
    communication disorders 18
    emotionally disturbed 30(T), 31, 98-99
    hearing impaired 39, 41, 44(T), 96-97, 163
    learning disabled 9, 98-99
    mental retardation 21, 23T, 24-25, 26T, 98-99, 253
    physical disabilities 58, 59T, 61(T), 64(T), 94, 95T, 97-98, 253, 284
    visually impaired 51, 52, 53T, 93, 94, 95- 96, 239, 238, 253
  Training 84, 85
  Use in increasing attention 131

Peer Tutoring 101-108(T), 102(T), 103T, 104(T), 105(T), 107T, 171, 215(T), 228, 232, 253, 266, 276, 291-292
  Suggestions for
    emotional disturbances 32(T)
    hearing impairments 39
    learning disabilities 10
    mental retardation 26(T)
  Training 103T-105(T), 104(T)
  With textbook and activities oriented approaches 106-108(T), 107T

Pegwords 153(T)-157
    Combined with keywords 155(P)-156(P)
    Numbers eleven to nineteen 156(P)
    Numbers greater than twenty 157(P)
    Use with ordered information 154-155(P)

Physical Disabilities 55-64
    Accessibility 58-61
        aisles 60
        auditory 190T
        class 56, 60-61
        computers 61
        curbs, stairs 61
        displays 61
        door knobs 61
        exhibits 61
        floor surface 60
        materials 58, 61(T)
        restrooms 61
        teacher presentations 61
        water fountains 61
    Adaptive devices 55
        communication 63
        felt boards 64
        flap switches 64
        little octopus suction holders 64
        magnetic boards 64
        manual grasp 61
        orthotics 55
        positioning 58
        prosthetics 55, 59T
        reachers 64
        reading 63
        suction disks 64
        wedges 55
        writing tasks 62
    Attributes/characteristics 56T
        attention 56T
        behaviors 56T
        intellectual/cognitive 1, 56T
        language 1, 16, 56T
        mental retardation 56T
        motor (fine) 2, 56T
        motor (gross) 2, 56T
    Auditory accessibility 202T
    Classroom environment 122
    Communication 57
    Communication boards 63
    Comprehension strategy adaptations 163
    Computer adaptive devices 211(T)-212
        speech synthesizers 63
        text reader 169, 210T
        voice recognition 212
    Cooperative learning 78, 80, 89, 90T, 97
    Definitions 56T
        arthrogryposis 56T
        cerebral palsy 56T
        head injury 56T
        hydrocephalus 56T
        meningomyelocele 56T
        muscular dystrophy 56T
        myelomeningocele 56T

        osteoarthritis 56T
        osteogenesis imperfecta 56T, 58
        osteomyelitis 56T
        rheumatoid arthritis 56T
        scoliosis 56T
        spina bifida 56T
    Field trip/demonstration 98, 219(T)-220, 223
    Fine motor skills (disabilities) 97, 98, 117, 238, 253,
        268, 276, 293
    Gross motor skills 98
    Incidences 55
    Instructional media accessibility 188, 191T
    Instructional media adaptations 62-64(T), 194
    Laboratory suggestions 63-64(T), 227-229, 234, 237,
            240-242, 253-254, 256, 261-263, 265-267,
            270-271, 274, 276, 284, 289-298
        accessibility 60(P)-61(P), 63-64(T)
            heights 63-64(T)
            stabilizing equipment 63-64(T)
        classifying 241
        earth science (landforms) 284
        force and motion 291-292
        graphing 238
        human anatomy 256
        magnetism and electricity 289, 290
        mapping 243
        measuring 234
        microscope use 267
        mobility 63-64(T)
        observing 239
        peer assistants 64(T)
            recording data 64
            secretarial tasks 64
        plants and animals 261, 261-262, 263
        powders, mixtures, and solutions 273
        predicting 241-242
        recording 263
        rocks, minerals and fossils 284
        solids, liquids, gases 298
        water 270, 271
        weather 277
        utilize adaptive material 64
        see also Stabilize Materials
    Mainstreaming techniques 57(T)-59T, 58(T)
        access 58, 60(P)-61(P), 201T, 202T, 203T
        medical considerations 57(T), 59T, 62(T)
        mobility 59(T)
        nonmedical considerations 58(T), 59, 63
        student (peer) assistants 58
    Manipulability and task performance needs 63, 203T
    Medical considerations 57(T)
    Mobility aids 57, 58, 59T
        braces 59T
        cane 59T
        crutches 59T
        prothesis 59T
        special shoes 59T
        walking chair 59T
        wheelchair 59T, 60(P)-61(P), 219
    Motor difficulties 199
    Nonmedical considerations 58(T)
        communication 57

Physical Disabilities (cont.)
    positions 57
    self-care help 57
    transportation/movement 57
  Note-taking, study skills 171, 174
  Peer assistants 57, 58, 59T, 64(T), 94, 95T, 97-98
    field trips 98
    manipulations (fine motor) 97, 234, 239, 270
    materials (dangerous) 97
    mobility 97-98
    secretarial 98
  Resources 55, 57
  Safety 57, 58(T), 59T, 60, 61, 62(T), 97, 98, 243
  Seizures 57T, 59T, 62
  Source of attention problem 139
  Visual accessibility 201T

Physical Science
  Assembling kits or models 251
  Force and motion 291
  Light and color 299
  Magnetism and electricity 289
  Powders, mixtures, and solutions 273
  Solids, liquids, and gases 297
  Sound 295
  Water 269

Plant Activities 260-261
  Adaptations for
    length of time 260
    observing 261
    planting seeds 261
    separating seeds 261
    recording growth 261
    reinforce stems 261
    visually impaired and sunlight 261
    watering 260
  Adaptive equipment
    braille numbers 261
    clay models 261
    closed circuit television 261
    magnifying lenses 261
    plant sticks and wire ties 261
    raised line graphs 261
    rubber band around dowel 261
    screenboard 261
    sorting trays 261
    syringe 260
    Wisconsin Fast Plants 260
  Commonly used species 257-258
  Practice, need for 260-261
  Process skills needed 257
  Selecting and keeping plants 258T
  Student self-esteem 257

Positioning 58, 63
  wedges 58

Positive Feedback 94, 140, 191-193(T), 196
  Behavior management 114T
  Mental retardation,
    mainstreaming techniques 24
  Reinforce attending 140

Pouring 232-234, 260

Pouring Activities 232-234
  Adaptations for 232-233
    scooping water 232
    spills 232
    supervision 232
  Adaptive equipment
    funnel 232
    paper towels 232
    partitioned trays 232
    plastic tub 232
    popcorn 232
    receptacle anchors 232
    rice 232
    solid volume indicator 232
    syringes 232

Powder, Mixture, and Solution Activities 273-276
  Adaptations for 274-276
    concept development 276
    cooperative learning 276
    heating substances 276
    labeling containers 275-276
    peer assistant 276
    pouring activities 276
    senses, use of all 274-275
    spills 276
    tactile observation of filtering & dissolving 276
    visually impaired 276
  Adaptive equipment 275-276
    Big Eye Lamp 276
    braille descriptions 276
    coffee stirrers 276
    color-coded containers 276
    descriptive video or audiotape 276
    funnels 276
    language cards 276
    light sensor 275
    magnifying lenses 276
    microphone 275
    sand 276
    simplified balances 276
    spoon handles 276
    strainers with handles 276
    syringes 276
    weights 275
  Color coding 275
  Dissolving 275
  Filtering 275
  Funnels, use of 276
  Recommendations 273-276
  Recording observations 275
  Spills 275
  Use of hearing 275
  Use of touch 275
  Uses 273

Prediction Activities 241-242
  Inferences 241
  Relevant variables 242
  Testing of 241

Presentation/Delivery 5(T), 10, 63-65(T), 81T, 96, 191-193(T), 213
  Activities/hands-on 10, 13, 30, 195, 203T, 227-229
    see also specific activity types
  Computer assisted 213, 214(T)
  Cooperative learning
    see Cooperative Learning
  Demonstration 10, 40T, 44, 48(T), 194-195, 217-225
    auditory accessibility 202T
    describing 48T
    rate of presentation 222(T)
    visibility 38, 39T, 41, 201T
  Discovery 25, 26(T)
  Discussion 10, 12T
    pictures, tables, and diagrams 10, 21, 39, 40T, 41, 165
  Enthusiasm 10, 193-194(T)
  Lecture 179-181
    auditory accessibility 202T
    concrete example use 21, 40T, 50, 168
    new information 64-65(T)
    rate of presentation 112, 222(T)
    visibility 38, 39T, 41, 201T
  Nonverbal cues 41
  Question and Answer 17, 25(T)-26, 40-41, 46T
  Suggestions for
    communication disorders 17(T)
    emotional disturbances 30
    hearing impairment 38T, 39-43(T), 221-222(T)
    learning disabilities 10-11, 12(T), 222-223(T)
    mental retardation 21-24, 222-223(T)
    physical disabilities 219(T), 223
    visual impairment 48(T)-50, 49T, 220(T)-221
  Textbook-oriented
    see Textbook-Oriented Approaches

Presentation Format 49T, 122(T)-123, 162(T)-172(P)
  Alternatives 162(T)-172(P)
    advance organizers 162T, 170
    audio formats 162T, 164-165
    audio-visual demonstrations 162T, 169-170(T)
    computer programs 162T, 169
    concrete manipulatives 10, 21, 23T, 162T, 168
    illustrations 11, 12(T), 162T, 165-166
    modified printed materials 162(T)-164
    pictures, maps, diagrams 10, 21, 41, 162T, 166-167
    preview/preteach text/media organization 162T, 171, 179-180(T), 183-184(T), 205(T)
    preview/preteach vocabulary and concepts 10-11, 39, 41, 162T, 171, 231
    summary charts and tables 11, 12(T), 162T, 167-168
    see also specific activity types
  Instructional media 199-207
    audio-visuals 10, 21, 22, 38, 41, 49, 50
  Suggestions for
    communication disorders 18
    emotionally disturbed 31, 32T
    hearing impairments 38, 39(T), 41, 42, 43(T), 163, 165
    learning disabilities 9, 10, 11, 12T
    mental retardation 21, 22, 23T
    physical disabilities 164

    students with reading difficulties 163, 164, 165
    visual impairments 162, 163, 164, 165
  Testing
    see Testing
  see also Mnemonics
  see also Language Cards

Preview/Preteach
  Concepts 39, 162T, 171, 231
  Suggestions for
    hearing impairments 38, 39, 43T
  Text organization 162T, 171
  Vocabulary 10-11, 162T, 171, 231

R

Radios 199T

Reading 63, 89, 161-178
  Adaptive equipment
    page turner 63, 164
    tape recorded text 9, 163, 164, 165
  Comprehension enhancement 162-177
  Demands
    textbook approach 9, 87
  Hearing impairment 37
  Learning disabilities 8, 9, 12(T)
  Peer assistants 96, 163, 164, 165
  Presentation format modification 10, 162(T)-172
  Students with difficulties 163, 164, 165
  Visual impairment 50, 96
  see also Text Adaptations

"Rebus" Writing 165

Regular Education Teacher
  As mainstreaming resource 69(T)

Resource Management
  see Mainstreaming

Response Format 117, 118T, 119, 122(T), 162
  Computers 117
  Oral reports 117
  Performance-based measure 117, 118T
  Secretaries 117, 118T
  Tape recordings 117, 118T

Reviewing 5T, 10, 21, 73, 165, 207, 218, 224, 231
  Learning Disabilities 8, 10-11
  Suggestions for
    hearing impairments 38, 39, 41, 44
    mental retardation 21, 26T

Reward System 91T, 196, 198, 216
  Attending 125
  Group systems 126(T), 136, 137
  Individual accountability 84, 86
  Token system 133, 134T

Rheumatoid Arthritis 56
see also Physical Disabilities

Robotic Workstation Attendant 212

Rocks, Minerals, and Fossils 279-281
Adaptations for 279-281
commercial samples 280
"mock rock" activities 279
models of sedimentary rocks 279
visually impaired 280, 281
Adaptive equipment
braille labels 280
closed circuit television 280
magnifying lenses 280
overhead projector 281
plaster of paris 280
segmented trays 280
Types of activities 279

Role-Play 79, 80T, 99, 100T, 104T
Hearing impairments
mainstreaming techniques 40, 41, 43T
Social skills 223-224

S

Safety 94, 95, 223, 273-274, 277, 279
Bomb scare 47
Fire 42, 47, 58
Laboratory safety
chemicals 273-274
fear of dark 300
fear of getting wet 233
heat sources 273-274, 276
microscopes 265
safety contract 81T
sharp edges 243
Peer assistants 95
Suggestions for
emotional disturbance 31, 32T, 99, 233, 288
hearing impaired 42, 95, 96, 97
learning disabilities 13, 99
physically disabled 57(T), 58(T), 59T, 60-61, 62(T), 97, 98, 223, 243
students with behavior problems 277, 279
visually impaired 47, 49T, 95, 96, 243, 273-274
Tornado 42, 47, 58

Scales and Balance Activities 233-234
Adaptations for
counting small objects 234
pretraining specific skills 233
Adaptive equipment
braille spring scale 233
large, simple balances 233
plastic guide at scale 233

Science Skills/Processes Activities
Assembling kits and models 251-254, 252T
Charting, graphing, recording data 235-238
Classification 240-241
Discovery 247-250
Invention 247-250, 249T
Mapping 243-245
Measuring 231
Observation 239-240
Pouring 232
Prediction 241-242

Science Projects
Procedure checklist 185T
Strategies for 185-186

Science Specialist 69

Scoliosis 54T
see also Physical Disabilities

SCREAM 5T, 74, 75T

SEH
see Emotional Disturbance

Seizures 62(T), 223

Self-Monitoring 127T, 130-133T, 131T, 132T, 142-143(T), 173,174
Suggestions for
learning disabilities 13
mental retardation 24

Self-Questioning 172-173, 178T, 183

Self-Recording 142(T)-143(T)

Senior Citizens
As mainstreaming resource 71(T)

Sensory Impairments (disabilities)
Cooperative learning 89
Peer assistance 94
Test-taking strategies 186
see also Hearing Impairments
see also Physical Disabilities
see also Visual Impairments

Severe Emotional Handicap (SEH)
see Emotional Disturbance

Slate and Stylus 162, 183

Social Skills 81, 91T, 99, 100T, 108T, 223-224
Behavior problems 73, 79
Emotional disturbance 31
Hearing impairments
characteristics 37
Learning disabled 9

Social Skills (cont.)
  Mental retardation
    laboratory techniques 21, 24, 26T
  Social acceptance 2, 9, 21, 37
  Social behavior 89, 100
  Social interaction 2, 9, 21, 24, 26T, 29, 31, 82, 94, 95T, 99, 100T, 107T, 108T, 223-224

Solids/Liquids/Gases Activities 297-298
  Adaptations for 297-298
    physically handicapped 298
    states of matter 297
    visually impaired 297
  Adaptive equipment
    braille thermometer 297
    ice cubes 297
    light sensor 298
    raised line thermometer 297
    stethoscope 298
  Types of activities 297

Solution Activities
  see Powders, Mixtures, and Solutions Activities

Sound Activities 295-296
  Adaptations for
    hearing impaired 295-296
    pitch and volume 295
    vibrations, observations 295, 296
    visually impaired 295
  Adaptive equipment
    amplifying devices 295
    bell system in vacuum chamber 296
    oscilloscope 296
    piano 296
    rubber bands and gongs 295
    tactile markers 296
    tuning fork 296
    watch spring 295

Speech and Language Difficulties
  Computer adaptive devices 212-213
  see also Communication Disabilities

Speech-Language Teacher 16, 17

Speech Disorders
  see Communication Disorders

Speech Synthesizer 16, 18, 210T

Spina Bifida 56T
  see also Physical Disabilities

Stabilizing Materials 62, 64, 232, 237
  Felt pads 64
  Slatted trays 64
  Velcro 64, 232

Student Attribution
  Negative 196-198, 197T
  Positive 196-198, 197T
  see also Motivation and Affect

Study Skills 78, 177, 178T, 183-184(T)

Summarizing 165
  Peer assistant 163
  Student 185-186
  Teacher 206

Syringe 232, 276

T

Talking Telephone Directories 210T

Tape Recorder/Player 164, 165, 173, 175, 186, 200, 204, 294

Teacher Effectiveness Variables 171

Team Teaching 68(T)

Television 199T, 204

Test-Taking Skills 186-189(T)
  Learning disabilities 11, 12T
  Objective tests 186-187(T)
  Promoting test-taking skills 11, 12T, 118, 177, 178T
  Short answer and essay 188-189(T)

Testing (evaluation) 11, 109-119
  Accountability 83
  Adaptations for students with disabilities 109, 116-119
    alteration of written format 117
    charts 11, 12T
    extra time 11, 12T, 23T, 24, 50, 51T, 83, 117
    individual 11, 23T, 24, 42, 43T
    major modifications 119T
    oral 11, 12T, 42, 43T
    partial credit 11, 12T
    presentation modification 118
    promote test-taking skills 11, 65, 118, 177, 178T
    scoring procedure modification 119
    spelling 11
    test format familiarization 117
    vary response format 117, 118T
  Applications for students with disabilities 109, 116(T)-119(T), 118(T)
  Continuous measurement, samples 116(T)
  Curriculum based measurement 110(T), 113-114(T)
    mental retardation 23T
  Formative evaluation 76, 83, 110(T)-111(T), 228T
    cooperative learning 83, 91
    effective instructional technique 5T
    inclusion in portfolio assessment 115T
    mental retardation 23T, 24
    peer tutoring 103T
    use with performance based measure 115
    use with summative evaluation 113
  Identification format 42, 43
  Motor or written abilities 117

Testing (cont.)
  Performance-based assessment 11, 23T, 24, 42, 43T,
      50, 83, 110(T), 114
    hearing impairment 42, 43T
    inclusion in portfolio assessment 115T
    learning disabilities 11, 12T
    mental retardation 23T, 24
    use in curriculum based measurement 114T
    use with alternative response formats 117
    use with summative evaluation 112
    visually impaired 50, 51T
  Portfolio assessment 110(T), 115(T)
    sample portfolio items 115T
    use with alternative response formats 117
  Promote test-taking skills 11, 118, 177, 178T
  Response format 117
  Suggestions for
    hearing impaired 42, 43T
    learning disabilities 11, 12T
    mental retardation 23T, 24
    visually impaired 50, 51(T), 111
  Summative 110(T), 112(T)-113
    examples of 112
    use in portfolio assessment 115T

Text Adaptations 9, 161-172(T)
  Braille 162
  Controlled vocabulary and syntax 163
  High interest, low vocabulary 163
  Various reading levels 163

Textbook-Oriented Approaches
  Cooperative learning 86-87, 90T
  Evaluation 111, 113, 114T
  Learning disabilities 9, 10
  Peer assistance 101, 163
  Peer tutoring 106, 107T
  Teaching suggestions 165
  Visual impairments 49
  see also Reading

Textured Materials 237, 254, 256, 268, 294

Thinking and Reasoning Skills 247-250

Time Management 65-71
  Allocated time 67
  Engaged time
    calculating 67
    strategies to increase 67T
  Possible resources 66(T)
  Sample schedule 66T
  Time, effective use of 66-67
  see also Mainstreaming

Token Systems 127T, 133, 134T, 141, 143, 196

Touch Screen 212

Typewriters 199T, 200, 204

V

Variable Speed Cassette 164, 204

Velcro
  dots 237
  gloves 254
  strips 254

Video Camera 294

Video Players 200

Videotapes 277
  see also Adaptations

Visual Impairment 45-53
  Adaptations for reading materials 161-178
  Attention problem 139
  Attributes/characteristics 46
    academic achievement 45
    intellectual/cognitive 1-2, 45
    language 1, 45, 50
    mobility 46
    motor (fine) 2
    sixth sense 45
    social adjustment 45
    stereotypic behavior 46
    tactual 46
  Audio-visuals 50, 51T
    closed circuit television (CCTV) 52, 53(T)
    describers 96
    descriptive video 50
    preview 50
    tape recording 49, 50
  Auditory accessibility 202T
  Classroom environment 122
  Computer adaptive devices 211T
  Cooperative learning 78, 89, 90T, 227
  Definition
    legally blind 45
    partially sighted 45
  Describing to 48(T), 49(T)
  Evaluation of 111, 117, 118
  Field trip/demonstration 96, 208-209(T), 212
  Incidence 45
  Instructional media adaptations 200, 201T, 202T,
    203T, 206, 226
  Laboratory suggestions 52-53, 233, 234, 236, 237,
    238, 244, 253, 256, 260, 261, 262, 268, 270, 271,
    274, 275, 276, 277, 278, 279-281, 284, 286-287,
    290, 292, 293, 296, 297, 298, 299, 300
    animals and plants 260, 261, 262
    astronomy 285
    braille 52, 53T
    charting and graphing 236, 237, 238, 260
    classifying 240, 241
    equipment 53(T)
    force and motion 292-294
    human anatomy 256
    light and color 299-300

Visual Impairment (cont.)
    magnetism and electricity 289
    mapping 243-245
    measure, mix, pour 233, 234
    microscope use 266, 268
    models and kits 253-254
    observing 52, 53(T)
    peer assistants 51, 53T
    physics of sound 296
    powders, mixtures, and solutions 274, 275, 276
    rocks, minerals and fossils 279-281
    room arrangement 47, 51(T), 52
    segmented trays 52
    solids, liquids, gases 297, 298
    spills 52
    stabilize materials 52, 53T
    water 270, 271
    weather 277, 278
  Low vision 52, 220, 234, 240, 244, 300
  Mainstreaming techniques 47-51(T), 48T
    classroom organization 47(T), 51T
    teacher presentation 48(T)-50, 49T
    testing 50, 51T, 111
  Manipulability and task performance 203T
  Mastering concepts 50
  Mobility 46, 47, 52, 85
    adult guides 46, 47
    cognitive mapping 46
    guide dogs 46
    laser cane 46
    long cane 46
    peer guides 51T
  Notetaking skills 183
  Observing
    closed circuit television (CCTV) 52, 53(T)
    light sensors 53
    microprojectors 53
    monitors 53
    peer assistance 52
    tactually defensive 52, 53T
  Peer assistants 51T, 52, 93, 94, 95(T)-96
    audio-visuals 52, 96
    field trips 96
    handling materials 96
    movement 51T, 95
  Reading 50, 96, 174-176
  Safety 47, 51T, 96, 243, 273-274
  Tactual 46
    analytic touch 46
    synthetic touch 46
    tactually defensive 52
  Verbalisms 50
  Visual accessibility 201T

Vocabulary
  Activities curricula 228
  Description and example/illustration 165, 291
  Force and motion 291
  Hearing impaired 40(T)-41, 228, 241, 255, 262, 299
  Language cards 18, 228, 236, 255, 276
  Language impaired 241, 255, 262

  Learning Disabilities 8, 10, 12(T)
  Mnemonics, use of keyword 18, 148(P)-153
  Pre-teaching 10, 162, 171, 231
  Science 40(T)

Volunteers
  Graduate interns 70
  Parents 71(T), 262
  Practicum students 70
  Senior citizens 71(T)
  Student teachers 70

Voyage of the Mimi
  see Instructional Media

Voyage of the Mimi II
  see Instructional Media

W

Water Activities 269-271
  Adaptations for
    clay boat activities 271
    drops, size and shape 271
    evaporization 270
    measurement and comparison 269
    objectives 269
    sound of 269
    spills 269
    surface tension experiments 271
    water drop models 270
    water level experiments 270
  Adaptive equipment 270-271
    aluminum foil 271
    clay 270
    magnet 271
    tactile markers 270
  Spills 269
  Types of activities 269, 295
  Uses 269

Weather Activities 277-278
  Adaptations for
    air pressure 278
    barometric pressure 278
    charts, use of 278
    clouds 278
    humidity 278
    supervision of 277
    visually impaired 277-278
  Adaptive equipment
    adapted rainfall gauges 277
    adapted thermometers 277
    cotton or polyester stuffing 278
    Voyage of Mimi 278
  Types of activities 277

Wisconsin Fast Plants 260

Wheelchairs 59T, 60(P)-61(P), 219

Writing Implements 62

Written Materials
  Development of 69

Written Work
  Demands
    textbook approach 87
  Note-taking 179-183
  Suggestions for
    communication disorders 17, 278
    hearing impairments 37, 278

Word Processing Skills 213, 214(T)

Word Processors with Synthesized Speech   210T

Appendix A:

Science Products/
Adaptations

Addresses and telephone numbers of companies and distributors are located after this product list.

Adapted thermometers, graduated cylinders and tactile
    floating scales
        Lawrence Hall of Science, University of
           California, Berkeley

Adaptive Firmware Card
    TASH Inc.

Adjustable Table
    adapt**Ability**
    FlagHouse REHAB
    Resources For Industry

Apple Joystick
    Developmental Equipment Inc.
    Fred Sammons, Inc.

Augmentative Communicators
    Prentke Romich Co.

Beok Grip Kit and Dyna-Form-It
    Wendell Foster Center, Inc.

BEX-Apple IIe
    Raised Dot Computing, Inc.

Big Eye Lamp
    Big Eye Lamp, Inc.

Biological Models: Pull-Apart Cell, Insect
    Identification Kits
        Carolina Biological Supply Co.
        Frey Scientific
        NYSTROM

Braille Blackboard/Slate/Stylus/Writer
    American Printing House for the Blind, Inc.

Braille Computer Programs
    Raised Dot Company

Braille Dog Tags
    Lawrence Hall of Science, University of
        California, Berkeley

Braille Labeler
    American Foundation for the Blind

Braille Rulers
    American Foundation for the Blind
    American Printing House for the Blind, Inc.

Braille Spring Scale
    American Printing House for the Blind, Inc.

Braille or Raised Line Thermometer
    American Printing House for the Blind, Inc.

Braille Timer/Clock
    American Printing House for the Blind, Inc.

Brailled Keyboard Overlays
    American Printing House for the Blind, Inc.

Braillemate
    SPEC TECH
    TeleSensory

Brock Microscope
    Brock Optical, Inc.

Closed Caption Television
    Wayne Distributing, Inc.

Closed Circuit TV Scanner
    SPEC TECH
    TeleSensory

Closed Circuit TV
    SPEC TECH
    TeleSensory
    The Caption Center

Computer Magnification Systems
    SPEC TECH
    TeleSensory

DECtalk
    Prentke Romich Co.

Descriptive Video Service
    Descriptive Video Service, Public Television

Desktop Rear Projection Screen
    American Printing House for the Blind, Inc.

Dudley, Me Now Series
    HUBBARD

DYCEM (Non-slip Materials)
    Wendell Foster Center, Inc.

Easy Build Rockets
    Estes Industries

Easy Listener
    Phonic Ear, Inc.

Echo II (IBM) and IIc (Apple)
    Edmark Corporation

Echo IIb
    Cambridge Development Laboratory, Inc.

ESS-Elementary Science Study
    Delta Education, Inc.

Facilitated Communication: Crestalk
    Crestwood Company

Flap Switches
    ABLENET

Food Facts, software program
    American Printing House for the Blind, Inc.

FOSS-Full Option Science Series
    Encyclopedia Britannica

Handi-Cassette Recorder/Player
    American Printing House for the Blind, Inc.

High Interest, Low Vocabulary Reading Materials
    Children's Press
    Phoenix Learning Resources
    Steck Vaughn Co.

Individual Study Screen (Desk Top; Rear Projection)
    American Printing House for the Blind, Inc.

Keyboard Adaptations
    Hooleon Corporation

Keyboard Emulators
    Prentke Romich Co.

Keyguards
    Developmental Equipment, Inc.
    Fred Sammons, Inc.
    Prentke Romich Co.
    TASH Inc.

Large Print Books
    American Printing House for the Blind, Inc.

LEGO
    LEGO Dacta
    Creative Learning

Light Probe
    American Foundation for the Blind

Light Sensor
    American Printing House for the Blind, Inc.

Light Talkers
    Prentke Romich Co.

Little Octopus Suction Holders and Stay Put Suction Disk
    Wendell Foster Center, Inc.

MacSema-Voice Express
    MacSema

Magnetic Models
    The Magnetic Way

Magnifier Hook-up to Video and CCTV
    KEN-A-VISION
    Leica Inc.

Magnifier Lamp, high intensity
    American Foundation for the Blind

Magnifiers
    Bossert Specialties, Inc.
    Ideal School Supply Co.
    Learning Things, Inc.

Miner's Cave, software
    MECC

Models (i.e., solar system, cells, etc.)
    ACCENT! SCIENCE
    Carolina Biological Supply Company
    Connecticut Valley Biological
    Frey Scientific
    HUBBARD

Modified Input Devices
    Prentke Romich Co.

MPrint
    SPEC TECH
    TeleSensory

Multiple Switch Box
    Developmental Equipment, Inc.

National Science Teachers Association Supplement of
    Science Education Suppliers
    National Science Teachers Association

Navigator Systems
    SPEC TECH
    TeleSensory

Optacon Systems
    SPEC TECH
    TeleSensory

OsCaR Systems
    SPEC TECH
    TeleSensory

Outspoken
    SPEC TECH
    TeleSensory

Oversized Desk or Workspace
    Arizona Teaching Tools

Paint Box Snap Keyboard Cover
    Developmental Equipment, Inc.

Phonic Ear
    Phonic Ear, Inc.

Pointer Stick
    Prentke Romich Co.

Projecting Microscope
    Frey Scientific
    Ken-A-Vision
    Resolution Technology

Raised Globes
    ACCENT! SCIENCE
    Frey Scientific

Raised Line Paper
    American Foundation for the Blind

Raised Line Drawing Kit
    American Foundation for the Blind

Recorded Textbooks
    Recording for the Blind

Relief Maps
    Frey Scientific

SAPA-Science...A Process Approach
    Delta Education, Inc.

SAVI/SELPH-Science Activities for the Visually
    Impaired/Science Enrichment for Learners with
    Physical Handicaps
    Delta Education, Inc.

SCIIS-Science Curriculum Improvement Study
    Delta Education, Inc.

Sewell Boards
    Tactile Learning Concepts

Sidiki Transparent Writing/Activities Table
    Wendell Foster Center, Inc.

Slatted Trays
    Lawrence Hall of Science, University of
        California, Berkeley

Sorting Trays
    Lawrence Hall of Science, University of
        California, Berkeley

"Space Hop"
    Delta Education, Inc.

Speaqualizer-IBM
    American Printing House for the Blind, Inc.

Speech Synthesizers
    American Printing House for the Blind, Inc.
    Developmental Equipment, Inc.

"Sticky Bears", software
    Cambridge Development Laboratory, Inc.

Switches
    Adaptive Communication Systems, Inc.
    Prentke Romich Co.

Tactile Markers
    Tactile Learning Concepts

TactilLiner Paper (raises up)
    Tactile Learning

Talking Typewriters
    American Printing House for the Blind, Inc.

Talking Calculator
    American Foundation for the Blind

Teacher's Pet (Talking Software)
    American Printing House for the Blind, Inc.

TeleBraille II
    SPEC TECH
    TeleSensory

Telescoping Mouthstick
    Wendell Foster Center, Inc.

Telex's PAS-1
    Phonic Ear, Inc.

Textalker-Apple
    American Printing House for the Blind, Inc.

Touch Talkers
    Prentke Romich Co.

Touch Window
    Developmental Equipment, Inc.
    Edmark Corporation

Turbo Mouse
    Fred Sammons, Inc.

Utensil Grips
    Fred Sammons, Inc.

Variable Intensity Study Lamp
    American Printing House for the Blind, Inc.

Variable Speed Cassette Player
    General Electric Co.

Velcro Closure Tape
    Joan Cook Housewares

Velcro, felt pads
    Fred Sammons, Inc.

Verapoint Braille Embosser and Software
    SPEC TECH
    TeleSensory

Videodisks
    Britannica Centre
    Optical Data Corporation
    Video Discovery

Voice Recognition
    Adaptive Communication Systems, Inc.
    Articulate Systems

"Voyage of the Mimi" and "Voyage of the Mimi II",
    multimedia, integrated kits
    WINGS for learning/Sunburst

Wisconsin Fast Plants
    Carolina Biological Supply Co.

Zygo-Digital Recording/Playback Aids
    Zygo Industries, Inc.

Adaptive Equipment and Science Publishers/Companies

ABLENET, AccessAbility, Inc.
360 Hoover St. N.E.
Minneapolis, MN 55413

ACCENT! SCIENCE
P.O. Box 1444
Saginaw, MI 48605
(517) 799-8103
FAX: (517) 799-8115

adapt**Ability**
P.O. Box 515
Colchester, CT 06415-0515
1-800-243-9232

Adaptive Communication Systems, Inc.
Box 12440
Pittsburg, PA 15231
(412) 264-2288

American Foundation for the Blind
15 West 16th St.
New York, NY 10011
(201) 862-8838

American Printing House for the Blind, Inc.
1839 Frankfort Avenue
P.O. Box 6085
Louisville, KY 40206-0085
1-800-223-1839
FAX: (502) 895-1509

Apple Computer, Inc.
20525 Mariani Ave.
Cupertino, CA 95014
(408) 996-1010

Arizona Teaching Tools
1356 S. Gilbert Rd.
Mesa, AZ 85204
(602) 892-7705

Articulate Systems
2380 Ellsworth St.
Berkeley, CA 94704
(415) 549-1013

Big Eye Lamp, Inc.
68 Yellowbrook Rd.
Farmingdale, NJ 07727
(201) 938-2490

Bossert Specialties, Inc.
P.O. Box 15441
Phoenix, AZ 85060
1-800-776-5885

Britannica Centre
310 S. Michigan Ave.
Chicago, IL 60604
1-800-554-9862
FAX: (312) 347-7903

Brock Optical, Inc.
P.O. Box 940831
Maitland, FL 32794
1-800-780-9111
FAX: (407) 260-5637

Cambridge Development Laboratory, Inc.
214 Third Ave.
Waltham, MA 02154
1-800-637-0047

Carolina Biological Supply Company
Main Office and Laboratories
2700 York Road
Burlington, NC 27215
1-800-334-5551
FAX: (919) 584-3399

Children's Press
5440 North Cumberland Ave.
Chicago, IL 60656
1-800-621-1115
FAX: (312) 693-0574

Connecticut Valley Biological Supply Co., Inc.
P.O. Box 326
82 Valley Rd.
Southhampton, MA 01073
1-800-628-7748
FAX: (413) 527-8286

Council for Exceptional Children
1920 Association Dr.
Reston, VA 22091-1589
(703) 620-3660
FAX: (703) 264-9494

Creative Learning Systems, Inc.
16510 Via Esprillo
San Diego, CA 92127
1-800-458-2880
FAX: (619) 566-2897

Crestwood Company
Communication Aids for Children & Adults
6625 N. Sidney Place
Milwaukee, WI 53209-3259

Delta Education, Inc.
P.O. Box 915
Hudson, NH 03051-0915
1-800-258-1302
FAX: (603) 880-6520

Descriptive Video Service
WGBH
125 Western Ave.
Boston, MA 02134
(617) 492-2777 Ext. 3490

Don Johnston Developmental Equipment, Inc.
P.O. Box 639
1000 N. Rand Rd.
Bldg. 115
Wauconda, IL 60084
1-800-999-4660
FAX: (708) 526-4177

Edmark Corporation
P.O. Box 3903
Bellevue, WA 98009-3903
1-800-426-0856

Encyclopedia Britannica Educational
    Corporation
310 South Michigan Ave.
Chicago, IL 60604

Estes Industries, Inc
1295 H Street
Penrose, CO 81240
(719) 473-9686

Fisher Scientific Co.
30 Water Street
West Haven, CT 06516
(203) 934-5271

FlagHouse REHAB
150 No. MacQuesten Pkwy.
Mt. Vernon, NY 10550
1-800-221-5185
FAX: (914) 699-2961

Fred Sammons, Inc.
145 Tower Dr.
Burr Ridge, IL 60521
1-800-323-5547
FAX: (708) 323-4602

Frey Scientific
905 Hickory Lane
P.O. Box 8101
Mansfield, OH 44901-8101
1-800-225-3739
FAX: (419) 589-1522

General Electric Co.
Consumer Relations
1 College Blvd.
Portsmouth, VA 23705

Hooleon Corporation
P.O. Box 230
Dept. CW91
Cornville, AZ 86325
(602) 634-7515
FAX: (602) 634-4620

HUBBARD
P.O. Box 104
Northbrook, IL 60065
1-800-323-8368

IBM
1133 Westchester Ave.
White Plains, NY 10601
1-800-222-7257

Joan Cook Housewares
3200 S E 14th Avenue
Fort Lauderdale, FL 33350

KEN-A-VISION Manufacturing Co., Inc.
5615 Raytown Rd.
Kansas City, MO 64133
(816) 353-4787
FAX: (816) 358-5072

Lawrence Hall of Science
University of California
Berkeley, CA 94720
(415) 642-8941

Learning Things, Inc.
68A Broadway
P.O. Box 436
Arlington, MA 02174
(617) 646-0093
FAX: (617) 646-0135

LEGO Dacta
555 Taylor Rd.
Enfield, CT 06082
1-800-527-8339
FAX: (203) 763-2466

Leica Inc.
P.O. Box 123
Buffalo, NY 14240-0123
(716) 891-3000
FAX: (716) 891-3080

MacSema
29383 Lamb Dr.
Albany, OR 97321
1-800-344-7228

MECC
6160 Summit Drive North
Minneapolis, MN 55430-4003
(612) 569-1500

National Science Teachers Association
1742 Connecticut Ave. NW
Washington, DC 20009
(202) 328-5800
FAX: (202) 328-0974

NYSTROM
Division of Herff Jones, Inc.
3333 Elston Ave.
Chicago, IL 60618-5898
1-800-621-8086
FAX: (312) 463-0515

Optical Data Corporation
30 Technology Dr.
Warren, NJ 07059
1-800-524-2481
FAX: (908) 668-1322

Phonic Ear Inc.
250 Camino Alto
Mill Valley, CA 94941
1-800-227-0735

Prentke Romich Company
1022 Heyl Road
Wooster, OH 44691
1-800-262-1984
FAX (216) 263-4829

Raised Dot Computing
408 South Baldwin
Dept. 902
Madison, WI 53703
1-800-347-9594

Recording for the Blind
20 Roszel Rd.
Princeton, NJ 08540
1-800-221-4792
FAX: (609) 987-8116

RESNA Press
Dept. 4813
Washington, DC 20061-4813

Resolution Technology
26000 Avenida Aeropuerto #22
San Juan Capistrano, CA 92675
(714) 661-6162
FAX: (714) 661-6162

Resources For Industry
R.D. 3, Box 12
Prospect Ave.
Walton, NY 13856
(607) 865-7184
FAX: (607) 865-7129

SPEC TECH
P.O. Box 1369
Greenwood, IN 46142
1-800-765-7483
(317) 888-1159

Steck Vaughn Company
P.O. Box 26015
Austin, TX 78755
1-800-531-5015

Tactile Learning Concepts
P.O. Box 1471
Boerne, TX 78006
1-800-633-3018

TASH, Inc.
70 Gibson Dr., Unit 12
Markham, Ontario, Canada
L3R 4C2

TeleSensory
455 North Bernardo Ave.
P.O. Box 7455
Mountain View, CA 94039-7455
1-800-227-8418
FAX: (415) 691-0637

The Caption Centre
125 Western Ave.
Boston, MA 02134
(617) 492-9225

The Magnetic Way
Division of Creative Edge, Inc.
2495 North Forest Rd.
Getzville, NY 14068
1-800-626-5052
FAX: (716) 689-6712

Video Discovery, Inc.
1700 Westlake Ave.
N. Suite 600
Seattle, WA 98109-3012
1-800-548-3472
FAX: (206) 285-9245

Wayne Distributing, Inc.
8219 Zionsville Road
Indianapolis, IN 46268

Wendell Foster Center, Inc.
P.O. Box 1668
815 Triplett St.
Owensboro, KY 42302-1668
1-800-323-5547
FAX: (502) 683-0079

WINGS for Learning/Sunburst
1600 Green Hills Rd.
P.O. Box 660002
Scotts Valley, CA 95067-9908
1-800-321-7511
FAX: (408) 438-4214

Zygo Industries, Inc.
P.O. Box 1008
Portland, OR 97207-1008
1-800-234-6006

Appendix B:

Related Organizations and Resources*

Learning Disabilities

Council for Learning Disabilities
P.O. Box 40303
Overland Park, KS 66204
(913) 492-8755

Division for Learning Disabilities
Council for Exceptional Children
1920 Association Drive
Reston, VA 22901
(703) 620-3660

Learning Disabilities Association of America (LDA)
4156 Library Road
Pittsburgh, PA 15234
(412) 341-1515

National Center for Learning Disabilities (NCLD)
99 Park Avenue, 6th Floor
New York, NY 10016
(212) 687-7211 or
(703) 451-2078 (Washington, DC office)

Orton Dyslexia Society
724 York Road
Baltimore, MD 21204

Mental Retardation

Administration on Developmental Disabilities
200 Independence Avenue, SW
Washington, DC 20201

American Association on Mental Retardation
1719 Kalorama Road, NW
Washington, DC 20009
(800) 424-3688
(202) 387-1968

Association for Children with Retarded Mental
  Development
162 Fifth Avenue, 11th Floor
New York, NY 10010

Association for Retarded Citizens of the United States
National Headquarters
P.O. Box 6109
2501 Avenue J
Arlington, TX 76006
(800) 433-5255
(817) 640-0204

Division on Mental Retardation
Council for Exceptional Children
1920 Association Drive
Reston, VA 22091
(703) 620-3660 Voice/TDD

* Disability areas listed in same sequence as found in the table of contents.

National Association for Down Syndrome
P.O. Box 4542
Oak Brook, IL 60522
(708) 325-9112

National Association for Retarded Citizens
2501 Avenue J
Arlington, TX 76006

National Down Syndrome Congress
1800 Dempster Street
Park Ridge, IL 60068-1146
(800) 232-NDSC
(708) 823-7550

National Down Syndrome Society
141 Fifth Avenue
New York, NY 10010
(800) 221-4602
(212) 460-9330

National Tay-Sachs & Allied Diseases Association
2001 Beacon
Brookline, MA 02146
(617) 277-4463

President's Committee on Employment of the Handicapped
Regional Office Building #3
7th and D Streets, SW, Room 2614
Washington, DC 20201
(202) 245-7634

Emotional Disturbance/ Behavioral Disorders

American Association of Psychiatric Services for Children
1133 15th St. NW Suite 1000
Washington, DC 20005
(202) 429-9713

American Psychiatric Association
1400 K Street, NW
Washington, DC 20005

Autism Society of America
1234 Massachusetts Avenue, NW
Suite 1017
Washington, DC 20005
(202) 783-0125

Children with Attention Deficit Disorders (CHADD)
1859 North Pine Island Road
Suite 185
Plantation, FL 33322
(305) 384-6869

Council for Children with Behavioral Disorders
Council for Exceptional Children
1920 Association Drive
Reston, VA 22091
(703) 620-3660 Voice/TDD

Federation of Families for Children's Mental Health
1021 Prince Street
Alexandria, VA 22314

National Association of School Psychologists
1511 K Street, NW
Suite 716
Washington, DC 20005
(202) 638-4750

National Mental Health Association
1021 Prince Street
Alexandria, VA 22314

National Society for Children and Adults with Autism
621 Central Avenue
Albany, NY 12206

Hearing Impairments and Communication Disorders

American Cleft Palate Association
331 Salk Hall
University of Pittsburgh
Pittsburgh, PA 15213
(412) 681-9620

Alexander Graham Bell Association for the Deaf
3417 Volta Place, NW
Washington, DC 20007
(202) 337-5220 Voice/TDD

American Society for Deaf Children
841 Thayer Avenue
Silver Springs, MD 20910
1-800-942-2732

American Speech, Language & Hearing Association
10801 Rockville Pike
Rockville, MD 20852
(301) 897-5700

The Caption Center
WGBH
125 Western Avenue
Boston, MA 02134
(617) 492-9225 Voice/TDD

Captioned Films for the Deaf
Special Office for Materials Distribution
Indiana University
Audio-Visual Center
Bloomington, IN 47401

Communication Outlook
Artificial Language Laboratory
Michigan State University
405 Computer Center
East Lansing, MI 48824
(517) 353-0870

Division for Children with Communication Disorders
Council for Exceptional Children
1920 Association Drive
Reston, VA 22091
(703) 264-3660 Voice/TDD

Helen Keller National Center for Deaf-Blind Youths
   and Adults
111 Middle Neck Road
Sands Point, NY 11050
(516) 944-8900

Modern Talking Picture Service
5000 Park Street, North
St. Petersburg, FL 33709
(800) 237-6213 Voice/TDD

National Association for Hearing and Speech Action
10801 Rockville Pike
Rockville, MD 20855
(800) 638-TALK

National Association of Parents of the Deaf
814 Thayer Avenue
Silver Spring, MD 20910

National Association of the Deaf
814 Thayer Avenue
Silver Spring, MD 20910
(301) 587-1788

National Captioning Institute
5203 Leesburg Pike
Falls Church, VA 22041
(703) 998-2400 Voice/TDD

National Center for Stuttering
200 East 33rd Street
New York, NY 10016

National Foundation for Children's Hearing, Education
   and Research
928 McLean Avenue
Yonkers, NY 10704
(914) 237-2676

National Hearing Aid Society
20361 Middlebelt
Livonia, MI 48152
(800) 521-5247

National Information Center on Deafness
Gallaudet University
Carnegie Hall, Room 205
800 Florida Avenue, N.E.
Washington, DC 20002
(800) 672-6720 Voice/TDD

National Student Speech Language Hearing Association
   (NSSLHA)
10801 Rockville Pike
Rockville, MD 20852
(301) 897-5700

Self-Help for Hard of Hearing People
7800 Wisconsin Avenue
Bethesda, MD 20814
(301) 657-2248
(301) 657-2249 TDD

Speech Foundation of America
5139 Lingle Street NW
Washington, DC 20016

Telecommunications for the Deaf, Inc.
814 Thayer Avenue
Silver Spring, MD 20910

Tourette Syndrome Association
42-40 Bell Boulevard
Bayside, NY 11361
(718) 224-2999

The Washington Area Group for the Hard-of-Hearing
P.O. Box 6283
Silver Springs, MD 20916
(301) 942-7612 Voice/TDD

Visual Impairment

American Council for the Blind
1010 Vermont Avenue, NW
Suite 1100
Washington, DC 20005
(800) 424-8666, 3-5 pm
(202) 393-3666

American Foundation for the Blind, Inc.
15 West 16th Street
New York, NY 10011
(800) AFBLIND
(212) 620-2000

American Printing House for the Blind
P.O. Box 6085
1839 Frankfort Avenue
Louisville, KY 40206-0085

Association for the Education & Rehabilitation of the Blind
  and Visually Impaired
206 North Washington Street
Suite 320
Alexandria, VA 22314

Blind Children's Fund
International Institute for Visually Impaired, 0-7, Inc.
230 Central Street
Auburndale, MA 02166-2399

Braille Circulating Library
2700 Stuart Avenue
Richmond, VA 23220

Descriptive Video Service
WGBH
125 Western Avenue
Boston, MA 02134
(617) 492-2777

Division for the Visually Handicapped
Council for Exceptional Children
1920 Association Drive
Reston, VA 22091
(703) 620-3660 Voice/TDD

Helen Keller National Center for Deaf-Blind Youths
  and Adults
111 Middle Neck Road
Sands Point, NY 11050
(516) 944-8900

National Aid to the Visually Handicapped
3201 Balboa Street
San Francisco, CA 94121
(415) 221-3201

National Association for the Deaf-Blind
12573 S.E. 53rd Street
Bellevue, WA 98006

National Association for the Visually Handicapped
22 West 21st Street
New York, NY 10010
(212) 889-3141

National Braille Press
86 St. Stephen Street
Boston, MA 02115
(617) 833-4000

National Federation of the Blind
1800 Johnson Street
Baltimore, MD 21230
(301) 659-9314

National Library Services for the Blind and Physically
  Handicapped
Library of Congress
1291 Taylor Street, N.W.
Washington, DC 20542
(202) 287-5100

National Retinitis Pigmentosa (RP) Foundation, Inc.
1401 Mount Royal Avenue
Baltimore, MD 21217

National Society for the Prevention of Blindness, Inc.
79 Madison Avenue
New York, NY 10016

New Eyes for the Needy
549 Milburn Avenue
Short Hills, NY 07078

Perkins School for the Blind
175 N. Beacon Street
Watertown, MA 02172

Recording for the Blind, Inc.
20 Roszel Road
Princeton, NJ 08540
(609) 452-0606

Society for Visual Education
1345 W. Diversey Parkway
Chicago, IL 60614
(312) 525-1500

United States Association for Blind Athletes
33 N. Institute Street
Brown Hall, Suite 105
Colorado Springs, CO 80903
(719) 630-0422

Physical Disabilities and Other Health Impairments

American Academy for Cerebral Palsy and
  Developmental Medicine
2405 Westwood Avenue
P.O. Box 11083
Richmond, VA 23230

American Cancer Society National Headquarters
1599 Clifton Road, NE
Atlanta, GA 30329
(404) 320-3333

American Diabetes Association
1819 H Street, NW
Suite 1200
Washington, DC 20006

American Epilepsy Society
179 Allyn Street
Suite 304
Hartford, CT 06103

American Heart Association
7320 Greenville Avenue
Dallas, TX 75231
(214) 750-5300

American Juvenile Arthritis Organization
1314 Spring Street, NW
Atlanta, GA 30309

American Lung Association
1740 Broadway
New York, NY 10019
(212) 315-8700

American Occupational Therapy Association
1383 Piccard Drive, P.O. Box 1725
Rockville, MD 20850
(301) 948-9626

American Physical Therapy Association
1111 North Fairfax Street
Alexandria, VA 22314
(703) 684-2782

American Rehabilitation Counseling Association of the
   American Personnel and Guidance Association
5999 Stevenson Avenue
Alexandria, VA 22304
(703) 823-9800

Association of Birth Defects in Children, Inc. (ABDC)
3526 Emerywood Lane
Orlando, FL 32806
(407) 859-2821

Association for Persons with Severe Handicaps
7010 Roosevelt Way, N.E.
Seattle, WA 98115
(206) 523-8446

The Candlelighters
Childhood Cancer Foundation
Suite 1001
1901 Pennsylvania Avenue, NW
Washington, DC 20006
(202) 659-5136

Cystic Fibrosis Foundation
6931 Arlington Road
Bethesda, MD 20814
(800) 344-4823

Division on the Physically Handicapped
Council for Exceptional Children
1920 Association Drive
Reston, VA 22091-1589
(703) 620-3660 Voice/TDD

Epilepsy Foundation of America
4351 Garden City Drive
Suite 406
Landover, MD 20785
(800) EFA-1000
(301) 459-3700

Juvenile Diabetes Foundation
60 Madison Avenue
New York, NY 10010
(212) 689-2860

The Kids on the Block, Inc.
9385-C Gerwig Land
Columbia, MD 21045

KIDS Project, Inc.
1720 Oregon Street
Berkeley, CA 94703
(415) 548-4121

Leukemia Society of America
733 Third Avenue
14th Floor
New York, NY 10017
(212) 573-8484

March of Dimes Birth Defects Foundation
1275 Mamaroneck Avenue
White Plains, NY 10605
(914) 428-7100

Muscular Dystrophy Association
810 Seventh Avenue
New York, NY 10019
(212) 586-0808

National Amputation Foundation
12-45 150th Street
Whitestone, NY 11367
(718) 767-8400

National Association for Sickle Cell Disease, Inc.
3345 Wilshire Boulevard, Suite 1106
Los Angeles, CA 90010-1880
800-421-8453
(213) 936-7205

National Ataxia Foundation
600 Twelve Oaks Center
15500 Wayzata Boulevard
Wayzata, MN 55391
(612) 473-7666

National Birth Defects Center
c/o Kennedy Memorial Hospital
30 Warren Street
Brighton, MA 02135
(800) 322-5014

National Cystic Fibrosis Foundation
6000 Executive Boulevard
Rockville, MD 20855
(800) FIGHTCF
(301) 881-9130

National Easter Seal Society for Crippled Children
 and Adults
2023 West Ogden Avenue
Chicago, IL 60612

National Epilepsy League
6 North Michigan Avenue
Chicago, IL 60602

The National Foundation for Ileitis and Colitis
444 Park Avenue South
New York, NY 10016

National Head Injury Foundation, Inc.
333 Turnpike Road
Southborough, MA 01772
(800) 444-NHIF
(617) 485-9950

National Heart Institute
9000 Rockville Pike
Building 31, Room 4A21
Bethesda, MD 20892
(301) 496-4000

National Hemophilia Foundation
The Soho Building
110 Greene Street, Room 406
New York, NY 10012

National Kidney Foundation
2 Park Avenue, Suite 908
New York, NY 10016
(212) 889-2210

National Multiple Sclerosis Society
205 42nd Street
New York, NY 10010
(718) 986-3240

National Rehabilitation Information Center
4407 Eight Street, NE
Washington, DC 20017
(800) 43-NARIC
(202) 635-5826

National Spinal Cord Injury Association
149 California Street
Newton, MA 02158
(617) 965-0521

National Wheelchair Athletic Association-Junior
Division
3617 Betty Drive
Suite S
Colorado Springs, CO 80907

Orthotic and Prosthetic Specialties, Inc.
9811 Mallard Drive
Suite 112
Laurel, MD 20708
(301) 470-3344

Scoliosis Research Society
444 North Michigan Avenue
Chicago, IL 60611

Shriners Hospitals for Crippled Children
2900 Rocky Point Drive
Tampa, FL 33607
(813) 885-2575

Spina Bifida Association of America
1700 Rockville Pike
Suite 540
Rockville, MD 20852
(800) 621-3141
(301) 770-SBAA

Spinal Cord Injury Hotline
American Paralysis Association (APA)
c/o Montebello Hospital
2201 Argonne Drive
Baltimore, MD 21218
(800) 526-3456

Spinal Network
Spinal Associates, Ltd.
P.O. Box 4162
Boulder, CO 80306
(303) 449-5412

Telephone Pioneers of America
22 Cortlandt St.
RM 2588
New York, NY 10007
(212) 393-2955

United Cerebral Palsy Association
666 E. 34th Street
New York, NY 10016
(212) 947-5770

Other

ABLEDATA
Newington Children's Hospital
181 E. Cedar Street
Newington, CT 06111
(800) 344-5405 Voice/TDD

Advocates - Resources - Counseling
ARC of King County
2230 Eighth Avenue
Seattle, WA 98121
(206) 622-9324

Alliance for Technology Access
1307 Solano Avenue
Albany, CA 94706-1888
(415) 528-0747 Voice/TDD

American Academy of Neurology
2221 University Avenue, SE
Suite 335
Minneapolis, MN 55414
(612) 623-8115

American Academy of Pediatrics
141 North West Point
Elk Grove Village, IL 60009-0927
(312) 869-9327

The American Association for the Advancement of Science
1333 H Street, N.W.
Washington, DC 20005
(202) 326-6630 Voice/TDD

American Association of School Administrators
1801 North Moore Street
Arlington, VA 22209
(703) 528-0700

American Bar Association Child Advocacy Center
1800 M Street, NW Suite 200
Washington, DC 20036

American Council on Rural Special Education
National Rural Development Institute
Western Washington University
Bellingham, WA 98225
(206) 676-3576

American Educational Research Association
1230 17th Street, NW
Washington, DC 20036
(202) 223-9485

American Humane Association
Children's Division
9725 East Hampden Avenue
Denver, CO 80231
(303) 695-0811

American Medical Association
535 North Dearborn Street
Chicago, IL 60610
(312) 645-5000

American Personnel and Guidance Association
5999 Stevenson Avenue
Alexandria, VA 22304
(703) 823-9800

American Vocational Association
1410 King Street
Alexandria, VA 22314
(703) 683-3111

Apple Computer's Office of
  Special Education Programs
20525 Mariani Avenue
Cupertino, CA 95014

Bilingual Special Education
Department of Special Education
EDB 306
University of Texas
Austin, TX 78710

Black Child Development Institute
1463 Rhode Island Avenue, NW
Washington, DC 20005
(202) 387-1281

Children's Defense Fund
122 C Street NW
Washington, DC 20001

Citizens Alliance to Uphold Special
  Education (CAUSE)
313 South Washington Square
Suite 040
Lansing, MI 48917
(800) 221-9105 Voice/TDD

Clearinghouse on the Handicapped
Office of Special Education and Rehabilitative Services
U.S. Department of Education
Switzer Building, Room 3132
Washington, DC 20202-2319
(202) 732-1214

Clearinghouse and Research in Child Abuse
  and Neglect
P.O. Box 1182
Washington, DC 20013
(703) 821-2086

Closing the Gap
P.O. Box 68
Henderson, MN 56044
(612) 248-3294

Collaboration Among Parents and Health Professionals
Project (CAPP)
P.O. Box 992
Westfield, MA 01086
(413) 562-5521

Coordinating Council for Handicapped Children
20 East Jackson Boulevard, Room 900
Chicago, IL 60604
(312) 939-3513

Council of State Administrators of Vocational
Rehabilitation
P.O. Box 3776
Washington, DC 20007
(202) 638-4634

Council for Disability Rights
343 South Dearborn, #318
Chicago, IL 60604

Council for Exceptional Children
1920 Association Drive
Reston, VA 22091
(703) 620-3660

Disability Rights Center, Inc.
1616 P Street, NW
Suite 435
Washington, DC 20036

Disability Law Center, Inc.
11 Beacon Street, Suite 925
Boston, MA 02108

Education Commission of the States
1860 Lincoln Street
Denver, CO 80295
(303) 830-3600

Father's Program
Merrywood School
16120 NE 8th Street
Bellevue, WA 98008
(206) 747-4004

Federation for Children with Special Needs
312 Stuart Street, 2nd Floor
Boston, MA 02116
(617) 482-2915

The Genesis Fund
30 Warren Street
Brighton, MA 02135
(800) 225-5995

HEATH Resource Center
Higher Education and Adult Training for People
with Handicaps
One Dupont Circle, Suite 670
Washington, DC 20036-1193
(800) 544-3284
(202) 939-9320

International Reading Association
800 Barksdale Road
P.O. Box 8139
Newark, DE 19714
(302) 371-1600

Migrant Education Resource List Information Network
(MERLIN)
Pennsylvania Department of Education
8th Floor, 333 Market Street
Harrisburg, PA 17018
(800) 233-0306
(717) 783-7121

National Academy of Sciences
2101 Constitution Ave., NW
Washington, DC 20148
(202) 334-2300

National Association for Bilingual Education
Room 407
1201 16th Street, NW
Washington, DC 20036
(202) 822-7870

National Association for the Education of Young
Children
1834 Connecticut Avenue, NW
Washington, DC 20009
(202) 323-8777

National Association of Private Residential Resources
6400 HT Corners Place
Falls Church, VA 22044
(703) 536-3311

National Association of Protection and Advocacy
Systems (NAPAS)
300 I Street, NE
Suite 212
Washington, DC 20002
(202) 546-8202

National Association of Secondary School Principals
1904 Association Drive
Reston, VA 22091
(703) 860-0200

National Association of State Directors of Special Education, Inc.
1800 Diagonal Road, Suite 320
Alexandria, VA 22314
(703) 519-3800

National Center for Education in Maternal and Child Health
38th and R Streets, NW
Washington, DC 20007
(202) 625-8400

National Center for Research in Vocational Education
The Ohio State University
1960 Kenny Road
Columbus, OH 43210-1090
(800) 848-4815
(614) 486-3655

National Clearinghouse for Bilingual Education
11501 Georgia Avenue
Suite 102
Wheaton, MD 20902
(800) 647-0123
(301) 933-9448

National Committee for Citizens in Education
10840 Little Patuxent Parkway
Suite 301
Columbia, MD 21044-3199
(800) NET-WORK
(301) 997-9300

National Council for the Handicapped
800 Independence Avenue, SW
Washington, DC 20008

National Education Association
1201 16th Street, NW
Washington, DC 20036
(202) 833-4000

National Information Center for Children and Youth with Handicaps (NICHCY)
P.O. Box 1492
Washington, DC 20013
(800) 999-5599
(703) 893-6061 Voice/TDD

National Institute of Neurological and Communicative Disorders and Stroke
National Institute of Health
U.S. Department of Health and Human Services
Building 31, Room 8A-16
Bethesda, MD 20814
(301) 496-5751

National Legal Resource Center for Child Advocacy
1800 M Street, NW
Washington, DC 20036
(202) 331-2250

National Ocean Access Project (NOAP)
P.O. Box 33141
Farragut Station
Washington, DC 20033

National Rehabilitation Information Center (NARIC)
8455 Colesville Road
Suite 935
Silver Spring, MD 20910-3319
(800) 346-2742 Voice/TDD

National Rural Development Institute
Western Washington University
Bellingham, WA 98225
(206) 676-3576

National Science Foundation
1800 G Street, NW
Room 516
Washington, DC 20550
(202) 357-7078

National Science Resources Center
Smithsonian Institution
Arts and Industries Building, Room 1201
Washington, DC 20560
(202) 357-2555

National Science Teachers Association (NSTA)
1742 Connecticut Ave., NW
Washington, DC 20009
(202) 328-5800

National Support Center for Persons with Disabilities
IBM (software)
P.O. Box 2150
Atlanta, GA 30301-2150
(800) 426-2133

PACER Center, Inc.
Parent Advocacy Coalition for Educational Rights
4826 Chicago Avenue South
Minneapolis, MN 55417
(800) 53-PACER
(612) 827-2966

Parent Information Center
P.O. Box 1422
Concord, NH 03301
(603) 224-7005

Parents Helping Parents, Inc.
535 Race Street, #220
San Jose, CA 95126
(408) 288-5010

PEAK Parent Center, Inc.
6055 Lehman Drive, Suite 101
Colorado Springs, CO 80918
(800) 426-2466, ext. 423
(713) 531-9400

Pilot Parents
Central Palm Plaza
2005 N. Central Avenue
Suite 100
Phoenix, AZ 85004
(602) 271-4012

Preader-Willi Syndrome Association
6439 Excelsior Boulevard, E-102
St. Paul, MN 55426
(612) 926-1947

President's Committee on Employment of the
 Handicapped
U.S. Department of Labor
Washington, DC 20210
(202) 523-4000

RESNA, an Association for the Advancement of
 Rehabilitation and Assistive Technologies
1101 Connecticut Avenue, NW
Suite 700
Washington, DC 20036
(202) 857-1140

Ronald McDonald House
500 North Michigan Avenue
Chicago, Il 60611

Sibling Information Network
Connecticut's University Affiliated Facility
University of Connecticut
249 Glenbrook Road u-64
Storrs, CT 06268
(203) 486-4034

Technical Assistance Resource Center
1101 Connecticut avenue, N.W.
Washington, DC 20036
(202) 857-1140 Voice/TDD

Travel Information Center
Moss Rehabilitation Hospital
12th Street and Tabor Road
Philadelphia, PA 19141

Very Special Arts
1825 Connecticut Avenue, NW
Suite 417
Washington, DC 20009
(202) 662-8899

Voyageur Outward Bound School
10900 Cedar Lake Road
Minnetonka, MN 55343
(612) 542-9255

Wilderness Inquiry II
1313 5th Street S.E.
Box 84
Minneapolis, MN 55414
(612) 379-3858 Voice/TDD

Appendix C:

Guidelines for Curriculum Adoption Committees and for Publishers of Science Curriculum

These guidelines are intended to assist curriculum adoption committees select curricular materials that better meet the needs of all students, including students with disabilities. Furthermore, these guidelines are intended to provide publishers of science curricular materials with critical information that can be incorporated into revisions of existing curricular materials and the design and development of new curricular materials.

The guidelines can be used during the adoption process while completing the evaluation of science curricular materials. Throughout adoption committees' deliberation processes, these guidelines can be used to determine whether or not the curricular materials being considered adequately address the needs of students with disabilities who will be mainstreamed into general education science classes. Further, it is recommended that reviewers select only a few of the relevant areas from specific science activities listed in Part III to complete.

These guidelines are intended to help the curriculum adoption committee in the following ways:

- focus on issues relevant to mainstreaming instruction in science

- provide information on characteristics of students with disabilities that may interact with science instruction

- provide information on adapting laboratory techniques and procedures for students with disabilities

- provide information on key instructional strategies that have been validated as successful mainstreaming strategies

- provide information on adaptive techniques, materials, and procedures that have been reported to be effective in facilitating mainstreaming of students with disabilities into science classes

In order to facilitate the mainstreaming process and to aid general education science teachers in instructing students with disabilities, it is necessary that specific information on teaching students with disabilities be addressed in the curriculum materials.

These guidelines provide an overall evaluation form that can be employed while examining curriculum materials. The evaluation forms follow the same organizational pattern as the guidelines developed for use by general education science teachers. The intent is that members of curriculum adoption committees who are unfamiliar with the guideline area can refer to the corresponding section in the manual for additional information. The evaluation form has three major parts. The first part addresses characteristics of students with disabilities, the second section addresses general mainstreaming strategies, and the third section addresses specific science activities.

It is recommended that evaluators complete the worksheet as they are reviewing materials. Comments from a particular series can then be summarized to provide valuable information describing the extent to which science curricular materials provide essential information on instructing students with disabilities.

Since many districts employ text-based approaches to science instruction a supplementary evaluation worksheet has been provided that provides a more detailed listing of guidelines for assessing reading and accompanying writing components of text-based approaches. This additional worksheet may also prove beneficial for evaluating the reading and writing components associated with activities-oriented approaches to science instruction.

Overall Worksheet for Evaluators

Publisher _____ Year _____ Grade _____ Program _____

Guidelines Chapter	Comments on Teacher Materials	Comments on Student Textual Materials	Comments on Student Worksheet or Workbook Materials	Comments on Student Laboratory Materials	Overall Evaluation
PART I: Characteristics of Disabilities and Implications for Mainstreaming in Science Classes					
General Characteristics					
Learning Disabilities					
Communication Disorders					
Mental Retardation					

1

Guidelines Chapter	Comments on Teacher Materials	Comments on Student Textual Materials	Comments on Student Worksheet or Workbook Materials	Comments on Student Laboratory Materials	Overall Evaluation
Emotional Disturbance					
Hearing Impairments					
Visual Impairments					
Physical Disabilities					
PART II: General Mainstreaming Strategies					
Time and Resource Management					
Effective Instruction					

Guidelines Chapter	Comments on Teacher Materials	Comments on Student Textual Materials	Comments on Student Worksheet or Workbook Materials	Comments on Student Laboratory Materials	Overall Evaluation
Cooperative Learning					
Peer Assistance and Peer Tutoring					
Evaluation					
Managing Classroom Behavior					
Attention					
Memory					

Guidelines Chapter	Comments on Teacher Materials	Comments on Student Textual Materials	Comments on Student Worksheet or Workbook Materials	Comments on Student Laboratory Materials	Overall Evaluation
Students With Reading Difficulties					
Improving Study Skills					
Improving Motivation and Affect					
Instructional Media					
Computer-Assisted Instruction					
Field Trips and Demonstrations					

PART III: Guidelines for Implementing Specific Science Activities in Mainstream Settings

Guidelines Chapter	Comments on Teacher Materials	Comments on Student Textual Materials	Comments on Student Worksheet or Workbook Materials	Comments on Student Laboratory Materials	Overall Evaluation
Introduction to Specific Science Activities					
Measuring and Pouring					
Charting, Graphing, and Recording Data					
Observing, Classifying, and Predicting					
Mapping Activities					
Invention and Discovery Activities					

Guidelines Chapter	Comments on Teacher Materials	Comments on Student Textual Materials	Comments on Student Worksheet or Workbook Materials	Comments on Student Laboratory Materials	Overall Evaluation
Assembling Kits and Models					
Human Anatomy					
Plants and Animals					
Activities with Microscopes					
Water Activities					
Powders and Mixtures					

6

Guidelines Chapter	Comments on Teacher Materials	Comments on Student Textual Materials	Comments on Student Worksheet or Workbook Materials	Comments on Student Laboratory Materials	Overall Evaluation
Weather Activities					
Rocks, Minerals, and Fossils					
Earth Science/ Landform Activities					
Astronomy Activities					
Magnetism and Electricity					
Force and Motion Activities					

Guidelines Chapter	Comments on Teacher Materials	Comments on Student Textual Materials	Comments on Student Worksheet or Workbook Materials	Comments on Student Laboratory Materials	Overall Evaluation
Physics of Sound					
Solids, Liquids, and Gases					
Light and Color					

Reading and Writing Components Worksheet for Evaluators

Publisher _____

Year _____　Grade _____　Program _____

Components	Comments on Teacher Materials	Comments on Student Textual Materials	Comments on Student Worksheet or Workbook Materials	Comments on Student Laboratory Materials	Overall Evaluation
General Characteristics of Students with Disabilities (see Part I of manual)					
General Mainstreaming Strategies (see Part II of manual)					
Presentation Format Guidelines					

Components	Comments on Teacher Materials	Comments on Student Textual Materials	Comments on Student Worksheet or Workbook Materials	Comments on Student Activities and Laboratory Materials	Overall Evaluation
Audio Formats					
Large Print Formats					
Supplemental High Interest, Low Vocabulary Materials					
Controlled Vocabulary and Terminology					
Representational Illustrations					
Organizational Illustrations (maps & diagrams)					

2

Components	Comments on Teacher Materials	Comments on Student Textual Materials	Comments on Student Worksheet or Workbook Materials	Comments on Student Activities and Laboratory Materials	Overall Evaluation
Supplemental 3-Dimensional Illustrations					
Mnemonic Illustrations					
Mnemonic Strategies for Learning Unfamiliar Vocabulary and Terminology					
Summary Charts and Diagrams					
Supplemental Concrete Materials to Illustrate Concepts					
Supplemental Computer-Assisted Instructional Programs to Illustrate Concepts					

Components	Comments on Teacher Materials	Comments on Student Textual Materials	Comments on Student Worksheet or Workbook Materials	Comments on Student Activities and Laboratory Materials	Overall Evaluation
Supplemental Video and Videodisc Programs to Illustrate Concepts					
Clear Organizational Structure to Reading Materials					
Advance Organizers					
Highlighted Information					
Adequate Review and Practice Activities					
Comprehension Strategies					

Components	Comments on Teacher Materials	Comments on Student Textual Materials	Comments on Student Worksheet or Workbook Materials	Comments on Student Activities and Laboratory Materials	Overall Evaluation
Self-Questioning					
Self-Monitoring					
Summarizing					
Clarifying					
Predicting					
Outlining					

5

Components	Comments on Teacher Materials	Comments on Student Textual Materials	Comments on Student Worksheet or Workbook Materials	Comments on Student Activities and Laboratory Materials	Overall Evaluation
Note-Taking					
Highlighting					
Visual Imagery					
Constructing Study Guides (graphic organizers, maps)					
Reviewing					
Study Skills					

6

Components	Comments on Teacher Materials	Comments on Student Textual Materials	Comments on Student Worksheet or Workbook Materials	Comments on Student Activities and Laboratory Materials	Overall Evaluation
Test-Taking Skills					
Writing a Research Report					
Using a Library and Reference Materials					
Completing Oral Presentations of Written Work					
Completing a Science Fair Project					
Word Processing Skills					